EDDIE SHORE

and That Old Time Hockey

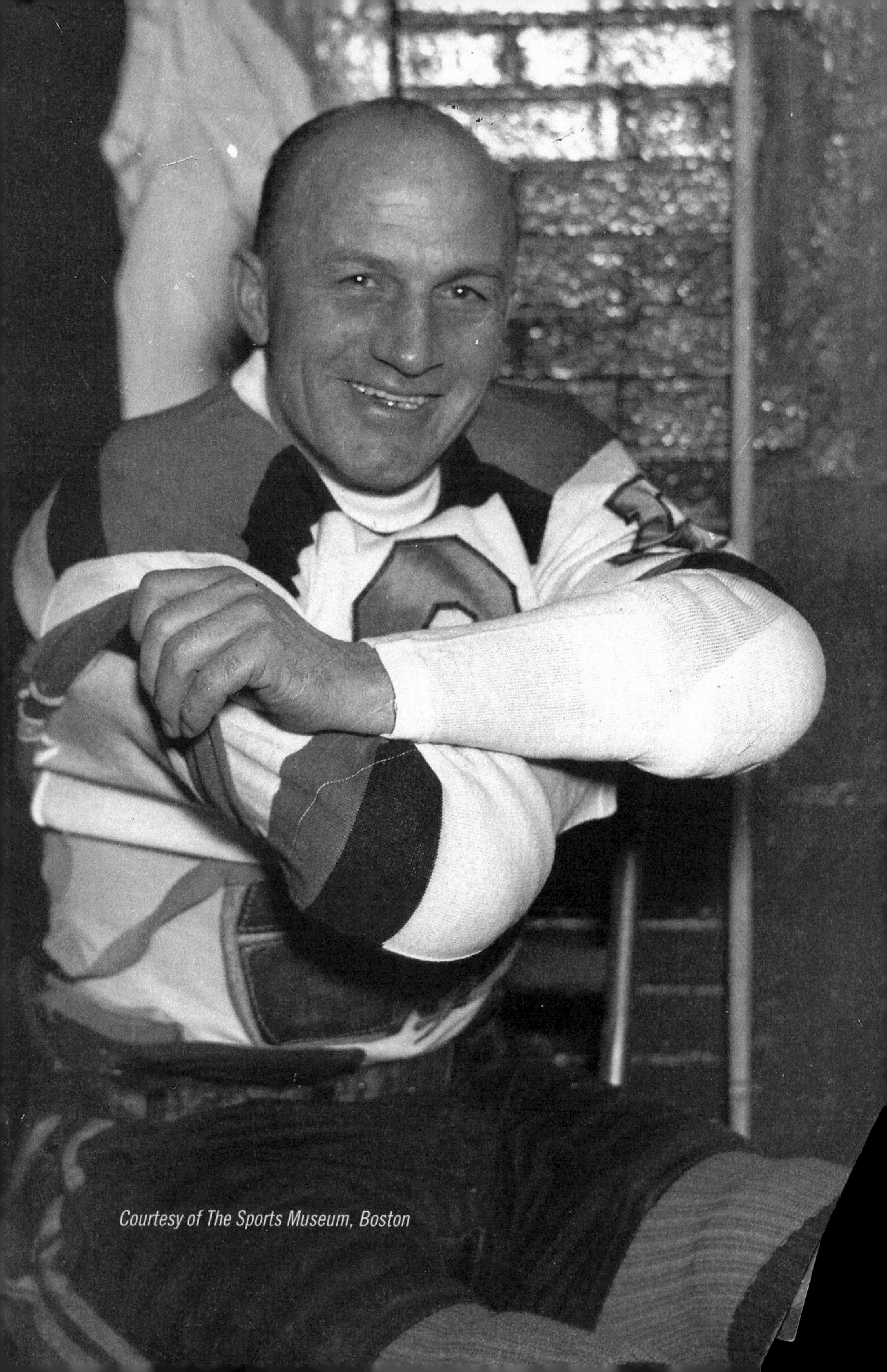
Courtesy of The Sports Museum, Boston

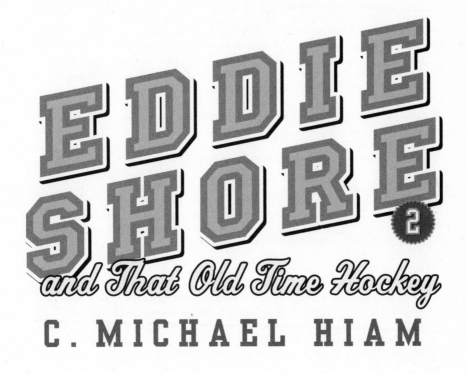

EDDIE SHORE

and That Old Time Hockey

C. MICHAEL HIAM

McClelland & Stewart

Cloth edition published 2010
Paperback edition published 2011

Library and Archives Canada Cataloguing in Publication

Hiam, C. Michael
    Eddie Shore and that old-time hockey / C. Michael Hiam.

ISBN 978-0-7710-4129-7

    1. Shore, Eddie, 1902-1985. 2. Hockey players – Biography. 3. Sports team owners – Massachusetts – Biography. 4. Springfield Indians (Hockey team) – Biography. 5. Boston Bruins (Hockey team) – Biography. I. Title.

GV848.5.S56H52 2011   796.962092   C2011-901988-4

We acknowledge the financial support of the Government of Canada through the Book Publishing Industry Development Program and that of the Government of Ontario through the Ontario Media Development Corporation's Ontario Book Initiative. We further acknowledge the support of the Canada Council for the Arts and the Ontario Arts Council for our publishing program.

Published simultaneously in the United States of America by McClelland & Stewart Ltd., P.O. Box 1030, Plattsburgh, New York 12901

Library of Congress Control Number: 2011925624

Typeset in Dante by M&S, Toronto
Printed and bound in the United States of America

McClelland & Stewart Ltd.
75 Sherbourne Street
Toronto, Ontario
M5A 2P9
www.mcclelland.com

1   2   3   4   5   15   14   13   12   11

For my Kid Line: Hannah, Eliana, and Daniel

Whatever your hand finds to do, do it with all your might.

— ECCLESIASTES 9:10

CONTENTS

INTRODUCTION

FRESH FROM AN OIL RUBDOWN, his naked body glistened under the harsh glare of the dressing-room lights. This was the great Eddie Shore, and by the popular standards of his day, the 1920s and '30s, he was the very picture of an athlete. He had light blond hair (what remained of it), sparkling blue eyes, clear skin, square shoulders, muscular arms, solid trunk, tapering waist, and powerful, stocky legs. Shore stood five feet, eleven inches, weighed 190 pounds, and, to opponents who lay awake nights thinking of ways to bust him with skate or stick, was made of iron.

Protection from injury in those days was minimal, and before each game he did the best with what he had. After putting on his underwear and pulling on an undershirt, he wrapped himself in yards of felt, stuffed cotton in his crotch, put papier-mâché pads kept in place by bicycle tape over his shins, and strapped leather armour across his shoulders. Then he donned wool stockings, canvas pants held up by a piece of rope, and a white woollen jersey trimmed in the brown and yellow of the Boston Bruins. Next, he laced his chromium-tipped skates, slipped on his leather gloves and, finally, he performed certain rituals, known to him alone, which had to be completed before every battle—because for Eddie Shore, every game was a battle, a battle that must be won.

As usual, Shore was the last player to dress, and as the Bruins' trainer, Win Green, threw a blanket over his broad shoulders for warmth, he exited the dressing-room door. Now out in the corridor and on top of the wooden planks, the burly Bruin walked slowly, determinedly, towards the rink.

For fourteen NHL seasons, 1926 to 1940, Eddie Shore of Saskatchewan was the most watched man in hockey. In Boston, he kept his adoring fans waiting, worrying, before suddenly appearing at the edge of the frozen surface to the orchestral swell of "Hail to the Chief." At the sight of Shore, fifteen thousand throats roared in thunderous unison while Win Green, with a fatherly pat on the back, lifted the blanket off his shoulders and then handed him a talcum-powdered hockey stick. With horns blaring, bells ringing, and a lone fire siren wailing, Shore propelled himself majestically out to centre ice. There, head held high, body erect, and with the stick at rest by his side, he paused for a moment—an Olympian on the podium, a thoroughbred horse at the post.

During the depths of the Great Depression, when money was tight, millions paid for the right to see the mighty Shore in action. In Boston, they did so for the sheer joy of cheering him and revering him; in other cities, they did it for the dark pleasure of spitting on him and hating him intensely. Shore invaded every arena in the National Hockey League like a runaway locomotive on a downgrade. He was mayhem on skates. "My memories of Shore come through a haze of red," the columnist Jimmy Powers once said. "He bled almost every night. Shore's blood dripped on the ice of Chicago, Montreal, Boston, and countless other rinks. Shore took it all with his battered jaw set in a grim line. He bounced up time and time again after being knocked down, to skate on wobbly legs to the bench, take a brief rest, and then go storming back into action."

Shore was thrilling on ice, and he had only to touch the puck and the spectators were on their feet, because everyone knew that with Eddie on the move, something fantastic was bound to happen . . . that he would bash somebody . . . or get into a fight . . . or score a goal . . . or start a riot.

The man from Saskatchewan was the Babe Ruth and Ty Cobb of hockey, a brilliant athlete with a temper to match, and his importance to the history of the professional game is immense. In the hockey vernacular of his age, Shore was a "superstar" who gave the NHL visibility in new markets south of Canada, saw it through the Great Depression, and sent it on its way to be the highly profitable sports empire it would become.

Shore decided one day to study hockey "as seriously," he said, "as others studied law or medicine." He first skated at age twelve, and only took up the game at sixteen, but he vowed to make it his profession. He dedicated himself to hours upon hours of lonely practice. "No man ever coached him," his friend and the future president of the NHL, Red Dutton, explained. "He was a self-made player in every way, the architect of his own destiny."

Shore went from beginner to professional in just five years. His knowledge of hockey was unparalleled, and his training techniques and theories of play, at first derided, were decades ahead of their time. In his later years, Shore was as controversial as he had been in his youth, yet his passion for hockey remained undiminished. After retiring as a player, he went on to introduce thousands of youngsters to the sport and, as owner and mastermind of the Springfield Indians, won championship after championship.

It would be hard to overemphasize the dominance that Shore in his heyday had over hockey, or how important and valuable he was to both the Bruins and every club in the NHL circuit. Whenever the visiting Bruins came to town, the marquee would read BOSTON BRUINS AND EDDIE SHORE, and the arena manager, expecting an overflow crowd, would have dollar signs in his eyes. "What makes Eddie Shore the greatest drawing card in hockey," Kyle Crichton famously wrote in 1934, "is the hope—entertained by spectators in all cities but Boston—that he will some night be severely killed." Shore was entertainment personified, and after every bout, his body would be black and blue, having given all it had. During his two-decade professional career, Shore was cut a hundred times, receiving 978 stitches. Newspaper artists gave up trying to diagram his sprains, tears, and fractures because the sketch became a blur.

Wildly popular as an object of worship and loathing, Shore's fame had its dark side. This was his penchant for retaliatory violence, making him among the most penalized men in hockey. Shore received numerous fines and suspensions, and in the NHL he spent the equivalent of more than twenty hockey games sitting in the penalty box. It was the "Ace Bailey affair," however, for which Shore was most heavily penalized. At the time, 1933, the tragedy was considered the most infamous incident in hockey history, and he was exiled from the league for sixteen games—a third of the season. In his absence, the fans chanted "We want Shore!" and attendance at Boston Garden dropped like a stone.

In keeping with his notoriety, Eddie Shore was always rumoured to be the highest-paid player in the NHL, and if so, he earned his pay many times over. He was elected to the league's First All-Star Team every year except one (the Ace Bailey year), and, in a record for a defenceman that will probably never be surpassed, won the Hart Trophy as the NHL's most valuable player four times. Shore propelled the Bruins to greatness and twice, in 1929 and 1939, he and his teammates drank champagne from the Stanley Cup. Then, only a few years after retiring, and at the insistence of his fans, Shore was inducted into the new Hockey Hall of Fame, becoming only its second living member. That same year, 1947, his Bruins jersey number, the celebrated Number 2, was sent aloft to the rafters of the Garden, never to come down. In 1970, the NHL afforded Shore its final tribute by awarding him the Lester Patrick Memorial Trophy in recognition of his outstanding contribution to hockey in the United States.

Almost a hundred years have passed since a young cowpoke named Eddie Shore first wobbled out onto the Saskatchewan ice to try his hand at hockey, and today, more than a quarter-century since his death in 1985, Shore is widely recognized as one of the great legends of the game. Yet it is also true that very few hockey fans today could say specifically who Shore was or what he did that made him famous, and most hockey books mention Shore only in passing, if they bother to mention him at all. This is unfortunate, because the man undisputedly deserves the full historical recognition that is his due, and in the pages that follow I attempt to address this wrong by telling the Eddie Shore story in its entirety. It is nothing less than the story of one of the best and most courageous hockey players ever to lace up a pair of skates.

ONE

=====

THE MONTREAL FORUM, built in 1924 specifically for that greatest of sports, ice hockey, was a place where both French and English Montrealers could come together to yell, jostle, bet, fight, argue, and drink as one people—at least when the despised Bruins came to town. The Forum could hold more than eleven thousand spectators (in a tight fit), two hundred red-capped ushers, and as many plainclothes and undercover police officers as were deemed necessary. Thousands of fans that day, November 23, 1929, had spent hours outside in a line for tickets, keeping warm by lighting small bonfires, and now, once inside, they joined other spectators who were settling themselves into the expensive box seats, the regular seats, the overflow seats, the standing-room areas, the windowsills, and, for a spectacularly good view, the rafters. Everyone was in a boisterous mood, particularly those at the far end of the rink who had paid fifty cents for the right to "rush" the wooden benches of "Millionaires' Row." The Forum's wooden benches held only two thousand, but there was always room for one more because there was always one more who could be pushed to the floor.

The Montreal Maroons were playing the roughest kind of game against Boston that night, and taking advantage of the roughness were Reginald "Hooligan" Smith and Dave Trottier, both having decided to make a sandwich out of Eddie Shore and, while they were at it, to give him plenty of the butt ends of their sticks. The crowd roared its approval at this, and seconds later roared even louder when Shore was sent reeling to the Forum's near-perfect sheet of ice. Shore groggily picked himself up, blood spurting from his eyes, and the manager of the Bruins, Art Ross, rapped his fists violently against the boards of the rink to get Shore's attention. Ross demanded he go off for repairs, but Shore refused, insisting on remaining in the game. When the Forum fans saw that Eddie was going to stick it out, they greeted this display of raw courage with hoots and cheers in both French and English.

The whistle blew, play resumed, and Shore dashed into combat again and was met by the Maroons' up-raised sticks. Two well-placed jabs to his face tore open his cheek and sliced deeply into his chin. Then the Maroons dropped all pretense of civility and really let Shore have it. "He was," according to an observer, "hammered, pounded, cut; and just at the end, a Maroon player cut across Shore and deliberately gave him a sickening smash in the mouth, which knocked out several teeth and felled the Bruin in his tracks." The final wallop was delivered by Babe Siebert, and it sent Shore reeling to the ice once again. This time, though, Shore did not get up; he lay motionless in a pool of his own blood and teeth.

Montrealers were the most sophisticated hockey fans in the world, and they knew true talent when they saw it, even if that talent wore the hated brown and yellow of the Boston Bruins. And so, as Shore, apparently dead, was borne away, everyone in the Forum rose in respect, putting their hands together in polite applause. Meanwhile, the referee, naturally, had been looking in some other direction and missed everything. Siebert and the rest of the Maroons escaped without penalty.

Five minutes after the game ended, the legendary Montreal hockey writer Elmer Ferguson ventured into the visitors' dressing room to see if Shore really had been killed. To his relief, Ferguson was told that the Bruin was still among the living. He found Shore "standing silently beneath the showers. Expecting an outburst I said, 'Rough going, Eddie.' Through bloody, swollen lips he answered laconically, 'It's all in the game. I'll pay off.'"

Eddie Shore was one tough hombre, and he got his moxie from his upbringing in the "wilds" of Canada. "I have heard him talk," the Boston sports columnist Austen Lake wrote in 1934, "with a trace of suspicious mist in his eye and a faraway look, about the winter moon over the tips of fir forests and the frozen void of nature that fairly throbs with loneliness, in which the distant howl of a wolf was a perfect soul note."

In reality, Eddie grew up far removed from any trees, fir or otherwise, because in the heart of Saskatchewan, where he was born in 1902, trees had yet to be planted. Most of the land had also yet to be tilled, and back then the area was a barren but beautiful landscape covered by grass so short that when

Shore was a little boy it barely came up to his knees. In the wintertime, the wind whipped across the prairie and a small Eddie, aged five and heading out to the unheated barn to milk the cows, could feel its cold sting.

Eddie Shore's paternal grandparents were among the first European settlers in Saskatchewan's Qu'Appelle Valley, arriving from Ontario in 1870. Those were the days of roaming buffalo, of Indian teepees, of Hudson's Bay Company trading posts, and the watchful (of the Americans to the south) eye of the North-West Mounted Police.

Made a province in 1905, Saskatchewan was bristling with opportunity, and the Canadian Pacific Railway was luring immigrants from eastern North America and Europe with the promise of free land if they would settle the prairie; thousands were taking the railway up on its offer. By 1910, when Eddie was eight years old, his father, Thomas John "T.J." Shore, had moved his wife, Kate, sons Aubrey and Eddie, and daughters Lizzy and Irene from Fort Qu'Appelle in the valley to a newly opened area twenty miles northwest. The son of pioneers, and therefore not an average homesteader, T.J. had a jump-start on everyone else, and in only a few short years he somehow leveraged his quarter-section (160-acre) allotment into a ranch of nearly seventy thousand acres, thirty-five miles wide and thirty-six miles long. The Shore place held four hundred head of horses and six hundred head of cattle; the operation produced 100,000 bushels of wheat and shipped 100 to 150 head of stock a year. The enterprise was worth at least half a million dollars, making Eddie's father the richest man in the district.

Of Irish Protestant stock, T.J. Shore embodied the work ethic, and he made sure that his two sons, Eddie and Eddie's older brother, Aubrey, did too. Under his harsh tutelage, the boys were never idle. As they grew older, the chores became ever more onerous until there were, it seemed, a dozen tasks, such as wheat harvesting, wood chopping, stock tending, and team driving, all of which had to be done before bedtime.

To help their work on the ranch, the two boys were taught to ride almost as soon as they could walk. At age seven, Eddie had his own horse, and soon he was breaking in ponies and starting to display a unique ability to endure great pain. When he was nine years old, one of these ponies refused to be tamed, and, with Eddie aboard, the animal reared back and then suddenly snapped forward. The boy's face slammed into the animal's head and he held on for dear life. Spinning in the saddle with a bloody and broken nose, he could hear a friend's voice yelling in encouragement, "'Stick it out, Eddie, stick it out!'" remembered Shore years later, "And I stuck it out."

At twelve, Eddie was driving four-horse teams to the grain elevators in nearby Cupar, and folks in town noticed that T.J.'s young son possessed unusual strength. Eddie became known as the boy wonder who could remove a thousand-pound grain tank from a wagon unassisted, and who could also work in the wheat fields like a grown man and never wilt. At thirteen, Eddie, with his six-shooter at his side and a rifle across his lap for good measure, was entrusted by his father to herd the family's prize horses to a distant grazing area. During one trip, he put the rifle to his shoulder and laid out warning shots to keep some strangers at bay. Word of this incident got back to the ranch, and T.J. found no cause to censure his son. At fourteen, he was taking on his father's broncos, and these four-legged outlaws reared and stamped and lunged wildly in an effort to toss him clear into the next county. At fifteen, Eddie was an expert roper, and he could make the hemp loop spin at his wish—but not without incident. A steer once dragged him a quarter of a mile at the end of a lasso before he let go. At sixteen, he was riding herd on thousands of cattle and rounding up strays.

Eddie was competitive; he had to be, with a brother two years older who wanted to keep him in his place. One day, the two of them were doing some barnyard work when Eddie became tired of being bossed around by Aubrey. A tussle developed over who would use the spade and who would use the pitchfork. Aubrey, like his father, wouldn't countenance any insubordination, and punched his little brother solidly in the mouth. Stunned, Eddie shook his head to clear his brain, then caught his older brother flush on the nose with a direct hit.

"For the next twenty or so minutes," Shore said, "we went around and around, knocking each other down time and again, but neither could put the other away, nor would either of us give up."

The brothers wrestled on the dusty earth, both hoping to land the knockout punch, but they were too much in each other's clutches for either of them to break away and execute the final blow. Exhausted, dirty, and bloody, Eddie and Aubrey had to settle for a draw. Their father had calmly witnessed whole thing. "I hope you two are satisfied," T.J. said. "Now get back to work."

T.J. was a stern disciplinarian, and if it was for the good of his boys, he was not afraid to apply the sting of the whip. He also had a temper and, if provoked, could administer a sound thrashing, especially if Eddie or Aubrey ever made a mistake.

T.J. was a perfectionist who would not tolerate failure in himself or anybody else, and he once ordered Eddie to operate on the hernia of a bull, telling him that if he failed, he would get a beating.

There were adventures aplenty for a boy growing up on the infinite reaches of the prairie, and Eddie had his fair share of them. There was the time when he almost froze to death while herding cattle in the winter. The temperature was sixty-one degrees below zero Fahrenheit. "I say sixty-one," Shore qualified, "because our thermometers registered sixty below and they all broke. I had to drive twenty-three head of cattle thirty-two miles for my father. A hired hand went with me because we couldn't get the cattle out of the chutes it was so cold." The trail through the deep snow was narrow. "The cattle stayed in file all right," Shore said, "and we jog-trotted them so they wouldn't freeze. We got off the horses ourselves every so often so we wouldn't freeze also." On the return journey, Eddie's horse fell down. "I didn't realize it until then but I was probably frozen. My legs were frozen in the shape of a horse. I couldn't get off, but the horse got up again with me in the saddle." A hundred yards farther on, the horse went down once more. "I was thrown off. I had to get up. It took me about thirty minutes to get on the horse again." With effort, and a good deal of pain, Eddie managed to regain his mount and make his way home. "You could freeze to death in a very short time out there," Shore explained, "and freezing would be a pleasure, just a pleasant numbness."

Eddie had his closest call at age twelve, when he was ordered to corral some horses; those that failed to go peaceably were to be roped and dragged in. Eddie had a twenty-square-mile area to cover, and he grabbed off all the easy horses first, leaving the hard ones for last. "That was an awful mistake," Shore recalled, "because when a fellow has a fresh horse under him he should go to work on the tough horses first, and not tire his mount unnecessarily on the easy ones, and then find that the tough horses have it in their dizzy brains to have some fun." By late afternoon, he had gotten the horses corralled, except for the last one, which sped away. Eddie took off after the escapee, and the pursuit was on.

The fugitive maintained a lead of several lengths, but by early evening the boy had gotten the better of the renegade. Just as he was about to rope the horse, however, his own mount hit a hidden burrow and he was thrown to the ground as 1,200 pounds of horseflesh came crashing down on top of him. Eddie's horse rolled clear and patiently waited for its master, who lay motionless on the grass, to get up. When Eddie finally recovered his senses, nighttime had arrived, and he discovered, painfully, that both of his shoulders were cracked. His loyal horse was still waiting, and it would be another half-hour before Eddie could successfully manoeuvre his crippled body back into the saddle and make the eighteen-mile trudge back to the ranch house.

The doctor did not offer hope for full recovery because the shoulders, particularly the right one, were too badly smashed. For three months, the boy had to be dressed by his parents, but, determined to get better as soon as he could, Eddie exercised the wounded shoulders for several hours each day. In time, he was able to twirl a rope and ride the range again. It was six years, however, before he could raise his right hand above his head.

T.J. Shore did his business in Cupar (pronounced Q-par), where, among other things, he granted loans, owned a livery and feed store, and sold horses, land, and insurance. The frontier town had sprung up almost overnight as a result of a Canadian Pacific Railway dictate, and in Eddie's youth Cupar was just a bare-bones collection of wood-framed buildings and houses lining wide, unpaved streets. Thanks to the civic generosity of Mr. T.J. Shore, however, Cupar did have sidewalks, as well as a new ice rink in a substantial structure that cost T.J. four thousand dollars. In a farming community like Cupar, where there was nothing to do during the long winters, it was a generous gift indeed.

As the sons of the influential T.J. Shore, Aubrey and Eddie were given keys to the rink, and Aubrey became a star on the local junior hockey team. Eddie, by contrast, was, he remembered, a "very weak and wobbly" skater. The future NHL superstar had little interest in hockey, perhaps because he considered it his older brother's sport, and therefore not for him. By happenstance, though, Eddie did get a crack at hockey once. He had accompanied Aubrey and the Cupar team on the sleigh ride to neighbouring Markinch for a game, but when the players arrived, they realized they were one player short, and so Eddie Shore was given his first hockey audition. It did not go smoothly. "I was," he recalled, "terrible."

Baseball and soccer were Eddie's sports, as was horseback riding, which came naturally to him. He would roar his pinto pony down the main street of Cupar in any position imaginable, and once, while standing up with his bare feet clinging to the animal's back, the pony halted abruptly and Eddie did not. He landed face down in the dirt. He attended the school in town, but was no scholar. "If the class was assigned twenty words to spell," a classmate recalled, "Eddie would misspell eighteen of them." He skipped classes, got into disagreements with his teacher, and was suspended several times.

In Cupar, there were enticements not found back at the ranch, and once, when he was about twelve, Eddie stood in front of the butcher shop while the butcher was cutting up an assortment of cooked meats. The butcher offered the boy a slice. "How would you like this, Eddie? Beat up that boy over there and I'll give you this, but if he beats you up then I'll give it to him." The other boy was four years older and thirty pounds heavier, but to Eddie it seemed a fair proposition. A crowd gathered to watch as he pummelled his opponent into submission. The butcher kept his word, gave Eddie the meat, and promised him a bigger slice if he took on an even larger, older, opponent. This time, he lost. Licked, he picked himself up off of the ground and seethed as his better devoured the prize. There was a lesson here, one that Eddie Shore had learned twice already in just one day: the winner gets everything, and the loser gets nothing. He would remember this.

When Eddie turned fifteen, he was a strong and steady youth on the cusp of full manhood. His father could trust him with all aspects of ranching and gave him responsibilities, such as allocating stock and overseeing the tenant farmers, usually afforded men twice his age. Eddie fulfilled his duties with confidence and skill, and his future as a prosperous rancher was certain, just as certain as the fact that his father's land extended as far as the eye could see. Yet, within three years, Eddie Shore, that same fresh-faced youth who was once poised to be master of all that he surveyed, would be penniless. He would not have enough money even to buy food.

Eddie's mother, Catherine Spannier "Kate" Shore, died in 1918 at age fifty-two, following a daughter, Clara, who died in 1908, and several infant children who had died earlier, into the grave. Nothing more is known about Kate Shore, but it can be surmised that she had a strong and positive influence on her son. When Eddie got married, it would be to a woman named Kate, and throughout his life he was invariably a gentleman around women and treated them as equals.

Around the time his mother died, Eddie's father sent him to the Manitoba Agricultural College, where Aubrey probably was already enrolled. Eddie planned on becoming a veterinarian, but for sport he tried out for the school's football team, where he was placed in the fullback position and did most of the kicking. Eddie also tried out for, and made, the basketball team. In the newspapers at the time, he learned about the sensational Dick Irvin, Winnipeg's hockey hero and the kind of player who could lead his team to 9–0 victories by scoring all the goals himself. Reading about Irvin's exploits gave Eddie the "dim idea," as he described it, to play hockey in addition to football and basketball. Aubrey was already on the college hockey team, and he candidly informed his younger brother that his hockey ambitions were, simply, absurd. This not only did nothing to quell Eddie's hopes, but predictably it had just the opposite effect. He vowed to Aubrey that he would not only be playing hockey for Manitoba soon, but would be playing professionally in five years.

Eddie knew that hockey demanded good legs, so he started running five miles every day and spending hours in the gymnasium. He also spent time rinkside, where he studied the best skaters' moves as they strutted their stuff. When not observing others, Eddie would practise alone on the ice and, like a fighter shadow boxing, would imagine himself checking an opponent or being checked himself. Or, he would pretend that he was dribbling through three or four opposing players and, by feinting and shifting, outwitting them to advance the puck. "That sort of thing looks ridiculous," Shore said, "but it is valuable to any boy who wants to play hockey."

The college had three hockey teams, and Eddie got playing time on one of the minor ones. He was properly initiated into the sport at age sixteen, when he received his first body check. Eddie would dress for games in the dormitory, then go down to the open-air rink. "Often we played at thirty to forty below," Shore said. "Our ears, noses and cheeks used to freeze regularly, and we'd be playing a little while and you could scrape the hoarfrost off of our backs and our chests. I remember we once played a game when it was fifty-five below and our eyelashes froze so stiff we were almost blinded."

After just one year, the budding veterinarian left the Manitoba Agricultural College for an unknown reason (his academic records are no longer extant) and enrolled at St. John's College School in Winnipeg the following fall. St. John's was western Canada's oldest school, and it would become famous for turning out such hockey players as Andy Blair, Murray Murdoch, and Red Dutton. Generations of boys had learned the game on the school's tiny sheet of ice, and, amazingly, at one point in the 1930s there were no fewer than thirteen "Johnians" in the NHL. Whether Eddie went for the hockey or for another reason is not known, but he did catch on with the

St. John's team for the first two games of the hockey season before going home for Christmas, never to return. The only record St. John's (now the St. John's-Ravenscourt School) has on Shore is a brief one, and it ends cryptically: "Withdrawn, Christmas 1919."

In Cupar, the hockey club was nearing the end of its first real season after limping along shorthanded for the past several years. The Great War of 1914–18 had wreaked havoc on Canada's hockey leagues, both professional and amateur, because the legions of young Canadian men who would otherwise have been in hockey togs had instead been fighting across the ocean in Europe. Canada, a vast but sparsely populated country of only eight million, had sent a staggering number of its citizens, more than six hundred thousand of them, to war, and now, after the armistice, in towns large and small across Canada, memorials were being planned for the local boys who would never come back. Saskatchewan, with a population of half a million, had contributed forty-two thousand men to the war effort; from the rural Cupar district, vacant of almost everything except horses, cattle, and gophers, 126 men—fifteen of whom would never return—served with the Canadian forces. With peace came the Spanish influenza, which killed more people worldwide than had died in the war. The epidemic swept through Cupar, taking away entire families. Thankfully, by the conclusion of 1919, the dual calamities had ended and Cupar could once again devote time to leisure pursuits. The Cupar Hockey Club readied itself for the 1919–20 season.

In the United States, it was believed that all Canadians were born wearing ice skates, and in fact for many Canadians their earliest and most cherished memory was of getting their first pair. "I remember thinking what a great present these skates were," the Ottawa Senators' immortal great, King Clancy, said of his youth, "and couldn't wait to put them on that morning. I stepped out on the verandah but had taken one stride when I sailed right down the steps and landed on the sidewalk." Getting skates was, for Clancy, as it was for a multitude of little Canadians just like him, only the beginning. "Once a fellow wangled the skates and a stick, the river became a second home," Clancy explained. "The rest of the equipment you had to come by as best you could. We used to make our own shin pads out of sweeper sticks tied together. These were sticks we'd find along the streetcar tracks after the sweeper car had been by to clean the rails. If we couldn't find enough sweeper sticks, we'd use issues of the *Saturday Evening Post*. It was the next best thing."

King Clancy's childhood friend in Ottawa was Frank Boucher, who would later earn fame with the New York Rangers. "We played hockey morning, noon, and night when we weren't in school," Boucher recalled. "On Saturdays, for instance, the first arrivals would start a game around 8 o'clock [in the morning], dividing the available players evenly into two teams. As more boys came they joined one side or the other, always keeping the teams equal. Soon there'd be fifteen or twenty boys playing on each side, thirty or forty kids pursuing the puck."

The game that Frank Boucher and his chums were playing was "shinny," the basic version of hockey. The word *hockey* traditionally meant a curved wooden stick of some sort, but in the 1820s and '30s it came to be associated with an obscure game played in England, which apparently involved a *hockey*. The first recorded mention of "hockey on the ice" was made in 1843 in Kingston, Ontario, which would seem to place the birthplace of the sport in Ontario—but Nova Scotians will have none of that. They claim that ice hockey comes from the Halifax region, where, by the 1860s, "the match game of hockey," as it was called in old newspaper accounts, was a popular winter pastime. While Nova Scotians may well have been early and ardent adopters of hockey, their claims of exclusivity have to be weighed against evidence that similar games called hockey were also played in the United States, if not in other parts of the world, for at least as long as they had been played in Nova Scotia. Unquestionably, however, it was in Montreal that hockey as a modern organized sport, as opposed to a mere game, was conceived with the adoption of the Montreal Rules, written in 1877. Hockey flourished, and from then on it was just a matter of scattering the sport across the continent via the newly built railway lines.

In Saskatchewan, hockey followed the railway as it linked the distant outposts of Moosomin, Indian Head, Regina, Moose Jaw, and Swift Current together. The larger towns of Regina and Moose Jaw were playing each other in hockey matches as early as 1894, and a year later a wayward shipment of hockey sticks abandoned in Moosomin served to fertilize the growth of the sport there.

Ice hockey in the years before 1900 was different from the modern game in many respects. Despite the Montreal Rules, the sport varied from place to place, and sometimes quite dramatically, but in general it was played in two periods of thirty minutes each and, whether played outdoors or indoors, the games were cold for spectators and players alike. Hockey's first superstar, Cyclone Taylor, remembered the game of his youth in Ontario: "Fans in those days were an amazingly hardy lot, and they had to be. In those days of more than seventy-five years ago, it seemed that the winters were much colder and longer than they are now. The wind would howl and the temperature would get down way below zero, but out they'd come in the bitter cold, packing those draughty arenas, and loving every minute of it. They came on foot, by train, in sleighs and cutters, dressed in furs and mufflers, and sat huddled under blankets. And they'd stay right to the end." Sometimes, on those mean winter nights, Taylor would look at the packed stands and ask himself, "Why are they here? Why do they come out on a night like this? But of course," he said, "I knew why. They simply loved hockey."

Between periods, shivering fans would have ten minutes to get some hot coffee, brewed in big, steaming urns under the stands, or furtively buy liquor, at a dollar a bottle, to keep warm. Tie games went into two five-minute extra periods, and if after these two sessions there was still no winner, play continued indefinitely until someone scored. In those days, players were not fussy about their sticks, as long as they were solid and heavy, and the only shot known to man or woman was the wrist shot. Teams played seven-man hockey, which most differed from the modern game because of the rover position between offence and defence, and also because forward passing was forbidden in all circumstances. Depending upon who did the reminiscing, seven-man hockey was preferable to the later six-man version either because it encouraged individualism or because it discouraged individualism.

All seven players were expected to stay on the ice for the entire contest. No substitutions were allowed for any reason, and if someone had to leave due to injury or a broken skate (with the exception, perhaps, of the mishap occurring at the very start of the game), they could not return; the opposing side, out of fairness, would also have to drop one of its players. The "goal guarder" stood between fixed pipes, both of his skates firmly planted firmly on the ice at all times. The NHL's great stand-up netminders, like Georges Vézina, who learned the game in the early days, retained that stance and had all the angles down so perfectly, and were able to anticipate each shot so keenly, that they gave every impression of standing still the entire game.

Hockey then was a rough-and-tumble affair, despite efforts to keep it gentlemanly. By the first decade of the century, fisti-cuffs were common, timekeepers fiddled with the clock when it was in their team's best interest to either make or lose time, and the sprinkling of salt on the ice was considered a good way to slow up faster opponents. Players caught in the act of making mischief had to pay their penance by "sitting on the fence" for three minutes, and, with no delayed penalties allowed, a spate of violations could leave practically no men on the ice. Goalies had to serve their own sentences on the fence (which made for some dramatic minutes), and there was also a rule (which should be reinstated immediately) against "loafing," meaning that any player not moving forcefully with the puck was penalized.

Hockey games back then were run by three on-ice offi-cials. Two of these luckless individuals would be forced to serve as goal umpires by standing exposed on the ice sheet behind the goaltender, while the third one would skate around the rink to referee the play—and dodge the tobacco juice that streamed from the stands. There were no off-ice officials in those days, spectators were expected to keep count of the score, and the *um-pa* beat of live bands provided a musical backdrop to the action.

By the time the 1919–20 hockey season in Cupar got off to a slow start (so slow that it didn't even begin until late January), ice hockey in Saskatchewan had already developed into a well-organized affair, with leagues of differing levels of skill. The sport was overwhelmingly a boy's and a man's game, although there were a few girls' and women's squads in the province, as well as spirited co-ed jousts of shinny on sunny prairie days. Men's teams could vie for local and provincial trophies, and even dream of national ones like the Stanley Cup (although no team from the province ever became a Cup challenger).

In Saskatchewan, like most of Canada, seven-man hockey had given way by the end of the war to the newer six-man version. Also in Saskatchewan, as in the rest of the country, the pressure to bring money into the game was fast threatening the traditional amateur status of the sport. To the west, the Pacific Coast Hockey Association, formed in 1912, was paying all of its players, not just its stars, as was the National Hockey League, organized in 1917 from the remnants of the National Hockey Association in the east. Both pro leagues were angling to lure away the province's best players. Within a year, Saskatchewan would fight back with its own professional hockey clubs, but for the time being, hockey in the province was still played for the love of the game, and occasionally for a little money under the table.

With Aubrey Shore leading the way, by the end of the truncated 1919–20 season the Cupar squad had ripped through all local competition to face the Melville Millionaires in the Saskatchewan intermediate amateur playoffs. The Millionaires had gone undefeated all season, and interest in the two-game, total-goals series was running high. Everyone in Cupar was expected to attend the first match on February 26, even with tickets an expensive fifty cents for adults and twenty-five for children (at a time when, in Cupar, twelve dollars could buy a ton of coal). Eddie Shore, having left St. John's that December, asked to join the home team for the series, and he even promised to pay his own way for the second game in Melville so as not to be a burden. The Cupar manager, a man named Heeb Sellars, refused. Faced with a determined Eddie Shore, however, Sellars learned what other managers would later find out: that it was next to impossible to say no to Eddie. Aubrey Shore's kid brother did not disappoint, and in the first game against Melville he proved his worth as a strong and skilled skater on the right wing, and as an untiring and energetic player overall. He caught the attention of the crowd both by his staying power and by scoring the last four goals for Cupar to give the team a convincing 9–3 victory over the Millionaires.

A few days later, when warming weather, the bane of hockey in the days before refrigeration, threatened to end the season at any minute, the two clubs were assembled in Melville for the second and deciding match. As play was set to commence, word came that a wire from the Saskatchewan Amateur Hockey Association had just arrived. Three Cupar players, the SAHA had ruled, would be ineligible to play because of their unsportsmanlike conduct during the game in Cupar. The three had allegedly threatened referee Corky Stein of Melville with violence. The Cupar men denied this, although they allowed that Stein, in their opinion, was an incompetent who had never played hockey and had no idea of how to handle a game. What was more, Cupar argued, the players in question—two regulars and the new boy, Eddie Shore—were all three incapable of being the roughnecks that Stein claimed they were. Cupar offered to pay the SAHA's thirty-dollar fee to protest the suspensions on the spot, and to forfeit the game if the suspensions were later upheld. The Millionaires refused to go along with this plan, but they did permit Cupar to use a wounded war veteran with an amateur card in place of the three banished players.

At the end of the second period, the Millionaires were leading Cupar when Cupar's goaltender, Laurence Gordon, was struck in the face by the puck. Badly injured, Gordon had to leave the game, whereupon the referee, a man named Heywood, took the opportunity to write a new page of the hockey rule book by abruptly ending the match. Heywood (who was, incidentally, the Millionaires' vice-president) declared the Millionaires winners, and thus the Saskatchewan champions, based on their razor-thin 11–10 total-goals advantage over Cupar. Incredulous, the men of Cupar reminded Heywood that there was still more than a full period of hockey left in the game.

The following day, Cupar Hockey Club officers were in Regina, the provincial capital, to meet with Frederick E. Betts, president of the SAHA. They put forth their case that the officiating for the series had been suspect, and Betts concurred

The Cupar Hockey Club, 1920. Eddie Shore is seated in the second row, second from left. His brother, Aubrey, is seated directly in front of him. *(Courtesy of Edward W. Shore Jr.)*

by nullifying the results of both games and decreeing that the series be determined by a single sudden-death match to be played in neutral Regina on March 10.

T.J. Shore hired a train for the fifty-mile ride from Cupar to the capital, and aboard the special express as his guests were his two sons and their hockey team, assorted Shore relatives, and almost the entire population of Cupar. The Melville contingent arrived on its own hockey excursion, and the rival rooters made their separate ways to the Regina Arena, where admission for the contest was a pricey seventy-five cents, open seating. Inside the building, it was warm, and the ice was wet and sticky. Emotions were running high.

The imperfect playing surface seemed to be mostly to the detriment of the Cupar players, although they did manage to get off more shots than the Millionaires, even if none of them actually went into the net. Both teams tried their hardest, and the game turned out to be both exciting and clean. Eddie Shore proved not to be much of a factor, though, and his fans would later claim that the man who sharpened his skates before the game was a partisan of the Millionaires who had ground the blades backwards, causing Eddie to stumble around the ice as if drunk. True or not, it is fact that Melville won the game, 4–2, and with it, the championship.

The heartbreaking loss to the Millionaires did nothing to diminish Eddie's love for hockey, and the following winter he practised at the Cupar town rink, pushing himself hard. He tried out new tactics, intended to catapult his body past opposing defences. For one, he placed an oil barrel on the ice and stacked three willing youngsters on top of it. Then, taking a running start at the far end of the rink, he rushed forward at top speed, made an awesome jump, and cleared the obstacle with room to spare. Other times, to keep in shape, Eddie skated thirty miles up river to buy provisions for the ranch.

Aubrey Shore was still playing for Cupar that next season, 1920–21, which may have been one older brother too many on the team for Eddie's liking, and after a game or two with Cupar, Eddie moved the twenty or so miles to Fort Qu'Appelle. The town had been a trading post in pioneer days, and to commemorate its heritage the streets had names like Hudson Street, Bay Street, and Company Street. Shore was seriously injured after just two games with Fort Qu'Appelle, and although the nature of his injury is no longer known, it

Eddie Shore, about age eighteen. *(Courtesy of Edward W. Shore Jr.)*

was severe enough for the doctor to tell him that he would not be able to move for two months. The patient countered by saying he would be on his skates in a week. T.J. implored his son to give up hockey and return home to the ranching business, but Eddie had been terminally bitten by the hockey bug and could not see himself working for his overbearing father ever again.

A week after the doctor had given his prognosis, Eddie got out of bed and woke up an hour later on the hard wooden floor. He had fallen down and knocked himself out cold. Crawling back to bed, Eddie managed to put on his clothes. He tried to stand again, and this time he was more successful, even managing to go downstairs. Two weeks later, and against all advice, Eddie lasted through a very rough game where he received another bang to the head that left him dazed for twelve hours afterwards.

When the Fort Qu'Appelle hockey team's season had run its course, Shore caught on with the team from neighbouring Indian Head for a couple of its final games, but his performance there was not to everyone's liking. Shore remembered one of the Indian Head fans saying to him, "Too bad young fellow, but you won't be able to make a hockey player of yourself."

"That's your opinion," Shore replied, "not mine."

That summer, Eddie put his education in agriculture to work, growing wheat on a half section of his father's land. He did well enough to show a sizable net profit. But farming, to Eddie Shore, was just a summer job; his larger ambition was to make a real hockey player out of himself.

That November, the officers of the Cupar Hockey Club met at the Imperial Lumber Yards to discuss the upcoming 1921–22 campaign. According to the front page of the Cupar *Herald*, the lumberyard conference was "an enthusiastic gathering" at which "it was decided to try to arrange a league with western towns if possible, namely: Bulyen, Strasbourg, and Nokomis. We have," the newspaper reported optimistically, "considerable new material in town, and prospects are bright for a good season's sport."

Two weeks later, on December 15, the front page of the *Herald* was not devoted to recreation. The tidings were grim: T.J. SHORE FOUND DEAD.

> Under most painful circumstances Mr. Thomas John Shore came to his death on Monday last. Mr. Shore had been greatly stressed with financial worries for past year, but had been buoyed up with the hope that the crops this year would tide him over. The slump in prices however, with their consequent losses to the farming industry, only aggravated the situation and on Monday in a fit of depression and mentally unbalanced he evidently decided to end it all. The deceased left the house at about one o'clock and was not missed until he failed to put in an appearance at supper time. A search was immediately instituted and his lifeless body was found suspended from the rafter in the coal shed by his brother Sanford.

Unmentioned was the fact that T.J. had literally bet the ranch on a factory in British Columbia that made nuts and bolts, and had lost everything, including money given to him by his fellow investors. Whatever T.J. had planned on leaving his children was also gone, and his sons and daughters were now destitute. T.J.'s funeral was held at the house, and the burial, presided over by the Reverend J.C. Mathews, was at the Cupar cemetery.

Just three days after the death, and two days after the funeral, a large and buoyant crowd convened at the very same ice rink that T.J. had paid for a decade earlier. The team from Strasbourg were the visitors, and they opened the scoring a few minutes into the first period, but Cupar fought back, putting the puck into the back of the Strasbourg net three times. During the second period, Strasbourg battled through the Cupar defences for two goals of its own to tie the score. The third frame of the exciting contest proved to be the most thrilling, when, with the final bell not far off, Strasbourg beat the Cupar goaltender for the final tally of the game. By that time, however, the Strasbourg cause was hopeless. This was because, in the last minutes of play, "Eddie Shore," according to the *Herald,* had scored "no less than four goals."

Shore quickly became Cupar's best player, equally at ease at right wing or right defence. He had a hot shot that invariably bulged strings behind enemy goaltenders, and he could secure the puck at faceoff to have it in the rivals' net in ten seconds. And because of all this, Eddie was a marked man. Opposing players would gang up on him in twos and threes, but when the smoke had cleared Eddie would emerge, seemingly unharmed, to score the winning goal. The young Shore was unstoppable *and* unflappable. When his hip was severely injured in a fall to the ice, the doctor said he would never play hockey again. Eddie was back in only four weeks. He left hostile crowds gasping and he left the Cupar crowds, which were turning out in record numbers, singing and parading around the ice after each victory.

Cupar dispatched the little town of Lipton in the first round of the intermediate championship of Saskatchewan, and then soundly defeated the team from Lumsden in the second round. The third round would be a sudden-death match against the Cee Pee Rovers, and the contest was held at Moose Jaw, where spring had turned the playing surface to a slushy mush.

The game against the Rovers, according to the Moose Jaw *Evening Times,* was "not an afternoon tea affair by any means." Far from it: the game was more like the recently ended Great War, only fought on skates. Blows were exchanged in the first two periods before the match degenerated into a free-for-all in the third. While order was somehow restored so that the contest could proceed to a conclusion, the game was a reminder of just how violent hockey could be. It never happened in Saskatchewan, but in Ontario, men had actually died playing hockey. Alcide Laurin was cut down by the stick of Allan Loney in 1905 (at trial, Loney was acquitted by a jury), and Owen McCourt met a similar fate at the hands of Charles Masson two years later (Masson was also acquitted by a jury). The sport, then as now, was fodder for critics who said it was little more than boxing or cockfighting on ice. Periodic predictions that the latest hockey outrage would doom the game forever always proved false, because the rough stuff was what the fans wanted, and if the fans did not get their fill of the rough stuff from watching hockey, they could always slug each other.

One story told in the January 12, 1929, issue of the *Literary Digest,* of all places, by a minor-league player named P.J. "Spider" Fynan, reflected those bad old days. "The worst riot I ever saw took place up in the little town in Quebec where I started my career—Richmond," Fynan recalled. "We had an independent league and the race was a close one and the championship hinged on a final game to be played between our team, Richmond, and Waterville, which had in its lineup the three Blue brothers. Walter Blue was the oldest, the biggest, and the toughest."

The Waterville team arrived in a big bobsled, and their fans in a narrow-gauge train consisting of two dingy little passenger cars pulled by a worn-out engine. The rink was surrounded by boards twelve feet high, but there was no roof to the building because it had blown away in a blizzard. "All through the game there were little tiffs here and there," Fynan said, "but nothing serious happened until Bill Cook, one of our players who had 'taken the butt end' many times from the Blue brothers during the season, went over to Walter Blue and hit him on the head with his hockey stick. Instantly there was a riot. The 800 spectators were about evenly divided, half from our town and half from Waterville, so they came down off the seats onto the ice and went to it. The players were way ahead of them by that time, of course.

"First one side of the fence was kicked down," Fynan said, "and the other three followed. Two cast iron stoves, known as 'box stoves,' were kicked over and the place caught fire and burned to the ground. The Richmond fans chased the Waterville supporters to their 'special train' and then smashed the windows and wrecked the cars before the train pulled out."

Fynan did not pretend to have been a hero during the riot, known as the "Battle of Richmond," but Major McIvar and Bill Rarry, prominent Richmond citizens, were. "Each six feet, two inches tall," Fynan remembered, they "stood back to back and handed out 'one-two punches' until they were exhausted. Every man who came within their range was knocked down. Almost as many home folks as aliens became their victims because, in the excitement, there wasn't sufficient time to figure out who was friend and who was foe. Those two just socked for the pure love of socking."

By the time the bell rang in Moose Jaw, the hockey men of Cupar had eliminated the Cee Pee Rovers by a score of 4–2. Eddie and Aubrey Shore and their teammates had become the southern Saskatchewan intermediate hockey champions, and they stood just sixty minutes away from winning the provincial trophy, the Henderson Cup. All Cupar had do was beat the northern Saskatchewan intermediate champions—none other than the Millionaires.

The train left Cupar for Saskatoon at 11 a.m., packed tight with the Cupar team, which had just absorbed a number of players from neighbouring Strasbourg, and a mob of hockey-mad supporters from both towns. Along for the ride was the Strasbourg band, and it would be difficult to imagine a merrier crowd as all sang songs while the band played on. The train arrived in Saskatoon early in the evening. The fans prepared themselves for a night's entertainment, the music men tuned up for the game, and the Cupar team braced itself for the business at hand.

The Millionaires were always partial to an unfair advantage as long as it benefited them, and for that night's amateur hour, according to the Saskatoon *Phoenix*, they had retained the services of men who were "not playing purely for the love of the game." Cupar Hockey Club officials vigorously protested Melville's use of hired guns (whose identities were not divulged by the newspaper), but as outraged as it was, Cupar was hardly about to delay a game that 1,700 spectators were so looking forward to seeing.

Cupar dominated in the opening exchanges, and for the first ten minutes the speedy Melville forwards, even with their paid help, were bottled up. The Millionaires seemed nervous, their passes went wild, and Cupar got the first goal when the puck was batted into the Melville net through a flock of Millionaires. Soon, though, the Millionaires shook off their trepidation and evened the score.

There was some rough stuff in the second period, and the referee dished out the penalties in an equitable manner, such that both sides seemed to be a man short at all times. The shooting increased, the play opened up, and to keep the fans happy, there were some pretty end-to-end rushes—as well as an unusual incident. It occurred when a Melville player named Harris, who was carrying the puck on his stick, slipped, fell on his back, kept possession of the puck, slid into Cupar's goal-tender, and continued on his way right into the Cupar net. It was an innovative way to score, but the play judge disapproved of the technique on principle and the goal was taken back. Harris tried again, this time using more orthodox methods, and he put the Millionaires into the lead, 2–1. Eddie and his line-mates gave the Melville goaltender, a man named MacDonald, a lot of work to do, but despite their best efforts they were not able to lodge the rubber in the strings behind him.

The game was decided in the concluding stanza. Shore staged one of the neatest rushes of the night, right up centre ice to get off a good shot that beat MacDonald completely. The Millionaires retaliated by quickly scoring a goal of their own. This left Eddie with no other choice but to repeat himself and again beat MacDonald completely. However, Eddie's two goals were Cupar's last of the night, while Melville went on to build a four-goal lead. For the second time in three years, the Millionaires had cruelly dashed Cupar's hopes for higher hockey glory.

Shattered by the loss, Shore walked out of the arena into the Saskatoon night. It was March 18 and hockey was over until next winter. Eddie Shore, nineteen years of age, had to hang up the skates and find a job.

TWO

===

THE YOUNG SHORE WENT BOLDLY out into the world. His parents were dead and the ranch was no more, sold off to pay T.J.'s debts. Eddie thought he might become a titan in the mining industry, but instead he did a little mechanical work, tried his hand at selling automobiles, and found occasional work as a carpenter. He even had a go at barbering. "I could use clippers and scissors pretty well because I used to cut the cowboys' hair," Shore said, "but I couldn't learn to put a cutting edge on a straight razor. I guess I mutilated a lot of faces before they waved me out of that league."

These were such lean times for Eddie that he skipped meals—and not by choice. There is no record of his having played for Cupar, or any other local hockey club, during the winter of 1922–23, likely because hockey in Cupar did not pay. Shore gave serious thought to becoming a prizefighter because there was real money in that, and he was expert with his hands, which were enormous. His fingers had a crushing power, and when he made a fist, it was deadly. Once, when Shore was working one of his various jobs, someone lunged at him with a crowbar. "I reached up," he said of his assailant, "disarmed him, picked him up and held him over a pot-bellied stove to warm his bottom, and then I punched him so hard he went through the closed doors and into the street."

Hockey, though, must have remained uppermost on Shore's mind, and he probably dreamed of becoming a star in the new Western Canada Hockey League, joining the likes of Dick Irvin in Regina or Newsy Lalonde in Saskatoon. The chances of that happening, though, were essentially nil because there were legions of daydreaming Eddie Shores all over the land, while there were, at the very most, eighty positions in professional hockey, split between three leagues. Rarely were there any openings. Shore, therefore, had to put the fantasizing aside and soberly contemplate the future; he had to face the adult decision between what he loved and a wage-earning occupation. He did his thinking and arrived at a conclusion regarding hockey. "I decided," he said, "to make the game my profession."

The Melville Millionaires had come away from Saskatoon with the Henderson Cup, but they had also taken a lot of hard lumps from Shore. They knew that he was available, and they wanted him to play for them. They told him their club had stepped up to the senior circuit and that they had a good chance of winning Canada's premier trophy for senior amateur play, the Allan Cup. They also told the impoverished Eddie that as one of them, he would be (quietly) paid five dollars a game and given a job shovelling coal for Melville's largest employer, the Canadian

National Railway. The offer was attractive—as if Eddie needed any convincing. "Even if I was firing an engine and only playing in my spare time," Shore later explained, "there was nothing I wanted so much as to be a professional. I was sure I'd make the grade. They couldn't stop me if they wanted to."

The senior circuit was brutal. For instance, Melville and the 10th Saskatchewan Battery felt a particular hatred towards one another, and whenever the two teams met to see who was best in the province, battle lines were drawn and curious spectators watched from a safe distance. Knowing that Shore had joined the Millionaires, the 10th Battalion had come prepared for combat. The date of the game is no longer known, but the moment the puck was dropped, the soldiers brought out their heavy artillery, with the aim of putting the civilian out of commission. "So they started just clubbing me over the head," Shore recalled of his opponents' strategy. He was knocked out cold. "Someone threw a bunch of water at me," he said, adding, "I had twelve or fourteen stitches taken to my head." Stitched up, he went back into the game, where twice more he was battered unconscious by the soldiers, and twice more the water treatment was applied. But try as they might, it would take more than an army battalion to stop Shore. "We won the game," Eddie recalled, "three to one."

The Melville Millionaires also played the Winnipeg Monarchs, and fifteen minutes into the opening period, as Shore was flying down the ice, the Monarchs' centreman ran right into him, bounced off, went up in the air, and, while doing a kind of somersault, succeeded in giving Shore a skate to the left side of his head. Shore's scalp was opened up, and he collapsed. He was quickly spirited to the dressing room, where he was patched up with four stitches. His head neatly bandaged, Shore reappeared and played for the last half of the period.

In the second period, the Monarchs sent Shore flat onto the ice once again, and as he lay prostrate, the Monarchs thought they might as well finish the job, and took turns hitting him in the stomach. Shore could only remember going down and getting up and going down again, and also that the lights in the arena went dim, much as if the game was being played by candlelight. After this, though, Shore had no memory of the rest of the contest, even though he still managed to skate, pass, and shoot. "The fellows watching the game," Shore recalled, "said I looked all right but I seemed to act kind of funny."

In the third period, when the Monarchs once again sent Shore limp and insensible to the dressing room, it was for the last time. "I was lying on the rubbing table unconscious when the game ended," Shore recalled, "I heard the final bell and jumped up thinking the game was about to start." Shore's jaw had been broken, his nose was broken, six teeth were missing, and he had about a hundred bruises all over his body. The man was ready to play some hockey.

Shore was just tightening up his skates when his team-mates started coming into the dressing room. They asked Shore, as he was bounding out the door, where on earth he thought he was going. To the ice, Shore told them. But the game was over, they said. "The hell it is," Shore replied, and they had to argue the point with him at some length before he realized that it was true. As bizarre as this incident was, it was a proud moment for Shore. "Playing practically a full game without any recollection of it," he boasted, at a time when concussions were not taken at all seriously, "I would regard as the most outstanding experience of my career."

In Melville, when not playing hockey or practising at the rink, which was something he did for hours on end, Shore shovelled coal in the CNR yard to supplement his meagre Millionaires stipend. The sociable Shore was also settling into the community, joining the local lodge of the Freemasons, an organization he would belong to for many years.

In February 1924, the Millionaires, who by reports had been playing "consistent" although "unspectacular" hockey all season (their record for that year has been lost), sprang something of a surprise by beating the Saskatoon Nationals to become the northern Saskatchewan senior champions. Next up for the Millionaires were the mighty Regina Victorias, and now the men of Melville would have a real fight on their hands. That fight, to be contested in three parts, was scheduled to commence on February 27 in Regina.

The Millionaires bested the Victorias by one goal in the first game of the series, and Shore, now playing right defence, was the Melville star. Even as a defenceman, Shore was still a puck-rushing dynamo. He led his fellow Millionaires in the attack time after time, he tied the game up with a shot that almost broke the twine, and he also put up magnificent resistance when the play went the other way. Shore again performed superbly during the second game, which was held in Melville, yet the Millionaires went down to defeat by one goal, and the series was tied. The deciding game, March 7, 1924, would be held in the "hub" of Saskatchewan, Saskatoon.

"It was sixty minutes," the Regina *Morning Leader* reported, "of the most grueling, scintillating, and breath taking hockey."

For Eddie, though, the scintillation came at a price. In the first period, he received four bad cuts to the face, and then he got a nasty bump on the dome and had to be carried off. He returned to the ice in time for the second period, his face buried in plaster to protect the new stitches. Then he was knocked cold twice more, and each time he came to, he was greeted by same sight: someone standing over him with an empty pail of water.

The rough gentlemen of the Victorias had dedicated themselves to showing Shore up, and even though Shore was perfectly capable of dealing with them as he saw fit, he dutifully kept his fists and his stick down. Before the game, Shore had promised the Millionaires' manager, Goldie Smith, that he would avoid penalties at all costs. The genial Smith was the Melville postmaster, and he knew little about hockey (in Shore's opinion), but he thought highly of his rookie who was always on the ice practising for an hour or two before the other players. For this important game, Smith told Shore that he needed to play hockey and not be sitting on the fence, even if it meant that everyone might think he was "yellow."

The contest continued for two five-minute overtime periods, and in the third overtime the heavily plastered Shore dashed down the right wing and cut loose with a shot at McKinnon, the Victoria goaltender. The puck bounced back into play after bulging the twine behind McKinnon. The goal umpire ruled no goal, saying that the puck had hit the outside of the net. The Melville fans were furious and showed signs of devolving into a mob. The umpire was hastily escorted from the building, and someone else was recruited to take his place. When play resumed, Chester Harris, one of Melville's best

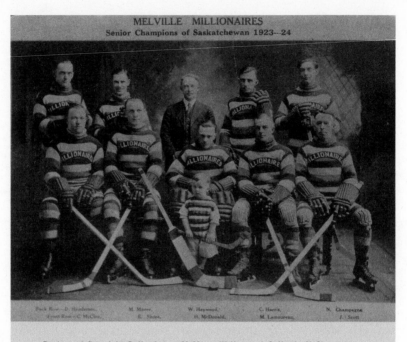

MELVILLE MILLIONAIRES
Senior Champions of Saskatchewan 1923–24

Back row, left to right: D. Henderson, M. Moore, W. Heywood, C. Harris, N. Champagne.
Front row, left to right: C. McCloy, E. Shore, H. McDonald, M. Lamoureux, J. Scott.
Boy in centre: Owen McDonald. *(Courtesy of Edward W. Shore Jr.)*

players, got lucky and had a clear path to the enemy's net. But in his excitement, Harris missed his shot and blew his chance. In the sixth overtime, it was the Victorias who got lucky and, unlike Harris, they made the most of it by sending the puck squarely into the strings of the Melville cage. The Victorias had won the game, and with it the right to advance to the western semifinal.

The Millionaires, if they were to have any chance at all of winning the Allan Cup that year, had to think of something fast. The Victorias' Shorty McNabb, they confided to SAHA officials, did not have an amateur card. The charge was substantiated, and the SAHA stripped the Victorias of their third-game victory and scheduled a make-up match, which the Millionaires handily won, 4–0. The Victorias, stunned by their shocking reversal of fortune, vowed action against Eddie Shore, alleging that he was being paid by the Millionaires, but their accusations went nowhere, and Melville's displacement of Regina as the 1924 Saskatchewan senior champion stood. For the men of Melville, it was on to Alberta to face that province's senior champions, the team from Bellevue, who, by a margin of 6–3, obstinately blocked Melville from advancing to the Allan Cup final. With no more tricks up their sleeves, the Millionaires were forced to accept final defeat. (If it was any consolation for the Millionaires, Bellevue was later bumped from contention; the Allan Cup eventually went to the Sault Ste. Marie Greyhounds.)

The season was over, and Eddie Shore once again sat himself down and gave his situation serious thought. If he was going make it to the pros, he reasoned, he had only a year or two, at most, in which to do it. Otherwise, he warned himself, he would be stuck playing in the bush leagues forever.

That summer, the young man headed west, travelling a thousand bumpy and dusty miles by automobile—an unusual and uncomfortable mode of long-distance travel in those days—to Vancouver, British Columbia. Shore arrived on a very hot, un-hockey-like day, and he set out to find the offices of the Vancouver Maroons, where he intended to ask to see Frank Patrick. This would have taken a lot of guts for a guy like Shore, who had played exactly one year of senior amateur hockey, because Patrick had been a renowned athlete at McGill University in his youth, had played years of professional hockey, had once scored six goals in a single game as a defenceman (at the time, a world record), and was now a savvy businessman of national repute. Frank, along with his older brother, Lester, controlled professional hockey west of Calgary, and he would have had no time to bother with every guy who came off the street thinking he was the greatest thing since Cyclone Taylor.

In their prime, the famous and dashing Patrick brothers had riveted thousands of roaring fans jammed inside packed arenas, while disappointing thousands more outside who could not get in. Their father, Joe Patrick, was, like T.J. Shore, of Irish Protestant stock and a self-made man. In the forested hinterlands of Quebec, Joe Patrick had built himself a fortune from wood. He was a no-nonsense, teetotalling Methodist. When Frank was seven, Joe showed that he had no patience with the finer points of skating instruction by throwing the boy out on the ice. "My immediate reaction was to get up and run on the skates," Frank remembered, "which I did. And that, incidentally, is how I skated throughout my school, college, and professional careers, always more like a sprinter than a skater."

When Frank was an adolescent, his father's business necessitated a family move from Daveluyville, sixty miles west of Quebec City, to bustling Montreal. Joe Patrick found a house in the railway district, where Frank and Lester were swept into the endless games of shinny played on the frozen river—or, when the river ice was too thin, on a vacant lot across from the house which was kindly flooded by the men of the local fire station. Hockey sticks were hacked from tree branches and pucks fashioned from blocks of wood or tin cans. "There is no hockey school on God's earth," Lester would later say, "to match that so innocently contrived by youngsters out on a frozen pond, learning to play by loving to play."

In the early years, before the family moved to Montreal, the Patricks had faced lean times. Potatoes were the mainstay of the evening meal, and family tradition was to dangle a small piece of meat above the table for all to look at as they took a mouthful of potatoes. Those days of poverty were well in the past, however, and as Joe Patrick's relentless commercial successes saw the family move several times to a neighbourhood that was better than the last, the clan ended up in the toniest of them all: the English-speaking suburb of Westmount. There had to have been something in the Westmount water supply, like strychnine or arsenic, because the district turned out some of the toughest hockey players in the world. The Patrick brothers were as tough as nails, and so were the other lads of the neighbourhood, children like the Cleghorn boys, Sprague and Odie; Walter Smaill; or "Mr. Big" himself, the cocky little Art Ross.

Lester Patrick and Art Ross, who were both destined to become Stanley Cup–winning players and managers, displayed their hockey business acumen early by creating a joint venture selling tickets—which they had bought earlier for thirty-five cents—outside the Montreal Arena for two dollars. Lester and Ross would also have the honour of being arrested together for participating in a riot between the French and English factions of the city. The two had seen the hockey sticks swinging and wanted in on the fun.

In 1908, Art Ross graduated from McGill, where he had once scored five goals against Harvard in a single game. After college, following the money trail, as Ross always would, he went on to earn cash as a "ringer" in the days when hockey was supposed to be a strictly amateur affair. He was not the only fraud in the circuit; organized gambling was known to pay even better money to take out a guy who just might be too good for his own good. Ross himself was nearly murdered one night in 1909, while playing against a team in the Colbalt mining region of northern Ontario, where local interests had seventy-five thousand dollars riding on the outcome. Ice goons had been brought in for the occasion and given up to two thousand dollars each to take care of the visitors' better players. Ross, as one of those better players (at a thousand dollars per game), was slashed across the forehead for eighteen stitches, and, before the battle was over, five of his teammates had to be hauled unconscious from the ice.

Unlike Ross, Lester had dropped out of McGill after just one year and, disappointing his father but yearning for adventure, gone west, where he worked in Calgary for the summer before moving to Brandon, Manitoba. There he survived the winter of 1903–04 on twenty-five dollars a month by playing hockey for the local club, the Brandon Wheat Cities. The club did well and, after winning the provincial title, went east to challenge the famed Ottawa Silver Seven in the Stanley Cup final. Lester, age nineteen, played cover-point (one of the two defensive positions of seven-man hockey), and although the Wheat Cities lost to the Silver Seven in the two-game series, Lester's performance was praised by the press as being exemplary.

Joe Patrick, restless after making several fortunes, and hankering after new opportunities, liquidated his Quebec lumber business and moved west to Nelson, British Columbia. There he embarked upon a grand scheme to harvest, with the muscle of imported Quebec labourers, millions of feet of virgin timber and send it south by river to the lucrative markets in the United States. Joe was a shrewd operator, but he was, above all, a family man. Having already moved his wife and the younger members of his large brood to Nelson, now he wanted his two eldest boys, by this time both in their early twenties, to be with him as well. Back east, Lester was holding a day job with a rubber company, while in his off-hours he was captaining the Montreal Wanderers to Stanley Cup wins in 1906 and 1907. Meanwhile, Frank was at McGill, where he was an all-around athlete and captain-elect of the hockey club.

Frank was allowed to finish school, but Lester obeyed his father's command and joined the family business out west. He had no sooner arrived in Nelson, however, than an urgent request for his services arrived from the Edmonton Eskimos. The team's challenge for the Stanley Cup had been accepted, and they were to play a two-game, total-goals affair against the Wanderers in December 1908. Lester agreed to the offer and played for Edmonton against his former team. After the two games, which Edmonton narrowly lost, 13–10, he had a friendly meal at a restaurant with his friend Art Ross, who had taken his old spot on the Wanderers.

"Lester," asked Ross, "how much did they pay you for the series?"

"Just expenses, why?"

"I got four hundred dollars for this series," answered Ross. "In advance. And I was cheated too. [Tommy] Phillips got six hundred from Edmonton and played less than half [a] game."

Ross explained to a surprised Lester that players were now raking in more than a thousand dollars per season, and perhaps this set Lester to thinking that there might one day be a place for legitimate money in the sport. When Lester returned to Nelson, his father asked him how much the Eskimos had given him for travel, meals, and lodging. "One hundred dollars," Lester replied, of which, he said, he had spent sixty-two. "Then," the upright Joe Patrick scolded, "you owe Edmonton thirty-eight dollars." Lester sent the remaining money back to the club, which had to have been astounded.

Frank completed his degree at McGill and joined the lumber company in Nelson, where his father sent him directly into the forest to learn the trade first-hand. Lester remained in town, keeping the books for the company. For both brothers, though, the pull of hockey and the incessant wires from professional clubs (the day of legitimate money had arrived earlier than Lester had expected) begging for their services was too strong a temptation, and they returned east in 1909.

The club that won them over was an extraordinarily well-financed team plunked down in an unlikely little spot, the small town of Renfrew, Ontario. The team, the Millionaires, was part of the new National Hockey Association and owned by a real millionaire named M.J. O'Brien, who had promised Lester three thousand dollars and Frank two thousand for the twelve-game NHA season. Lester thought the pay obscenely high, yet the money he and his brother were getting was nothing compared to what one of their teammates earned. This was the young but already fantastic Cyclone Taylor, who once wagered that he could skate through an opposing team backwards and score a goal (and won the bet). Taylor was paid five thousand dollars by O'Brien for his dozen games, which worked out to seven dollars a minute, which even by today's standards is pretty good pay.

Taylor's fame and compensation made him a target both on and off the ice. Once, he was sandwiched between two opponents and, falling over, hit his head on the ice. A rival fan yelled out at Taylor, "Get up! You're nothing but a chicken-livered, gutless coward!" Frank Patrick, who remembered the tirade well, said, "There was a lot more, all of it rotten, and I saw red. Taylor, as courageous a player as I've ever known, lay there perhaps very badly hurt, with this maniac baying obscenities at him. I skated to the screen, lifted my stick and let the pest have the butt-end right in the face. The blood gushed out of his nose and spurted over the boards, and the fellow just slid down out of view."

There would be no professional hockey for the Patrick brothers in 1910–11 because their father managed to keep them at work in Nelson while he arranged to sell the lumber company to an English syndicate for $440,000. Joe Patrick had once again made a fortune, and he shared the money with his sons, giving them $25,000 each.

Lester and Frank were suddenly rich, and their father suddenly had nothing to do except count his change, and so the next steps for the three men were obvious: to move to Vancouver; to build the world's largest, and most modern, indoor ice arena there for $210,000; to construct a smaller, but similarly modern, arena in Victoria for $110,000; to begin a new professional hockey league that would be the world's best; to add a third team representing New Westminster, with plans for a third arena to be built there; to invite hockey clubs in Edmonton and Calgary to join the new league; to raid the NHA of all its best players; and to accomplish all this in less than twelve months.

There was no time to waste. In Victoria, the Patricks put down $10,000 for land on which to build a 4,000-seat building, while in Vancouver they paid $27,000 for prime real estate on which to construct a 10,500-seat giant, large enough to accommodate more than 10 per cent of the city's population. Winters were too mild along the B.C. coast to rely on naturally frozen ice, so the Patricks adopted the system used in New York's famous St. Nicholas rink, where refrigerated coolant was piped under the playing surface to create an "artificial" surface. Despite the soundness of their business plan, when the family invited others to become part owners in the enterprise, the response, mysteriously, was a mere $5,000. The Patricks found this so insulting that Joe returned the money and took out a $100,000 mortgage so that the family could pay for everything itself.

Forging ahead, Lester and Frank readily accepted their own terms to play in the Pacific Coast Hockey Association, the name that they had chosen for their league, and then lured other top talent, including Newsy Lalonde, Walter Smaill, Tom Phillips, and, eventually, Cyclone Taylor, from an irate NHA to join them. The league opener, January 3, 1912, in Vancouver, was played in front of a disappointingly small crowd of just 2,300, and attendance grew only slightly as the season progressed. Still, remarkably, the PCHA lost only $9,000 that first year. After this inauspicious start, the Patricks' league quickly grew in stature, and the Stanley Cup, which had begun life as a challenge trophy, became the prize awarded to the winner of a yearly bout between the champions of the PCHA and NHA.

By the time Shore came calling in the summer of 1924, however, the Patricks, despite their many hockey successes (their league won the Cup in 1915 and 1917) and innovations (including the penalty shot and the red light above the goal), had failed in their efforts to establish the big-league game on the west coast. Their rival, now called the National Hockey League, with its base in the large metropolises of the east, was paying its players salaries the Patricks could never hope to match. Seeking shelter, Lester and Frank had given up their league's independence and merged it with the Western Canada Hockey League for 1924–25.

Once he had located the offices of the Vancouver Maroons, Eddie had some difficulty in the waiting room. It seemed there was a local ordinance that prohibited an honest fellow from being able walk in off the street to meet with the owner of a hockey club. Shore, however, was not to be dissuaded, and he put forth his case with such tenacity and persistence that it nearly drove Frank Patrick's secretary mad. Shore was shown in to see the big boss.

"Frank kept getting up and sitting down," Shore recalled. "He would walk a few steps, look at me, puff at his cigarette and sit down." Shore told Patrick that he wanted to play for the Maroons. "He didn't seem impressed," Shore recalled, but Shore turned on the talk and boasted to Patrick that he could equal any player in the league. "I told him I could play better than Gizzy Hart, who was then with Lester in Victoria, and that I'd like a trial." Patrick, who had a gift for sarcasm, and also the odd habit of blowing the ash off the end of his cigarette, responded to Shore's modesty by shrugging his shoulders and blowing some ashes Shore's way. Patrick then patiently explained that the Maroons did not play hockey in the middle of a heat wave, plus they did not pay money for guys to try out. Shore all but pleaded for a chance, saying that if he was allowed to give it a shot with the Maroons in the fall, he would do so for free and without a contract. Patrick could only reply wearily that if Shore happened to be in Vancouver when training started, "he'd," as Shore remembered the conversation, "look me over." The interview ended for Shore in frustration; for Frank Patrick, it ended in watching destiny walk right out the door.

Shore knew he would have no money for a return trip to Vancouver in the fall, especially as nothing of substance had been promised him by Patrick, so he attempted to hook up with the Calgary Tigers, also of the WCHL. The Tigers, though, failed to bite, and a dejected Eddie Shore returned to Saskatchewan. Meanwhile, Melville's postmaster, Goldie Smith, had convinced Wes Champ, owner and manager of the WCHL's Regina Capitals, to give Shore a look, telling him that if he did, he would not be disappointed. Champ invited Shore to do some practice skating with the Capitals on beautiful Wascana Lake, Regina's natural jewel in the heart of the city. It was early November and the ice was of questionable strength; passersby were shocked to see the hockey men on it so early in the season.

The Caps enjoyed the practices, and they also enjoyed pushing the new kid around, knowing that he was just a cowardly Millionaire on account of his yellow performance in last year's third Allan Cup playoff game against the Victorias. They also knew that Shore was the only amateur trying out for the team, meaning that if he made the payroll, Wes Champ would let one of them go.

Eddie was subjected to some terrific roughing, and every

practice left him black and blue and sore from head to toe. The treatment initially puzzled him, but then he caught on and retaliated with a ferocity rarely seen on placid Wascana Lake. It was once said of Shore that he could do to a man what a leap into the spokes of a thirty-foot flywheel could also do. In short order, Shore had set every single one of his mates straight, and they rapidly changed their tune when it came to dealing with the new kid.

On December 8, 1924, Eddie Shore, age twenty-two, saw his first professional hockey game. It was in Saskatoon—the Sheiks vs. the Regina Capitals—and Shore was dressed for the event in a striped red and white sweater that made him look like a human barber pole. He had signed a thousand-dollar contract with Champ for the season and was there to play as last substitute for the Caps. Dick Irvin, the hockey hero he had read about while in school, was now, unbelievably, a teammate. Along with Irvin, five of the other nine Capitals that year—Amby Moran, George Hay, Art Gagne, Rabbit McVeigh, and Puss Traub, were destined to join Shore in the NHL. But Shore did not know this then; all he knew was that he had finally made pro and, exactly as he had told Aubrey he would, had done so in five years.

The Capitals were given two good drubbings by the Sheiks in their first two games, and Shore got the first two penalties of his professional career. In Saskatoon, it was a 5–2 loss for the Caps, and then, at their home opener at the Regina Stadium, it was a humiliating 5–0 defeat. The Caps continued losing, and they took their beatings bravely—so bravely, in fact, that Wes Champ promised, as an early Christmas present to himself, he would trade away each and every one of them. The Caps turned things around and went on to crush the Edmonton Eskimos 7–0, and in that rout Shore both assisted on a goal and scored a goal unassisted.

The following game was in Calgary, where the Tigers' stalwart defensive duo, Mervyn "Red" Dutton and Herb Gardiner, played no favourites when it came to body-checking, and they gave the rookie the works. "We dropped him a dozen times," Dutton later said admiringly of Shore. "The forwards combed him with cross checks. We rode him every time he came down but he came back like a bull." In hostile Calgary, Shore caught the fancy of the capacity crowd. The new man had rosy cheeks, he had pluck, and he was full of fight. According to the correspondent for the Regina *Morning Leader,* "Dutton and Gardiner had Shore sprawling the ice time and again but the big fellow seemed to like it, for he never faltered under the heaviest fire, and always came up for more. Shore, in the opinion of this writer, is the most promising prospect that has broken into pro hockey since the organization of the WCHL, even better than Gizzy Hart of the Victoria Cougars, as he not only can stand the bombardment such as handed out by Dutton and Gardiner, but can give some himself."

Confident from their wins in Edmonton and Calgary, the Capitals strutted into the Regina Stadium on December 27 and promptly lost to Lester Patrick's Victoria Cougars, 5–0. Two days later, they lost a closer contest to Frank Patrick's Vancouver Maroons, 6–5. Shore's play was stellar, and Frank asked Wes Champ, "Who is that new guy you got there? I've seen him somewhere before this." Following their losses to the Patricks, the Capitals went on to lose still more games to enter the WCHL cellar, from which they would never emerge. The fans of the Caps, however, did have at least something to cheer about, and that was Eddie Shore. "The galloping cowboy," they called him, a player who never let league standings get in the way of his skating over somebody.

Champ promoted the rookie to a regular substitute position on right wing, and there he shamelessly robbed pucks from opponents and, by the end of the season, had scored six goals. Shore's shooting was fairly rudimentary, but he was able to launch the disc high and fast or send it in low and slow, and he once even fooled the brilliant goaltender George Hainsworth into letting his shot slide by. Shore may have lacked style and combination tricks, but he occasionally demonstrated a flashy move that would be remembered as the "big play" of the night. Sometimes he was even the Caps' best man on the ice, the spark plug who could get the team going again, and he would join with Puss Traub and Abbie Newell to add a world of punch to the Capitals' offence. On defence, which he also played, he was equally effective. He put up a bulwark that was not easily outguessed by opponents, and when he steamed into action, he was a thorn in the side of the league's best stars, men like Frank Fredrickson, stripping them of their effectiveness. Shore did not play the Sunday-school brand of hockey, and his face bore witness to this fact by often being freshly stitched up and decorated with green plaster. Always aggressive, Shore spent seventy-five minutes in the penalty box that season, and there were not many others in the league who could make such a claim.

The Capitals, with no chance of making the playoffs, lost their last game after ten defeats in a row. Fittingly, the final contest was disrupted when a dog wandered out onto the ice.

The dismal season now ended, Shore returned to the Melville train yards and Wes Champ withdrew the Capitals from the WCHL, thus ending big-league hockey in Regina for all time. Champ put his men up for sale, and Pete Muldoon, manager of the Portland Rosebuds, bought them in bulk, although he could not sign Shore, who held out for an additional five hundred dollars, which was two hundred more than Muldoon would agree to.

In Edmonton, Alberta, the big-league game also appeared destined for extinction when, with the 1925–26 Western Hockey League (as it was now being called) season about to commence, the owners of the Eskimos, together with manager Kenny Mackenzie and captain Duke Keats, announced plans to relocate the franchise. On a Saturday night, local boosters of the "blubber eaters," as the Eskimos were fondly nicknamed, met in strength to show their support. Not since its days as a Hudson's Bay Company trading post had such an enthusiastic meeting been held in Edmonton, and the fans pledged ten thousand dollars' worth of Eskimos ticket reservations. The gesture did not leave Mackenzie and Keats unmoved, and they announced that the "Esks" were not going anywhere. Mackenzie now had to find himself some hockey players, and his partner Keats had a suggestion regarding one candidate.

"I'd been worked over by some pretty good ones in my time," Keats recalled years afterwards, "but there was this little guy from Regina who didn't play much, but when he did, he gave it to me good. I told my partner Ken Mackenzie, 'Get that little runt. I want him on our club.'" Pete Muldoon still owned "that little runt," and so Mackenzie offered to take Shore off his hands in return for an Eskimo, Bob Trapp. The deal was made, and Mackenzie prepared to wire his new player, wherever he might be, enough money to get him to Edmonton in time for training camp.

The few Eskimos who had been signed so far began holding snappy workouts in the outdoor rink on 121st Street, and by November 30, the ice at the Edmonton Civic Arena had at last set and practices could be held there. The WHL season was already well under way, however, and the Eskimos still did not have enough players to hold a proper scrimmage. Mackenzie went on an expedition searching for more men. Eddie, for one, was nowhere to be found, and without the budding Regina star, hockey experts in Edmonton noted glumly, the Eskimos' chances were looking none too good. Then Mackenzie, with not a day to spare, returned home, accompanied by Shore, now safely signed to an Eskimos contract. "Mackenzie," according to the newspapers, "had to go as far as Minneapolis to round up this bird."

Thanks to the summer exercise regime provided free of charge by the Canadian National Railway, Shore, who had just turned twenty-three and had probably been in Minneapolis angling for a hockey job, was rail thin and worn out. Shore's diminished physical condition, though, was not obvious, and Edmonton sports reports were breathless in their enthusiasm. "Eddie Shore, the big husky player," one of them wrote after an Eskimos practice, "was on hand for the first time—and this gent will do, mark that down on your cuff. Shore uncorked a great burst of speed, stick-handled well, and was dead on target with his shots."

Mackenzie had, at the last minute, pulled a major-league hockey team out of a hat, and it was an impressive assemblage of talent. There was Duke Keats at centre, Art Gagne at right wing, Barney Stanley at left wing, Eddie Shore at right defence, Johnny Sheppard at left defence, and, in goal, Herb Stuart. (All six were destined for the NHL, although the chunky Stuart only played a few games for Detroit.)

The Eskimos' first game resulted in a narrow loss in Saskatoon against the Sheiks. Managed by the legendary Newsy Lalonde, the Saskatoon team contained an embarrassment of hockey riches. The Sheiks had no less than Cy Denneny, the brothers Bun and Bill Cook, Fred Gordon, and George Hainsworth on their roster. It was slushy going in Saskatoon, and Shore was not a favourite with the home crowd—or with Lalonde's crew, either. Every Sheik felt it his duty to take a crack at the new Eskimo, and they did everything they could to intimidate him, but he would not be intimidated. "Shore," reporter George Macintosh said, "has plenty of the stuff violin strings are made of." In order to prove this, Shore and his linemate Johnny "The Fighting Midget" Sheppard stepped into opposing forwards with utmost abandon.

A week later, at their home opener in Edmonton, the Esks again lost to the Sheiks, and Shore received a major penalty for taking a belt at Bill Cook with his stick after the two had exchanged bumps. The Eskimos' losing streak ended with their third game, a rousing 9–5 victory over the Vancouver Maroons. In the dressing room afterwards, the Eskimos broke into song, belting out "On Top of the World."

Accolades for Shore came quickly. In a game that saw the Eskimos beat Victoria, a Cougar by the name of Clem Loughlin had swung his hickory like a meat chopper down on Art Gagne's head, but that event, sensational as it was, was not the news of the game. The big story was "Eddie Shore bursting into the spotlight with a goal that fairly sparkled. Breaking up a rush at the blue line, Shore tore through the Cougars on a swerving rush that left all his opponents—and most of the spectators—dizzy, and finished by blasting a shot past Holmes that that cool customer hasn't seen yet."

Shore was soon known to zigzag down the ice on a raid and wind himself around defenders like a piece of tape. He could also fly down the ice as straight and as fleet of foot as an arrow shot from a powerful longbow. Shore was there and back, covering more territory in one period than most forwards did in an entire game, even though he was a defenceman. Shore's body had now filled out to make him bulky as well as muscular, and his hockey skills had become noticeably more sophisticated. Shore blocked well, he seldom lost possession of the puck, and he passed with good judgment. In every corner of the league, all eyes were on Mackenzie's amazing find. The young man was described by the Edmonton press as being "one of the brightest hockey gems that ever sparkled in western Canada," and his play "fairly glistened with brilliance." Shore's defensive ability, combined with his never-tiring aggressiveness, caused him to be picked by the sports press as one of the stars of the WHL. Under no circumstances did Shore ever wilt, and he withstood checks that sent him clear over his war club and into the boards. He survived sticks wrapped around his head that laid him out flat, and which would have killed a lesser man. During an Eskimos trip to the west coast, Shore's talents were on display during games against Vancouver and Victoria, and he earned himself the highest praise in both cities. In fact, Shore wowed them wherever he went, leaving folks talking about him for weeks afterwards.

The Edmonton fans, of course, thought the world of Eddie. In their opinion, he was the wildest and woolliest cowhand to ever lace up a pair of skates. Breaking up an attack, the galloping cowboy would circle his own net with the puck and then thunder off for the other end of the rink. Rounding check after check dished out by opponents, and leaving them all in turn as if they were standing still, Shore would split the defensive combination wide open and then, racing through the gap, and without slowing up for an instant, would fake the opposing goaltender out of position, smash the puck down the alley, and score. It was the kind of play that made the crowd in Edmonton leap up and holler as Shore leisurely skated back to his blue line, the noise sweet music to his ears. One reporter for the *Edmonton Journal* was so enraptured by Shore that he was moved to write verse: "It's been Shore, Shore, Shore / The boy who shows defencemen how to score / You can hear the foemen crackling / When young Edward is attacking / And the writhing, pop-eyed fans begin to roar."

In Edmonton, the young hockey star was readily accepted into the city's sporting fraternity, and, when not playing hockey, he would enjoy nights out on the town with friends. Once, Eddie and company went to see a Commercial Grads women's basketball game, which the Grads won. The Grads *always* won: their last defeat had been three years earlier, and over the past decade they had lost only four times. After the game, Shore met one of the players, Kate Macrae. She was a Scottish-born woman from Glasgow who had come to Canada with her family at age five in 1910. Kate was soft spoken, very confident, trim,

Kate Macrae in 1928. Women's basketball was not an Olympic event that year, but Macrae and the Edmonton Commercial Grads travelled to Amsterdam to play against men's Olympic basketball teams. *(Courtesy of Edward W. Shore Jr.)*

of about Eddie's height, and, like him, was a fantastic athlete. She was fast making a name for herself through her aggressive play, and that first encounter between the city's two young sports stars evidently sparked something, because within a few years, when Eddie was finally able to make enough money in the puck game to buy a house and some land just outside of Edmonton, the couple would get married.

In early March, when moderate temperatures had begun to melt the Civic Arena ice down to the sawdust, there was a mishap during the Eskimos' morning practice. "Bobby Benson was playing defence," Shore explained, "and as I came down the ice I tried to step around him and he hooked my skate and I went into the boards with my right leg under me. When I hit the boards my right skate went into my left leg. The skate was buried there—the worst slash I ever remembered." Luckily, no tendons had been cut, but fourteen stitches were required above Shore's left knee joint to close the wound. The doctors ordered him not to play hockey for six months.

Shortly afterwards, a train belching thick black smoke sped through some of the most awe-inspiring scenery in the world, carrying the Eskimos from the prairie to the Pacific coast for their Stanley Cup playoff appointment with Lester Patrick's Cougars, the defending Cup champions. The Eskimos had been forced to leave behind in Edmonton one of their own, Bobby Boucher, who had come down with a serious case of blood poisoning. "But what was more alarming" for the Eskimos, the press explained, "was the condition of their defensive star." At the Edmonton station, Shore had boarded the train—on crutches—directly from the hospital, and "was evidently suffering severe pain."

A rather weary looking Shore with three of his fellow "Esks." Left to right: Eddie Shore, Art Gagne, Barney Stanley, and Duke Keats. *(Courtesy of the Glenbow Museum, Calgary.)*

The wound had become infected, and it was all Shore could do to get his trouser leg over the swelling. Upon arrival in Vancouver, Shore went straight to the hospital to have a new dressing applied, and afterwards he hobbled up the gangway of a ship for the journey to Victoria for that night's game.

Leaning on his crutches, Shore moved slowly around the deck, trying to limber up the leg. It was hopeless. While Shore looked forlornly out to sea, he was greeted by an Edmonton man who was a doctor—and a rabid hockey enthusiast.

"Got to play tonight, Eddie."

"Yeah, but how?" Shore answered.

"Put the foot down and start walking," advised the doctor.

"So's your old man," was Shore's comeback.

Two of Shore's teammates, Art Gagne and Johnny Sheppard, joined Shore on deck. Like the good doctor from Edmonton, they wanted to get Shore exercising his bad leg. Gagne and Sheppard meant well, and their plan was as simple as it was crude.

"How's it coming, Eddie; make it all right?" asked Gagne.

"Yeah, I guess so, after a little time," said Shore.

"Well, we'll help you, Eddie. Here, let's see your crutches a minute."

"I wonder if a crutch would float," said Gagne when he got the crutches.

"Yeah?" asked Shore. "Well it might, but you don't need to try it."

"Aw, let's try it," urged Sheppard, and with that, Gagne tossed both crutches overboard.

"You've got enough stuff to walk even without any legs, Eddie," Gagne said in all honesty, "let alone crutches."

Shore was left staggering around on deck, and when the referee's whistle blew that evening, Shore was not in Kenny Mackenzie's lineup because he was still in the dressing room, having a large dose of painkillers shot into the gaping wound, which was now gushing gore. When Shore emerged onto the ice two minutes after the game had started, the Cougars gave him a rough ride. Eddie's condition was no secret, and Lester Patrick's men made sure to aim for the damaged leg. The stitches began to pop out, and Shore's canvas pants and woollen socks were soon soaked in blood, but he refused to come off the ice. Characteristically, every time the Cougars ripped into him, he only played harder. Although to the spectators, sitting comfortably in their seats, the injury did not appear to bother Shore any, his effectiveness as a player was compromised, and without his firepower the Eskimos went down to a 3–1 defeat. After the game, Shore blamed himself for the outcome.

A crowd of more than ten thousand awaited the start of the Eskimos' "home" game, which was held in Vancouver on March 22, 1926, as it would have taken the two teams too long to travel back to Edmonton. With less than forty-eight hours to recuperate from being the bull to Patrick's matadors, it was not certain whether Shore should risk another fight. A doctor in Vancouver told him that if he was crazy enough to play, he could lose the limb. Shore replied that that he knew that, but he had to help his teammates out somehow. Upon seeing Shore take to the ice, the Vancouver fans rose up and howled, and for sixty minutes Shore dove into the teeth of the Cougars in rush after rush. With his help, the Eskimos tied the game 2–2 at the end of three periods. Because of the total-goals format, however, the Cougars won the series, 5–3. Back in Edmonton, the losers were mobbed by their appreciative fans, and no one was the people's favourite more than the battered Eddie Shore, who looked to reporters "like a man who was not absolutely fit." This was true, and Shore's next move was to go to hospital.

While Shore was convalescing in early April, the Montreal Maroons snatched the Stanley Cup from the former champions, defeating the Cougars three games to one in a best-of-five series. It was an ignominious ending for Patrick's men, and it was also the last time a non-NHL team would vie for

Lord Stanley's rose bowl. The era of National Hockey League dominance had arrived.

During the summer of 1926, Kenny Mackenzie was non-committal about pro hockey returning to Edmonton in the fall. Only the playoffs, Mackenzie complained, had prevented the Eskimos from going into the hole financially. The problem facing Mackenzie and every WHL club was that the Canadian west, with its vast distances and small cities, could not support the big-money game, and no one knew this better than the Patrick brothers. They gave it another two seasons, at most, before the WHL would be forced to fold, and with no intention of waiting around for this to happen, the brothers easily convinced their fellow owners to close up shop.

Eddie Shore was once again without a team. His horse had been shot out from under him for the second time in two years, and, discharged from the hospital but still limping badly, he went back to his job shovelling coal for pennies an hour on the freight trains of the CNR.

THREE

===

CHARLES F. ADAMS, the owner and president of the Boston Bruins, shuffled out onto the soft, black ice to receive the presents: two bear cubs given to him by the loyal employees of his First National Stores, which, as advertised, was "New England's Own Grocery Chain." A balcony built to satisfy the public's hunger for hockey was a new addition to the Boston Arena this year, but tonight's season opener, November 16, 1926, was still sold out. Under the dim lights, a packed crowd of eight thousand, already wet from the rain outside and now sweating from the heat and humidity inside, cheered wildly. The presentation over with, the music from Win Green's band died down and Mr. Adams and the bewildered cubs left the ice to go their separate ways.

The first period was filled with the brutal stuff Boston fans had come to love, and Bruins Billy Coutu and Sprague

Cleghorn, both of them fighting types and former captains of tonight's opponents, the Montreal Canadiens, did not disappoint: the referee, Dr. Jerry Laflamme, promptly chased both to the penalty box for their misdeeds.

The red-shirted Canadiens launched repeated attacks, and Montreal's star player, Howie Morenz, made terrific runs at the Boston cage, but it was the Bruins that scored first. Percy Galbraith, a war veteran recently introduced to Bostonians as "a great wing, a big man," had come out of a Minnesota amateur club to earn his first NHL goal only minutes into the second period. Galbraith had sped past Montreal's fabulous winger, Aurèle Joliat, wormed his way by the Canadiens' outer defencemen, and whipped the disc into the strings behind their ace goalie, George Hainsworth. The crowd yelled itself hoarse and, moments later, yelled itself hoarse again when the goal umpire's flag was raised for a second time. This happened when the Bruins' Lionel Hitchman abandoned his defensive position and burned a shot at Hainsworth. Hainsworth managed to block but not clear, and Bruins winger Carson Cooper, a wicked driver of the puck, was in perfect position to gain the Boston lead, 2–0.

The furious Frenchmen increased their slashing and roughing, the Bruins responded in kind, and a virtual parade of players was delegated by Laflamme's whistle to the penalty box. Morenz partially redeemed the Canadiens by dashing in alone past Hitchman, closing in at speed on the Bruins' tiny goaltender, Dr. Charles Stewart (like Laflamme, a dentist), and, at the very last second, neatly jumping the puck over Stewart's stick to score.

By the third period, play was increasingly difficult due to

the heat, the melting ice, and low-hanging tobacco smoke so thick that it gagged the fans, Bruins, and Canadiens alike. Visibility had deteriorated to the point where, from the upper seats, it was hard to tell the two teams apart, or even to read the NO FAST SKATING sign, posted for the benefit of public sessions, along the boards. In his citadel at the west end of the rink, Hainsworth was completely enveloped in smog.

Into the murk, Cooper whizzed a long shot in Hainsworth's direction, and the goal umpire deemed it valid, but those in the press box, peering through the smoke, could not honestly tell whether the puck had landed against the curtain or not. Canadiens coach Cecil Hart was outraged by the playing conditions and vowed a protest to NHL president Frank Calder.

With fifteen minutes to go in the game, Cooper made a bid for his third goal, while Eddie Shore, a new man for Boston and someone who struck a local sports reporter as being "a heavy, husky, fiery chap," held possession of the puck. With not yet three full periods as a Bruin behind him, Shore, despite playing right defence, had already proven his ability to make, as the reporter put it, "opposing defenses look like whipped cream." Shore had "caught the fancy of the fans. The new defense man is tall," the reporter wrote, "yet sturdily built. His speed for a man weighing 190 pounds is exceptional and he handles both his body and his stick well. He is aggressive and quite agreeable to giving and taking the body bumps."

Shore retained hold of the disc and Joliat bore down on him to deliver, it was reported, "the hardest check of the night right at mid-ice and Eddie of Saskatoon went up in the air a yard or two and landed on his third vertebrae." A second before that, however, Shore had managed to move the puck toward the Canadiens net, and there "Dead Eye" Cooper met the rubber and put a shot past Hainsworth before the goaltender knew what had happened. The goal gave the Bruins the win, and a delirious horde emptied out of the Arena and onto Huntington Avenue.

Following Shore's introduction to Boston on that sultry night, the Bruins' manager, Lester Patrick's old friend Art Ross, thought he saw offensive potential in the man from Saskatchewan; and so, for the game against the Montreal Maroons in Boston a week later, Ross decided to bring Shore up to right wing. The contest commenced, and the action, as it always was with the Maroons, was dirty. Inevitably, there were casualties. The Bruins' Lionel Hitchman was one of the first to go, leaving the game with a leg injury and a cut over one eye. Then the Bruins' Red Stuart suffered a split lip, Montreal's Harry "Punch" Broadbent made for the dressing room to have his head patched up, and, thanks to some heavy-handed stick work by Boston's Sprague Cleghorn, an unconscious Merlyn Phillips had to be rushed off to the visitors' dressing room, trailing a stream of blood. The assault on Phillips was a little much even for Arena fans, and Cleghorn was booed lustily.

The game wore on and the Bruins, ragged from their first road trip, which had taken them to Detroit and Chicago in the past few days, began to falter. Ross decided to return Shore to the blue line. Back where he belonged, the defenceman, paradoxically, became an offensive threat once more. The crowd gave the big westerner a standing ovation, and, it was reported, "he made numerous dashes down the ice, showing speed and stamina, fine stick handling and rare judgment. On two of those rushes he passed the puck directly in front of the

Maroons cage, from points close up, but in neither instance was a teammate able to send it home." Finally, the Bruins managed to count on a Shore-inspired charge, and although not a fortnight had passed since his inaugural game, he became the favourite of local fandom. "The Boston fans didn't know hockey in those days," Charles F. Adams recalled, "but you didn't have to know hockey to get delirious over Shore."

That previous summer, when the WHL had gone bust, Adams had offered to buy the league roster, sight unseen, but he was not the only man in the NHL looking for former WHL talent, and the competition was intense. Tex Rickard, the boxing promoter and builder of Madison Square Garden, and his business partner, Colonel John Hammond, had just bought rights for New York's second NHL franchise, and they needed twelve players by the first game of the 1926–27 season. Then there was Bill Dwyer, who owned the original New York NHL franchise, the Americans; his illicit gains from bootlegging gave Dwyer the means to outbid Adams. There was also the anglophone elite of Montreal, whose money and influence had established the Maroons, and who could, and did, spend lavishly on their club. In addition, Adams faced competition from syndicates that had just bought NHL rights to Chicago and Detroit, who, like Rickard and Hammond, were looking to staff entire teams.

And so, after the breakup of the WHL, it had been a summer of unseemly squabbling in the east, as rich men fought like children over the hockey spoils of the west. When it was all over, Adams had failed to corner the market, but he and his manager, Art Ross, were probably satisfied that fifty thousand dollars had bought them Victoria's Frank Fredrickson,

Calgary's Harry Oliver, Edmonton's Duke Keats, and that other Edmonton player, Eddie Shore. The players, however, would not see anything like fifty thousand dollars in salaries. While it is not known how much Shore made in his first season as a Bruin, it was not enough, as he turned to the pool halls of Boston to make his real income. Fredrickson was so insulted by the offer he got that he refused to sign with the Bruins at all, and somehow finagled a contract with Detroit instead.

The Bruins' training camp prior to the 1926–27 NHL season had been a short, two-week, loosely run affair, reflecting the Art Ross philosophy that the strong will survive and others will die, and the players would sort it out themselves. Shore joined practice a few days late, on November 3, just twelve days before the first game against the Canadiens. The twenty-three-year-old brought with him to Boston few possessions other than a saxophone and, the Boston *Evening Transcript*'s A. Linde Fowler later remembered, "a reputation of being afraid of nothing."

Like Shore, Billy Coutu was a right defenceman and new to the Bruins, having come in a trade from the Canadiens. Unlike Shore, however, who was tough when he had to be, Coutu was simply vicious, and had earned notoriety for his role in a 1923 rampage at Montreal's Mount Royal Arena. The trouble had occurred during a game between the Senators and Canadiens, who were bitter rivals, that would determine which team would go on to the Stanley Cup final. From the first minute of play, Coutu and his partner in crime on defence, Sprague Cleghorn, assaulted any and all Ottawa players they could get their hands on. Courtesy of those two, the game quickly degenerated into a bloody farce. Coutu and Cleghorn, though, thrived in this kind of environment, and they saved their best for last. This came in the third period, when Cleghorn butt-ended Ottawa's Lionel Hitchman, knocking Hitchman out cold, and Coutu brought his stick down hard on Cy Denneny's head, felling Denneny and leaving him semi-conscious. As Denneny was carried off ice for stitches, Coutu, for some reason, went berserk, and his craziness spread to the other players. Soon, fights broke out everywhere, and then, like a flash fire, the madness jumped the boards and roared high into the stands. In an instant, there was complete pandemonium, as spectators in a blind fury poured onto the ice to get the referee, Lou Marsh, but slipped and fell all over each other. Marsh managed to skate to safety.

Coutu, an aging thirty-four-year-old in his tenth NHL season, knew that Shore was a threat and decided to do every-thing he could to prevent the westerner from making the club. Shore, though, who had survived similar treatment on Lake Wascana at the hands of the Regina Capitals, knew the score. "Hockey needs the constant infusion of new vigorous blood," Shore later explained. "Well, the youth eventually crowds out the veteran, doesn't he? And the old timer is desperately trying to hang on. He can hang on if he can retard the success of the kid. So some of the veterans very adroitly take care of the kid, by which I mean they aim to break his chances." Coutu was one of these veterans, and in training camp he sized up both Shore and another (unknown) rookie. "Coutu seized every chance he got to rough us under cover," Shore said. "He actu-ally broke the heart of my kid pal—made him quit the game." But not Shore. "I took what I had to take for a long time. Then it was a fight to the finish between that old timer and myself."

Ross was putting his men through a hectic workout one December morning, a month into the NHL season, when Shore and Coutu began bumping each other good and hard. It quickly turned ugly, and the other Bruins gave the combatants a wide berth. Coutu repeatedly lined Shore up for a smashing charge, and Shore repeatedly crashed into Coutu with sickening force. Shore would not back down, and Coutu, aiming to break Shore once and for all, skated to one end of the ice and flew forward in a bull-like rush. Shore knew how to deal with untamed animals, and he was ready for this one. As Coutu came towards him, he crouched down at the last second and pushed into his adversary with all his weight, power, and speed. The collision sent Coutu bouncing backwards, in Shore's estimation, "about eight feet." Coutu fell to the ice and then "got up and sank down, got up again, and went down again. This time he stayed there." Unlike his challenger, Shore was still upright on the blades of his skates—and, more important, "I knew that I was sticking around."

The victor, however, did not emerge from the encounter unscathed. Shore was bleeding profusely because Coutu's head "had smashed into my ear and torn it off. There was just a little piece of skin holding it on." The ear, Shore was told by team physician, Dr. Joe Shortell, could not be reattached. Shore wanted a second opinion, so he had the Bruins' trainer tape the dangling flesh and cartilage to his neck and apply some ice. Then, Shore put on his street clothes and went out looking for another physician. It was eleven o'clock in the morning.

Shore made the rounds of the medical offices in the city. "They all said just what the doctor told me," he later recalled. "It was not possible to save the ear. Just before office hours for the day ended, I ran across a fellow who was more encouraging. He asked me what type of anesthetic I wanted. I told him just to give me a small mirror. That way, I could watch the kind of stitching he did. I made him change the very last stitch. If I had not done that, he'd have left a scar. I told him I was just a farm boy who did not want his looks messed up."

By late December, the weather had turned bitterly cold and the soft, bumpy Arena ice of November had given way to a surface that was granite hard and marble smooth. The air inside the arena was no less frigid than outside, and the cold was a tonic to the Bruins. They tore loose against the visiting Pittsburgh Pirates, firing unceasingly at the net, and after sixty minutes had scored three unanswered goals. In terms of Stanley Cup contention, the thinking among the Boston sports press was that this year, the team, with players like Shore, "bids fair to be right up there."

Hockey had taken a firm hold in Boston, where the professional game was only in its third year, and the Arena continued to boast one overcapacity crowd after another, each more violently enthusiastic than the last. Games often became near riots, and anything that met with the fans' disfavour brought forth all manner of truck onto the ice: paper programs, bottles, eggs, pennies, fragments of wood, and, in a much-remarked-upon incident, a chair.

The season progressed, and the Bruins began climbing to the top of the American Division. Ross was a disciple of well-oiled combination play, and preached to his squad to labour seamlessly as a whole. But one of the new players preferred to work alone. In Toronto, Shore grabbed the puck down by his own net, whizzed solo up the ice at great speed, broke through the St. Pats' defence, blasted one at the goal, and then, one reporter wrote, "piled into the net on top of the goalie with the puck against the strings. It was a brilliant dash." During a game in New York, he acted alone once more, speeding through the opposition and firing a bullet-like drive at goalie Lorne Chabot, who caught the puck in his face and was cut badly. On another solo effort the same night, Shore was luckier. He flew up ice, tricked his way through the New Yorkers, neared Chabot, and, this time, avoided the goalie and punched the puck into the net to count.

The Boston press noted that Shore "'hogged the rubber" and failed "to vary his attack, that is, pass occasionally," but the crowds at the Arena, yelling like mad each time he appeared poised to begin one of his fantastic drives from deep in the Bruins end, could not get enough of the man from Saskatchewan. A spectacularly pretty attack occurred late in the final period of a contest against Detroit when, for the winning goal, "Eddie Shore made a brilliant romp up the ice, swung completely around the Cougars' cage and snapped home the puck before he could be covered or goalie Harry Holmes get any idea of just where the puck was coming [from]."

Eddie Shore and the Montreal Maroons would always have special feelings towards one another, and the start of this long but troubled relationship can perhaps be dated to Shore's first major NHL infraction. It was in Montreal, at the Forum, during a late December game, and in the second period play had become rough. Sprague Cleghorn and Merlyn Phillips had earlier gotten into fisticuffs, and a shot by Harry Broadbent had banged the Bruins' little goaltender, Dr. Charles Stewart, over the eye. It took the doc some minutes to regain consciousness before he could resume his place between the pipes. Then, one minute before the end of the second period, the recovering dentist had just caught a shot that had been driven in by a Maroon when, suddenly, another Stewart (no relation), this one the Maroons' lazy and lethal Nels "Poison" Stewart, lunged at the small Boston goalie. Nels Stewart, who it was said "had the proportions of a pachyderm," crashed into the dentist even though the whistle had blown, and this sat poorly with the Boston aggregation.

"Every man jack of the Bruins has a soft spot for Dr. Stewart," it was explained by the Boston *Evening Transcript* afterwards, "and every man would fight for him at the drop of the hat." Before waiting for any hats to drop, Shore floored Nels Stewart. A wild fight ensued, during which Art Ross's men held the sizable "Nellie," as the Boston press derisively called the Montreal Stewart, to the ice, while Eddie mercilessly pounded away. Shore drew the wrath of the crowd for his exertions, and league officials awarded him a major penalty and a fifteen-dollar fine.

Shore more or less behaved himself for the next three weeks before a slash to Detroit's John Walker, and abusive language to referee Lou Marsh, brought on another major penalty and an increased fine of twenty-five dollars. The fine probably had its intended effect on the cash-strapped Shore, because it would be his last of the season. His Boston fans, however, probably wished he would be fined some more. "Kill him, Eddie!" became their battle cry.

In the dead of winter, Boston's canny Boston manager, Art Ross, and shrewd owner, Charles F. Adams, were thinking of spring and of how beautiful the Stanley Cup would look on

Shore during his first season in Boston, 1926–27. *(Courtesy of Edward W. Shore Jr.)*

display in Boston, surrounded by tulips and daffodils. In planning for this happy day, Ross and Adams banished players like fan favourite Carson Cooper, who was sent northward to the Canadiens in a trade, and player favourite Charles Stewart, who drank and, because of too much—or too little—alcohol, had come down with the jitters. In their places, Ross and Adams welcomed three newcomers to the club: goaltender Hal Winkler, right winger Billy Boucher, and centre Frank "Freddie" Fredrickson (via a trade with the Detroit Falcons).

The Bruins immediately benefited from the mid-season personnel changes, and this was critical if Boston was to win the Cup. The clever and aggressive Fredrickson made a noticeable difference, and he and Shore sometimes rushed as a pair. For instance, in a January game against the New York Rangers, it was reported that "the greatest attack of the season was unloosed with Eddie Shore and Fredrickson going wild." Shore had been ragging the puck in enemy territory for a spell, and then did something out of character. He "suddenly skated into the middle zone where he passed to Fredrickson. The latter by clever stick handling and speed made a path, broke a shot between the defense men's legs, and counted." In general, however, Shore remained largely a one-man show; his evolution into a true team player was still a year or two away.

Fredrickson was instrumental in that win over the New York Blueshirts, scoring four of Boston's seven goals, and the victory was followed by a string of others that guaranteed the Bruins a berth in the playoffs. In late March, Adams proudly announced that all successful applicants for playoff tickets would be notified by mail. But there was still a bit of regular hockey to play, and a game pointless in terms of the standings promised to be a classic of the season: *les Canadiens* were scheduled to visit. Thousands of Boston Arena tickets were already in the hands of local French folk eager to see their sensational skating compatriots from across the border, and particularly to see the most thrilling skater of them all, the peerless Howie Morenz.

Morenz on ice was a sight to behold, and it was once said of the superstar that when he dashed forward at phenomenal speed, it was as if all other players were suddenly skating backwards. Morenz wore Number 7, but he skated by his opponents with such rapidity that, in the blur, they swore they saw 777. Morenz was so fast that he often struggled to properly set himself up for a shot. The man was a pest to his adversaries thanks to his ability to attack one second and then fly back the very next to be here, there, and everywhere. The "tireless" Morenz had, reporter Harold Krease wistfully remembered years later, "grace in every movement: a feather dart, a streamlined train, a swooping gull. There was poise, distinction, artistry in his skating form."

Inspired by his example, the flying French carved rings around the Bruins and were also superior defensively. Bruins fans did what they could do, booing and jeering and throwing paper from the stands, and in an effort to enliven his teammates, Fredrickson got into a scrum and uppercut his opponent. But it was all to no avail. The dashing Howie Morenz scored the contest's only goal, and it was impossible not to cheer the star. Late in the contest, when his work was done for the night and Morenz skated to the bench, everyone in the crowd gave him, it was reported, "a tremendous ovation."

It was late March 1927, and the Bruins had only to skate out the last road games of the regular season before the start of the playoffs, so Art Ross kept his three best men, Eddie Shore, Freddie Fredrickson, and Harry Oliver, at home and out of harm's way. The three would rejoin the team for the opening round of the "moneyed game," the Stanley Cup playoffs, when every Bruin would be on his own when it came time to grab a slice of the cash pie. The incentive to give it one's best during the playoffs was considerable, because 20 per cent of the total gate receipts would be set aside and apportioned out to individual players on the winning team of each division, according to quality of play. If they made it past the playoffs and won the world series of hockey, even more money awaited: the big purse. "Every Boston player can see $2,000 ahead of him," as the bonus system was explained to the public, "if the team can crash through to a title this week and next week." Unexplained—because it did not need to be in an era before the multi-year hockey contract—was that this might also be the last hockey money some of the Bruins would see, should they be cut after the season was over.

The "Rossmen" arrived at the Waldorf-Astoria in New York under instructions to avoid the nightlife and remain where they were. Fredrickson remembered of one such occasion that "Art Ross, Harry Oliver, Sprague Cleghorn, and myself were playing bridge and there was Shore alone in the hotel drawing room, playing his saxophone with the damnedest noise in the world coming out. Finally, Ross says to Harry Oliver: 'Jesus Christ, Oliver, go and tell that silly bastard to blow on the goddamned thing and not suck on it.'"

Boston's first-round opponent was Chicago, but the Black Hawks were just then without hockey facilities of their own, and so their "home" game was held at Madison Square Garden in New York. The Boston club was the favourite, and its players were in good health. Percy Galbraith was over a recent attack of ptomaine poisoning, and the thinking was that if the rest of the Bruins stayed healthy, and if Sprague Cleghorn could stay out of the penalty box, the Black Hawks would be in for a stormy time.

Earlier in the season, a promising young NHL player named Ace Bailey, new to the Toronto St. Pats, naively insulted Cleghorn just before the opening faceoff, and Cleghorn, without bothering to look, instinctively shot out a left hand that sent Bailey reeling to the ice. "Pop! His fist came from nowhere," Bailey remembered, "caught me right in the nose, and knocked me down. I struggled to get up. 'Stay down you crazy bastard,' Bill Brydge said, grabbing me. 'Do you want to get killed?'"

Brydge spoke from experience. At one time, he had been Toronto's supposed antidote to Cleghorn, back when Cleghorn was still with the Canadiens. "Bill Brydge was gonna give us some muscle," Toronto's Conn Smythe said in 1971, "he was gonna be our bad man. And when Cleghorn came down, he did give it to him, the knee, the elbow, the stick. But Cleghorn paid no attention; he just waited. Then the time came and, my, he did straighten out Mr. Brydge. He just made a mess of him. Fifty stitches."

During another game, in 1925 against the Senators, Cleghorn had broken loose with the puck and sped towards the Ottawa net, unaware that one of the true giants of the game, King Clancy, was in hot pursuit and gaining fast. When Clancy neared Cleghorn from behind, he shouted for the puck—an old trick, but it worked—and Cleghorn did as asked. Clancy scooped up the rubber. The Ottawa spectators loved it. "The crowd roared with laughter as Sprague did a slow burn," Clancy recalled. "He glared at me but said nothing at the time. When the period ended and the players were leaving the ice, I heard someone behind me shout, 'Oh King!'" Unbeknownst to Clancy, Cleghorn had already begun to swing from the floor. "I turned around," said Clancy, "and that's when every light in the rink went out."

Sprague Cleghorn was not only the master of the clenched fist coming out of nowhere, he was also the master of the skate to the groin, the elbow to the head, the stick across the face, the stick in the face, the stick over the head, the full-force frontal cross-check, the slam headfirst into the boards, the running charge from behind, and, his favourite move of all, the butt end in the ribs. "He'd skate over to the Montreal bench where they kept a big can of talcum powder," Clancy remembered, "sprinkle some of it on his hockey glove, and then run that glove up and down the shaft of his stick. Then he'd glare over at our bench and we knew that he was ready—ready to give us the butt end of his stick."

Cleghorn was a real bloodletter, and Detroit's Jack Adams called him an "unwashed surgeon." In the aftermath of a 1922 game during which Cleghorn had attacked Ottawa's Eddie Gerard and given him five stitches over the eye, butt-ended Cy Denneny, resulting in eight stitches in the forehead and nose, and charged Frank Nighbor and smashed him to the ice, referee Lou Marsh decreed Cleghorn a disgrace to hockey. The Ottawa police told Marsh they could have him arrested, but Marsh, perhaps not wanting to bring bad publicity down upon the league and anger his employers, the NHL club owners, respectfully declined.

Cleghorn and his younger brother Odie spent years playing together for Montreal, and the two would arrive at the arena, each dressed marvellously the same in top hat, spats, cane, and gloves. Sprague and Odie were as inseparable as twins, and the day of Sprague's funeral in 1956 was the day that Odie died. In 1912, the Montreal Wanderers, with the brothers Cleghorn on the roster, played an exhibition match against the Canadiens in Toronto in which Odie accidentally collided with Newsy Lalonde and both went down dazed. Sprague skated to the scene of the mishap and wreaked havoc with his stick. When it was all over, Lalonde lay unmoving on the ice, bleeding from the nose and head, and the spectators thought he was dead. Although Sprague and Odie were not always on the same team, the brothers kept in touch, taking time to compare notes on who in the league was due a good beating.

After his playing days were over, Sprague reckoned that he had "probably been in fifty stretcher-case fights and collisions." Not all of these were on the giving end. "You'd need a battery of adding machines," he said of his lesser injuries, "to tabulate all the minor cuts, bone bruises, torn ligaments and pulled tendons my quarter century of hockey gave me." Nowhere is it recorded that Sprague ever doubted that injury was a natural consequence of playing hockey, or questioned why it should be so.

Despite his dirty play, Sprague Cleghorn was also a superb hockey player. In eleven NHL seasons, playing defence, he managed to score eighty-seven goals, and over the course of his very long hockey career he demonstrated an ability to overcome great adversity. As captain of the Wanderers in 1916, for example, Cleghorn led his team through a succession of early victories before meeting up with Ken Randall. Randall's reputation as a "bad man" had come, according to reports, from "episodes in which he figured in the defunct Maritime League." During a game against Montreal, Randall united with the rugged Wanderer leader at an angle. Catapulted into the boards by Randall's check, Cleghorn shattered his ankle. It appeared that his hockey days were over; but Cleghorn surprised everyone when he announced his intention to play again next season. As luck would have it, that fall he slipped on an icy sidewalk and broke his other ankle, and any talk of a return to the sport now seemed utterly improbable. Yet, the following November, Cleghorn showed that he possessed physical resources and courage far above the ordinary, and, playing for Ottawa, he was paired on the defence with Eddie Gerard in front of Clint Benedict to form one of the greatest barricades hockey has ever known.

A veteran of many years of hockey by the time Shore joined the Bruins, "Old Man" Cleghorn, age forty-six, was generous enough to teach Eddie a thing or two. "I broke Shore into the big time and I claim some credit for making him the standout defenceman he became," Cleghorn said later. "He had a lot of stuff when he joined us, but there were still things he needed to learn and I taught him those things."

The New York–Boston rivalry went beyond just hockey (it had something to do with the Yankees and Red Sox), and the Madison Square Garden crowd had no qualms about siding with the Black Hawks and calling for the Bruins' heads. The Bruins, though, smeared the Black Hawks in the first of the two-game, total-goals series to lead the American Division semifinal. In that game, Fredrickson scored, and then it was Cleghorn's turn on a nice pass by Galbraith. "Sailor" Jim Herberts, he of a seafaring past, scored, and after Herbert's goal, Fredrickson counted on a Shore rebound. Finally, Oliver shot the disc into the cage to make it 5–1. "The rout was made complete," one newspaper reported, "when Eddie Shore who had been the recipient of the boos of the New Yorkers raced down the left side of the rink." With three Chicagoans holding on to him, Shore broke away, held possession of the rubber, "and whipped it home for the final goal. The crowd, which had been hostile to Shore, gave him a big reception." This was Shore's twelfth goal of the year, which, for the 1920s—or, for that matter, any other decade—was a high number for a defenceman. The following night, at the Boston Arena, and in a match with only spasms of high-class play, the Bruins won the game, and with it the right to face the Rangers.

Fourteen sportswriters from New York papers arrived in Boston the next day. Local fans had learned of the victory the night before by listening to the customary fifteen-minute summary of the action, called a "re-broadcast," which aired on WEEI radio immediately following Bruins games. Now, in anticipation of the upcoming series to decide the American Division winner, Boston went hockey mad. Three hours before the scheduled time of the opening faceoff, a line of five hundred souls had formed around the Arena reservations window, all hoping for any uncalled-for tickets. Some fans were bidding for tickets, with one pair going for an astronomical thirty dollars. Tex Rickard came up from Manhattan on an afternoon train and was without a pass; naturally, he was taken care of. Those in the standing-room contingent, two thousand strong, were permitted to rush the Arena gate just before the puck was dropped, and once inside, many stubbornly stood in the aisles, blocking the view of those who had paid good money for their seats.

From the outset, the Bruins and Rangers began bodying each other and going down like tenpins, and the crowd went wild, yelling, howling, and booing whenever anything happened. An errant disc was shot into the promenade, hitting a spectator; coming from the other direction, a wad of toilet paper was thrown at the referee. The Rangers and Bruins carried their sticks high and ruthlessly bumped, tripped, and board-checked each other, but, despite working like Trojans, neither side could score. Then the intimate combat of the first period gave way to distant bombardment as each side stood back and took long shots.

The air was now thoroughly fouled by tobacco smoke, and after the second period, Arena workers went out onto the deteriorating ice to do what little they could to make it ready for the third. The band struck up "Tessie," a mainstay of Red Sox baseball games, to get things going again, but when play began, it was clear that both teams were all used up, having been bounced around as if made of rubber for too long, and when the final bell rang, the score was 0–0.

The Boston and New York armies resumed the battle at Madison Square Garden on April 4, and the spectators, all sixteen thousand of them, were in a state of frenzy. Charles F. Adams, having never seen his team win in New York, decided to stay home so as not to be a jinx, and his superstition worked: the Bruins won, 3–1.

At the Garden, the Rangers had given it their all, twenty-seven penalties had been handed out (thought to be a record at the time), and the Bruins showed the effects of the game's ferocity by the collection of bumps, cuts, and bruises they had amassed. Every Bruin had been a star and, according to the Boston *Globe,* "Hitchman, Shore, Coutu and Cleghorn showed they are real money players by superlative defensive work." Sensational in goal, Hal Winkler proved to be a source of constant frustration for the Rangers, who could not get one by him. New Yorkers, however, love a winner, and, in the final minutes of the game, the crowd's hostility turned to admiration when it became undeniable that the Bruins were the better club. With its victory, Boston was now in the Stanley Cup final.

"Hockey lingered in the lap of spring here today," New York correspondent Seabury Lawrence reported from Boston two days later, "and fond hopes budded on historic Boston Common that the Boston Bruins would come home in front in the epochal hockey series for the Stanley Cup which starts tomorrow night at the Boston Arena." The Ottawa Senators, victors in the Canadian Division, had beaten the Canadiens and were already aboard their special sleeper train and expected at Boston's North Station by daybreak. League officials, including president Frank Calder, were arriving from Montreal, while NHL club owners, managers, and players began flocking into Boston from distant parts. "We all know that Ottawa has a wonderful hockey team," Ross told the press. "The Bruins will be in there battling with the same determination that brought victory over the Black Hawks and the Rangers. My players will give it everything they have." In front of the Arena, a seething crowd began pressing against the ticket window at 9 a.m. in preparation for its opening at twelve-thirty. The final would be a best-of-five series.

The Boston Arena, built in 1909, was one of the first in North America to have artificial ice, and likely the ice plant had not been updated since, because the only time there was good ice in the building was when outside it was well below freezing. Icemaker Henry Allen promised the fastest surface of the year, and he worked laboriously towards that end. When the Arena doors opened, his handiwork was on display: all marvelled at the smooth, perfectly frozen surface that lay before them—a surface so utterly black that, without the usual layer of white snow on top, it would be hard to see the puck.

Play benefited greatly from Allen's labours, and the action was fast and clean with excellent passing and smart headwork on the part of both teams. It was the best of winter hockey on an unusually balmy spring evening in a building packed to the rafters with thousands of warm bodies. Under such conditions, "It was not through any fault of his own," the Boston press explained the morning after, that Allen's ice did not last the night. Expanses of exposed concrete appeared a short time into the game, which made skating treacherous, and eventually the play literally ground to a halt. First, second, and third overtime sessions failed to produce any scoring chances, and Charles F. Adams, to prevent player injury, called the game off, saying that to continue would be "inhuman." NHL president Calder, who would never dare contradict a club owner, had no choice but to agree. The Arena customers were not prepared for a scoreless tie, but that is exactly what they got for their money.

Massachusetts governor Alvan T. Fuller, a Republican who had made a fortune selling Packard automobiles, was Adams's guest for the second game. Fuller had just decided not to commute the death sentences of the Italian immigrants and anarchists Nicola Sacco and Bartolomeo Vanzetti, a decision that paved the way to the electric chair for those two. Later that summer, when the condemned received their lethal doses of voltage at the Charlestown State Prison, the civilized world, which had implored Governor Fuller to commute their death sentences, reacted with revulsion, and massive protests erupted around the globe.

The executions would leave a black mark on the state of Massachusetts because Sacco and Vanzetti, a shoemaker and fish peddler respectively, had been convicted of a gangland-style robbery and murder of a type their supporters said they were incapable of committing. Their trials had been as much about the defendants' political views as about the crimes of which they were accused, and the judge in the case had tipped his hand when he told some golfing buddies that he would get the "anarchist bastards." The pressure on Fuller, both at home and abroad, to spare the lives of Sacco and Vanzetti, therefore, had been enormous, but Fuller's conscience on this April night was clear and he was looking forward to an enjoyable evening of hockey. The Bruins, happy to accommodate, provided what entertainment they could for His Excellency, and one bit of excitement, it was reported, occurred when "Eddie Shore carrying the disk in the middle zone, crashed into George Boucher so hard that the latter curled up on the ice."

George was not the only Boucher brother to find winter employment in the NHL. Another of them was Shore's teammate,

Billy Boucher, who had previously played for the Canadiens. With his old team, Billy had been in many a game against the Maroons at the Forum, where, whenever the two hometown teams squared off, the English fans sat on one side of the rink and the French on the other. These hard-fought and bitter intra-city contests were always, Montreal hockey writer Elmer Ferguson wrote, "classics of hockey hate, hockey fury." An example of this hate and fury occurred during a game in 1925, when Billy Boucher was lined with mighty mite Aurèle Joliat, a featherweight at 128 pounds. Near the end of a tense second period, Joliat was sure that his shot had entered the Maroons net, although Ernie Russell, the goal umpire, thought not. The extremely temperamental Joliat rushed at Russell, seated in the umpire's cage, and swung his stick savagely at him, but Russell managed to grab the stick. Behind Russell, enraged French fans fought to bust into his cage. One fan succeeded and pinned Russell's arms to his side while Boucher battered him bloody with his stick. Boucher's teammates pulled the furious Canadien away, and, now freed, Russell chased the fan who had held him into the stands and landed a solid punch. Meanwhile, at the other end of the rink, Nels Stewart scored for the Maroons.

Eddie Shore's problem was on vivid display during the first period of the game against the Senators. He had been sent to the penalty box four times in twenty minutes, not so much for what he'd done but for what the referees *thought* he'd done. The truth was that Eddie's reputation for being a bad man was such that he could not even dart a mean glance his opponents' way without being chased off the ice. To the referees of the NHL, Shore was a marked man, and he spent ten minutes of the sixty-minute game that night in the penalty box. It was during his penalties that Ottawa scored two goals and won the bout, 3–1.

The night after this discouraging defeat, the Rossmen left Boston on the long, hard train ride to Ottawa, where they arrived, the worse for wear, at noon. The tired Bruins went to their hotel, the noble Château Laurier next to the Parliament Buildings, hoping to get what little sleep they could before that evening's contest.

Awaiting them at the Château was a relaxed Eddie Shore.

Travelling solo, Eddie had left Boston on an earlier train so as to get his proper rest. It was this kind of behaviour that made him something of a mystery to the other players. Off the ice, Shore was a retiring, almost shy individual, showing up at the Arena just long enough to attend practice or play a game, then disappearing—to where, no one knew. He seldom mingled socially with his teammates, and he came to be called the "Lone Wolf."

Although thoroughly fagged, the Bruins got off to a sizzling start that evening and outplayed the Senators, quickly making it 1–0. Freddie Fredrickson and Sailor Herberts on offence and Lionel Hitchman on defence played remarkable hockey for Boston, although early in the second period the Senators evened the score. This came about when, according to the press, an Ottawa player "stepped into Eddie Shore from behind the Boston cage and for a minute or two Eddie was groggy. He had a bleary look in his eyes, but there was not a mechanical defect in his hockey." Shore then got into a mix-up with George Boucher and the two were waved off. The penalty was ruinous to the Bruins, as Sprague Cleghorn, who was now alone on defence without Shore, was tricked in a play that allowed Cy Denneny to score.

Knowing that Shore was the bane of NHL officialdom for his disdain of authority, the Ottawa skaters goaded him into taking additional penalties. It was a smart strategy, and with Shore regularly off the ice, whatever sizzle the Bruins had left was soon silenced. The contest dragged on, and after twenty minutes of unproductive overtime, Adams told NHL president Calder to call it a draw.

Presently, the Senators had four points in the series, one each from the two tied games, and two from the win in Boston. To prevail, the Bruins needed to win the two remaining games in Ottawa, while the Senators needed only to win one. A deadlocked series seemed possible, and NHL club owners were in a jam over what to do about it. Following their instructions, Calder warned of "the danger of dragging hockey out too long" and ruled that there would be no extra games. He also said (quite controversially) that if the series ended with no side victorious after the next two games, then there would simply be no Stanley Cup winner this year.

All the next day and into the wee hours, the wail of Eddie Shore's saxophone penetrated the thin walls of the hotel as he stumbled over "Blue Skies," "A Little Spanish Town," and his favourite, "Roses that Bloom in Picardy." Columnist Bill Grimes remembered, "Eddie's sour notes sure spoiled that trip for the hockey scribes for his saxophone solos completely neutralized the effects of all the Scotch and soda they had consumed, which was plenty." Telegrams wishing the Bruins well—and the referees ill—were pouring in from Boston, and word was sent out that, in regards to the do-or-die match with the Senators the next night, the Rossmen were in excellent spirits.

The game, after a clean start, turned into one of the dirtiest and roughest in the history of the sport. The Senators pressed the attack from the first moments of play, and their second-stringers, men such as Hec Kilrea and Frank Finnigan, demonstrated just how good the Ottawa club could be. Their skills that evening surpassed even those of Boston's first forward line, and Boston's bald goaltender, Hal Winkler, was kept busy by a dozen hard and accurate shots. But in the second period, the Bruins came back with Galbraith and Fredrickson to test Ottawa's goalie, Alex Connell, with a couple of good chances. It was Ottawa that scored first, though, when Finnigan aimed the disc at Winkler from behind a couple of players and managed to locate the corner of the Boston net.

Just after this goal, Sailor Herberts and Kilrea got into what appeared to be a hockey mating dance as they circled each other with sticks locked together up high. When this strange ritual ended and the sticks were freed, Herberts promptly turned around and gave Ottawa's Hooley Smith a solid whack over the head with the hickory. Referee Billy Bell was right there, but did not penalize Herberts because, just moments earlier, Smith had butt-ended him without consequences. Accounts, Bell figured, were now even. From the other end of the rink, however, sounded the shrill of referee Dr. Jerry Laflamme's whistle, which was followed by the doctor himself, who came dashing down ice to order Herberts off. Sailor Herberts turned as white as Moby Dick. He raised his harpoon and tried to spear Laflamme, and for this, as well as for using certain salty terms, he was sent to the "dry dock" for a five-minute major while a torrent of unprintable words from the Bruins bench were hurled at Laflamme. Taking advantage of the penalty, Cy Denneny practically clinched the championship for Ottawa by scoring the second Ottawa goal. With Herberts back in action, the Bruins later put one into the Senators net, but Ottawa succeeded yet again to lead 3–1.

The officiating all evening long only served to confirm the Rossmen's conviction that Laflamme was biased against them, a belief dating back to the end of the previous season, 1925–26, when Laflamme had ruined the Bruins' chances of making it to the playoffs. Now the Bruins were certain that Laflamme was going to ruin their chances of winning the Stanley Cup. They hadn't forgotten that, just two nights ago, during Stanley Cup game number three, when Ottawa's King Clancy slipped and fell of his own accord with not a Bruin in sight, Laflamme had punished Boston anyway. And in tonight's game, at the end of the third period, who should come rushing down centre ice on an excellent opportunity to count but good old Eddie Shore, when an Ottawa trip sent the big Bruin sprawling—but, surprise, surprise, Jerry Laflamme's whistle was not to be heard.

Angered to the point of seeing red, the Boston men tore the lid off, and during the final five minutes of the game, players on both sides banged, slashed, and cut each other down in a manner that was nothing short of brutal. The Bruins' giant defenceman Lionel Hitchman, who had formerly been with the Royal Canadian Mounted Police (and had been excused from the force because his "services were needed in hockey"), bumped George Boucher, sending him to the ice. The Ottawan, who reporters said, "Never did have too much control over his temper," got up and ran murderously into Hitchman on the left side boards and let the former Mountie have it with his stick. Hitchman was no stranger to swinging the lumber himself, and he retaliated in kind. The rink was in an uproar. Senators and Bruins wrestled with each other at centre ice, players dashed in from the sidelines to join the fray, and Ed Gorman, who was retained by the Senators for just such contingencies, raced over with aforethought to do Hitchman grievous bodily harm. Gorman and Hitchman went at it, but were tossed out of what remained of the game before they could kill each other. The Ottawa crowd, known for taking its hockey seriously but calmly, was appalled.

The players on both teams were now totally out of control. In the final seconds of the contest, Hooley Smith, who had loudly boasted before the game that he would get Shore no matter what, raised his stick and brought it down as if he was going to split the Bruin's skull from forehead to chin. In a case of mistaken identity, however, it was actually Harry Oliver's head that Smith bludgeoned. Oliver, who was a wonderfully clean player and would never intentionally hurt a flea, dropped in his tracks like a felled bullock. Big "Perk" Galbraith rushed to Oliver's aid and helped his stricken teammate, streaming blood and holding his hands to his face, to the dressing room. All the while, Laflamme's whistle was oddly silent.

The intended victim of Smith's attack was not far away, and Eddie Shore was at Smith from behind in less than half a dozen strides. "He lifted his stick," as a reporter later reconstructed the incident from what Shore had told him, "with the intention of bringing it down on Smith's head." But then, "In the act of swinging it, it flashed over him that out in the West, on his father's ranch, he had more than once killed a steer with a stick, and that thought stayed his hand." Sobered by the memory, Shore instead gave Smith a gentle tap on the noggin. This apparently was enough to remind Laflamme that he had a whistle and that, according to NHL regulations, he was allowed to use it. The referee sent Shore and Smith off the ice to serve matching minors. Shouting from the Boston bench, Ross and Adams demanded that Laflamme explain how Smith, after having almost murdered Harry Oliver, was deserving of a mere minor. Laflamme ignored their protests and rudely turned his back to them. Smith and Shore had only just begun to serve their two minutes of penance when the gong sounded.

"We lost the game—and the cup," Fredrickson remembered, "but after it was over Ross got us together in the dressing room and said, 'Okay, the first man who gets that referee gets a $500 bonus.'" From then on, it was every Bruin for himself. Laflamme was walking to his dressing room when a crush of brown-and-yellow jerseys encircled him in the passageway under the seats, and then Laflamme got what was coming to him.

Billy Coutu delivered three hard blows, and the referee was knocked stiff, tumbling to the floor where a knot of Bruins, abetted by rooters who had taken the train ride up from Boston, kicked at him. Ross held a few of his men back, but others were permitted to go about their work. Billy Bell stepped in to aid his stricken partner, but the Rossmen reached Bell first and he received the benefit of one healthy swing. Now he, too, was stretched out. A furious Charles F. Adams, his dream of bringing the Stanley Cup home to Boston ruined, dropped his cane, and, with a few choice words, rushed at Laflamme and, as Laflamme later complained bitterly to Calder, laid hands on him "roughly." Nonsense, Adams would say in his defence; he was never afforded the chance to throttle Laflamme because, by the time he had arrived upon the scene of this "unfortunate incident," the referee was already "flying through the door." The police pulled Laflamme from the Boston mob, but the damage was done and the doctor emerged with a painfully swollen face. Bruins players and management then stormed into their dressing room, vowing vengeance on all and sundry.

To thank the men for their outstanding work over the past season, the Bruins held a luncheon at Montreal's famous Windsor Hotel, birthplace of the NHL. Because all the Bruins were Canadian, there was no point in making them travel back to Boston just for a meal, and Adams could not have been a more gracious host. He warmly complimented Art Ross for his successes and expressed the hope that he would manage the Bruins for years to come. Then Adams distributed ten thousand dollars in well-earned bonus cheques to his men—which did not include the thousand dollars that each Bruin would receive as his portion of the playoff pool (and, in Billy Coutu's case, an extra, but confidential, five hundred).

Bruins training camp was eight months away, and Harry Oliver in particular could use the respite from hockey. His face was swollen, his nose was badly broken, and he would need time to recuperate. Hal Winkler intended to return west to his business selling insurance; Sprague Cleghorn had work at a Montreal racetrack awaiting him; and Billy Boucher, an automobile salesman in Ottawa, had been prospecting members of the Senators during breaks in the Stanley Cup games and hoped to close some deals. Hockey was Billy Coutu's main business, and with a family of four to support, he had good reason to look forward to next season. But for him, there would be no next season. Frank Calder had hung responsibility for the public-relations disaster that was the postgame riot around his neck, and banned him from hockey for life.

Regular-season statistics had been compiled earlier, and with 133 minutes, Nels Stewart was the NHL's most penalized player. Close behind in second place, with 130 minutes, was Eddie Shore. "There is no finer kid in the league," the Boston *Herald*'s Stanley Woodward remarked of Shore, "but he's still a little crude."

FOUR

===

THE HARD-WORKING AND FRUGAL Eddie Shore, now eleven
thousand dollars richer and with his sights set on a life with
Kate Macrae, as well as some prime farmland in Alberta for
the two of them, saved his money and returned to the CNR.
Shovelling coal was a far from glamorous pastime for a hockey
superstar like himself, but it was ideal for an athlete. Opening
the firebox to face the blazing heat, Shore would rhythmically
swing shovelfuls of coal into the engine, building up his arm
and back muscles and deepening his chest. "The average pro
lasts from three to five years in the game, and there are some
that are good for ten years or longer," Shore said. "The number
of a man's playing years depends, I believe, somewhat on his off-
season occupation. If he gets out of condition over the summer
the effort of putting himself back takes too much out of his
reserve strength, and tends to burn him out as an athlete."

In the fall of 1927, Shore arrived in Boston with a new contract in his hand and a new watch in his pocket. The contract was from the Bruins, and it was lucrative enough to convince him that he no longer needed to get his summer exercise shovelling coal: the watch was a retirement gift from the CNR. Immediately, the mighty Shore succumbed to the changes in water, food, and atmosphere. Abnormally warm November weather for New England laid him low, and practices for him and for his teammates were hot and unpleasant.

The Bruins were barely ready for the action when it came, but not so their fans, who had been delighted by their heroes' spectacular bid for the Stanley Cup the season before (and especially by the donnybrook up in Ottawa). On opening night the "slaughter house," as the Boston Arena was affectionately called, was fairly bubbling over with the enthusiasm of fans who could hardly wait for the show to begin. The Arena lights were brighter than the previous year, and the Bruins' new music man Leo Reisman, splendid in his brilliant uniform, was keyed up and eager to play. When the contest was about to start, Reisman and his twenty-two piece orchestra struck up "The Star-Spangled Banner."

There were new rules to the NHL game that season, the result of changes insisted upon by Charles F. Adams and Art Ross to speed up the sport for the benefit of the booming American market. Among other innovations, Ross and Adams saw to it that the greatest leeway was now given to forward passing, and that the rules would discourage interference with a rushing attacker. Additionally, to ensure that the paying customer was treated to enough scoring, Adams and Ross placed limits on the width of goalie leg pads. Ross took the reforms a step further by designing a new hockey puck and a new net. The old pucks had a habit of bouncing around like a thing alive, and Ross's solution was to deaden the rubber by making it denser (and more painful for goaltenders to catch). Then, to ensure that the new pucks stayed in the net, Ross patented a contraption of his own design, resembling a giant lobster trap. It had a bellied back and two semi-compartments covered with slack cord to snare the rubber. The innovation worked as advertised, and for pucks foolish enough to enter the "Ross net," there was no hope of escape.

The league's referees, including that night's judge of play, Mickey Ion, had been brought up to date on the new rules and were ready for another season of officiating. Ion, a competent referee in a league that seemed to have few of them (a constant complaint for the next decade), was honest and fearless, and a man with whom it was poor policy to argue. Ion loved to hand out fines. Skating up to an offender, the referee would reel off numbers. "Ten," "Twenty-five," "Fifty," or even "One hundred," he would say, indicating the dollar amount owed to the NHL. Ion made his decisions quickly and he enforced them rigidly. "When that whistle blows," Pete Muldoon of the Black Hawks once said of Ion's officiating, "it is not with any apology." Nothing that happened anywhere on the ice escaped Ion's notice, because it was impossible to deceive someone who was as expert in detecting foxy behaviour as he was. Appropriately enough, Ion owned a fox farm, reputed to be the finest of its kind in Washington State.

The visiting Black Hawks had been toughened by pre-season games against minor-league clubs and so should have easily carried the night. The seventy-degree temperature and melting ice inside the Arena, however, affected Chicago and Boston players equally, and with the score tied after sixty minutes neither team was proficient enough with Ross's new puck (which rolled around on the bumpy ice just like the old ones did) to take advantage of the overtime period.

Disappointed spectators filed out of the building and into the warm air, likely unaware that they had just seen a portent of the Bruins' greatness for a decade and more to come. It happened late in an extremely hectic second period, when a long-striding, long-legged Bruin recruit, age nineteen, cor-ralled the puck. The Chicagoans were down a man, and the remaining Black Hawks mobilized to stop the lone rush. The new Bruin, however, avoided the Chicago forwards and roared down ice towards the Hawk points, who readied to bash him, but instead bashed into each other. Scrambling through the failed ambush, the new Bruin momentarily lost the puck, regained it, and then, whirling around, took a sweeping back-handed shot to send the rubber flying into the Chicago net. The modest youngster—Aubrey "Dit" Clapper was his name—had not a second to celebrate before nearly losing the use of his right hand to Lionel Hitchman's congratulatory grip.

In the days following that game, Ross, who was not given to effusively praising his men, let it be known that he was pleased with his team, marvelling that the combination of Freddie Fredrickson, Percy Galbraith, and Henry Oliver was the smoothest-working forward line he had ever seen. To com-plement his veterans, Ross now had the versatile Clapper, who could play any of the three forward positions with ease.

The aging Sprague Cleghorn was thought by observers to have wasted too much time in the penalty box last season to be of much use to the Bruins. Ross may have thought the same way, because he intended to use his violent veteran as an assistant coach; but Cleghorn would not be denied a regular turn on the ice. He got off to a surprisingly clean start and resumed his place as a valuable member of the team. Behind forwards Fredrickson, Galbraith, and Oliver were the Bruins' "three musketeers" in the persons of Shore, Hitchman, and Hal Winkler. By the end of November, the lead musketeer had been fully acclimated, and Ross could once again count on Shore to go through enemy forwards as if they were balanced on paper skates.

The Maroons arrived a week later for their first game that season at the Arena, and Shore was the man to get things going in that spectacular way of his that always delighted the home crowd. He set sail for the Maroons net like the USS *Indianapolis* at full steam, and, leaping to their feet, the fans yelled, "Go it Eddie! Go it Eddie!" The demonic defenceman skated down the left side of the rink for a few strides, switched over to the right for a few more, swerved to the left, poked the puck through the Montreal points, swung around the defenders to rejoin the puck, and then took a deliberately played shot that Clint Benedict never even saw. The fans were ecstatic. "Now I ask you," one fan was heard saying to another, "ain't he a pip?"

The Maroons centre, Nels Stewart, had it in for Shore all night. He managed a stiff check, but otherwise could not get the Bruin. As Boston scored more unanswered goals (and would win 4–0), Stewart's frustration grew, and in the third period he took it out on Fredrickson, caught off balance from having just shot the puck near the rear boards. Stewart was known to be so lazy that he bothered to move his hefty frame only to take a shot on net or to hit somebody, and on this occasion, true to form, he leisurely shifted his bulk over a few inches to connect with Fredrickson. The Bruin went up into the air, hitting his head on the wire fence above the back boards, bounced off, and landed back on the ice, face down. He didn't move. Fans leapt onto the ice and Frederickson was carried off, comatose, by the faithful to the dressing room.

Shore continued to shine, and soon after, in a match against the Canadiens, found himself boxed in by *les Habitants* when a Bruins addition, right winger Fred Gordon, passed him the puck. Shore, not expecting the pass, was caught off guard but still somehow manoeuvred through the enemy ranks and let drive that valuable backhander of his to score. The capacity Arena crowd went hysterical, howling and stamping, then howling and stamping some more for the remainder of the game. Afterwards, the Bruins, nearing first place in the American Division, headed west for games in Chicago and Detroit.

The boys in brown and yellow won a December 11 game in Chicago, and the next day in Detroit, they were looking forward to a repeat. In a room high up in their hotel before the game, they were playing bridge when, at around two o'clock in the afternoon, Art Ross rose and closed and locked the door. What he had to say, he told his "kids," was important: there was a chance that tonight's game could be thrown for twenty thousand dollars. There were five gunmen behind the scheme who were, at this very moment, waiting down in the lobby, and their agent—a "little fat Jew," Ross called him—had come up to discuss the proposal. The agent was let in.

"How do you do, Mr. Ross," the agent said. "I want that you should tell me what you have decided about that little offer."

"You needn't ask me to decide anything," Ross responded. "Here are the players; put your proposition up to them."

The agent hesitated, apparently not willing to talk to a room full of strangers. "I tell you what we should do," he said. "Let me talk with one or two of your players and you in private."

"That's fair enough," said Ross. "Sprague and you, Freddy, come with me and let's hear what this bird has to say." There was the sound of talking and arguing from behind the closed door, and when it opened again, Cleghorn appeared before his teammates alone.

"Fellows what do you think!" he gasped. "That bird has raised his offer to $30,000 and what's more, he has the coin. I've seen it." There was silence. "What should I go back and tell him?"

Shore, whose face, according to an eyewitness, had turned the "color of a peony," said, before any of his teammates could speak, "You can go back and tell him that he can't buy this crowd for $30,000 or $100,000."

Accompanied by Ross and Fredrickson, the agent re-entered the room to get his answer—and he got it. Shore grabbed hold of him with both hands, lifted him high in the air, and headed towards the window, which was ten or twelve stories up. He was making to throw the agent through the glass when Ross, Fredrickson, and Cleghorn shouted: "Eddie! Eddie! No, no! Don't do that! Don't do that! He's only kidding! He's only kidding!"

The identity of the "agent" was not revealed by the press, but he was described as being a hockey fan and a friend of Ross, and also one of the world's foremost magicians. He had volunteered to help the men relax before their game, and Ross had come up with the idea of the little "joke." Even though he had nearly lost his life, for the next two hours the magician kept the players spellbound with card tricks. That night, the Bruins won, 2–1 in overtime.

A week later, in mid-December, the Bruins received a good walloping when the Canadiens trounced them by four goals. Like all games against the Canadiens, it was, as they said in those days, "a wow," especially since it was played in Montreal.

The spacious surface at the Forum was A-1, the ice almost as smooth and as fast at the end of the third period as it had been at the start of the first. The Canadiens flew around their rink at dazzling speed, and so elusively that bodily contact was at a minimum. Howie Morenz, plenty swift enough when he played elsewhere, was simply impossible to catch at the Forum, where he always played his best. Roger Kahn, writing in *Esquire*, provided a glimpse of the dashing Canadien in top form:

First Morenz is circling behind his own goal. Then a little hop signals the start of his charge down center ice. Skating from the hips with easy, long strides, Morenz gains speed with incredible swiftness. The crowd at the Forum rises to its feet in waves, as he skates past and the cheering comes down in waves too, rolling from the tiers of seats louder and louder. As if to match the crescendo's rise, Morenz drives himself still faster past the goal. In his path two defensemen brace and set their heavy frames. Suddenly, Morenz is upon them, hurling his body into the air as though he would jump over the two men. All the crowd is on its feet now and screaming. Somehow, Morenz breaks through. There is a final feint, a goalie's futile lunge, a hard, quick shot into the open corner of the cage. Morenz has scored. While the Forum rocks with sound, he skates easily back to center ice for the next face-off.

Morenz and the man who played to his left, Aurèle Joliat, teamed together with perfection. The tightly wound Joliat was capable of spectacular moves, artistic stickhandling, and a deadly wrist shot. "With that flick," one reported noted, "he can pack speed into a shot that is outstanding." Joliat, who detractors said "did his work in spurts," was an inconsistent player, but when his game was on, as it was this night, he was in a class by himself, and against the Bruins, he and Morenz were nearly invincible. The pair were adored by the Montreal fans and blessed by those in the cheap seats near the Forum roof, and when Morenz and Joliat stepped out together onto the gleaming ice at the start of the game, praise and pandemonium broke out among the "gallery gods" on high.

Everything went right for the Canadiens, who played just as strenuously after taking a good lead as they had when they were a goal behind after the start. The Bruins attacked in groups of three, had the puck stripped from them in the offensive zone, and back came Morenz, right into the teeth of their defence. "I can truthfully say that he is the hardest player in the league to stop," Shore said. "He comes at you with such speed that it is almost impossible to block him with a body-check. He crashes so hard that his opponent often gets the worst of it. Ask me—I can tell, for he's shaken me right to my toes many a time. Furthermore, he swerves so quickly when travelling at top speed that you may miss him entirely. Add his bullet shot to his speed, and you have, to my mind, the greatest offensive combination in hockey today. Everybody likes Howie. He's clean, fair, and sportsmanlike, and always gives his best. He's one player whom no opposing defense bears down on unnecessarily, because he doesn't deserve any unduly rough treatment."

It was Shore's delight and pleasure in the winter of 1928 to flatten opposing players left and right, and for this the peppery Bruin was the main butt of referee wrath, as he racked up the penalty minutes. Even his supporters acknowledged that he too often drew penalties that, as one reporter delicately put it, "were administered for no other reason than that there was a little crudeness, at times, to the energetic manner in which he put some opponents out of play." Cooper Smeaton, a long-time referee, recalled in the 1970s: "Hockey in the twenties and thirties was great, and I enjoyed the trips and the players . . . well, most of them. There were a few I could have done without, like Eddie Shore. Shore was nasty and, as far as I was concerned, a threat to the other players, a real danger. He was a madman when he got out on the ice."

By every account, Shore was a hothead who returned every slight with compound interest and who rarely passed up an opportunity to get into a fight. Also, by every account, Shore was not above a little theatrics.

Smeaton and his colleagues knew Shore and his little "acts," and they afforded the big Bruin zero leeway. Press reports from the era seem to have Shore forever "writhing" on the ice, only to recover miraculously moments later to regain his "zip." While fortitude and smelling salts accounted for many of Shore's speedy recuperations, this was not always the case. "Shore was

The Human Cyclone: A rendition of Shore submitted to reporter A. Linde Fowler
by a reader of the Boston *Evening Transcript. (Courtesy of Edward W. Shore Jr.)*

a very colourful hockey player," Fredrickson explained, "who
put everything he had into the game but also used every sub-
terfuge he could to win the sympathy of the crowd. He'd fake
getting hurt and would lay down and roll around in agony.
Then he'd get up and be twice as good as ever."

Always a terrific fighter, Shore sought to demolish those
who had wronged him or any of his mates, and he earned a
bad-boy reputation to match. He was sensitive about this, and

once answered hotly when asked if he was a hard guy: "Hard guy, bad boy—no, I'm not either one. Never started roughing anybody in my life—never will. But of course, if somebody is trying to knock me loose from my brains, trying to break my arm or leg, trying foul tricks to keep me from helping my team win—well, that makes it a little different."

It was apparently a little different late in February 1928, when the Pittsburgh Pirates' Duke McCurry, with both hands on the hickory, used his stick to smash Shore across the mouth. This was done directly in front of referee Dr. Eddie O'Leary, who, like most referees when it came to fouls made upon Shore, pretended not to have seen a thing. So the next time McCurry skated down ice, Shore took matters into his own hands. For this, he was banished, and as he was making his way to the "cooler," McCurry said something and swung his stick, and in an instant the two were at it. McCurry hit first, but from then on he was the underdog. Harold Cotton of the Pirates made the mistake of thinking it was a public fight and promptly landed on the middle of his back when Shore's right hand smacked him on the chin. Shore fights often degenerated into melees, and this one was no different. Six Pirates together could not easily tear the Bruin off McCurry. Finally overpowered, Shore was led away. Behind him, several Pittsburgh players lay kicking in agony.

Capable of superhuman feats of rushing and scoring, Shore was all too human when it came to making blunders. Two mistakes that he commonly made (and for which the Bruins commonly paid dearly) were being caught up ice when the play had reversed direction, and being confined to the cooler because of some pointless penalty that he had taken. "Errors made in a hockey game are heartbreaking," Shore said. "I have played in [lost] games this season and others for which I believe I was to blame. After these games I realized that I had done the wrong thing, or made a move that cost my team the game. Such thoughts stay with a player for a long time, and cost the player more in bitterness than all the censure he will get from the fans."

The truth was, though, that Eddie Shore's adoring fans rarely censured him, if at all. "He was the Babe Ruth of hockey," the Bruins' Milt Schmidt once said, "especially here in Boston, where he could do no wrong."

Shore still practised for hours at the Arena or, if the Arena was booked, in the public rinks or on the ponds of Boston. He was also watching the great players of the league, particularly Howie Morenz, his rival and his idol, and learning from observation was a key to Shore's success. "When you start to play hockey," he advised the young readers of the magazine *Open Road for Boys* in 1935, "use every opportunity to see the good players and study them. Observe how they lift their feet; how they set them down; how they shove them forward; how they sway their bodies; the spring of their legs; the angle of their knees and their body bend; all these things are important and count in playing the game." Perhaps too embarrassed to admit this to his readers, Shore also studiously watched ladies' figure skating, and learned a lot.

Glued to the puck, Shore could circle an opponent's net, round and round, with such speed that his pursuers became dizzy. He was intimidating. "Like a car with high-beams on," Schmidt explained. "He'd take the puck from one end of the ice to the other, and they'd all spread out as if he were some bowling ball." He was entertaining too. "He was the only player," Bruins trainer Hammie Moore remembered, "who had a whole arena standing every time he rushed down the ice." And he was, in his own way, likable. "There is no more hilarious and husky hoister in the league than Eddie Shore," John Kieran wrote from New York. "He's a hard player but a fair one. He can take a bump or give one with the same cheerful spirit."

Anyone who played against Shore would contest the notion that he ever played with a "cheerful spirit," because in reality he played more like the Grim Reaper, although it was not always Shore who did the reaping. One close call came sometime during the 1927–28 season, when Shore received a horrific gash from one of his former Capitals teammates, Charlie "Rabbit" McVeigh, now playing for the Black Hawks. While it was an accident, McVeigh was one tough customer— "so tough," it was reported, "that when he was a youngster in Winnipeg he used to chew tobacco and then roll it up and save it to smoke when dry. He spent twenty-two months in the trenches during the war, went over the top about twenty times, and killed one of the enemy 'Because,' he explains, 'he got in my way.'" McVeigh and Shore had both been rushing down the ice, in opposite directions, when Shore was tripped and went down. McVeigh could not stop in time to avoid him. He took a leap, but his skate cut right between Shore's eyes, spraying blood all over the ice. According to legend, Shore was sent to a hospital, from which he escaped in time to catch the train for the next Bruins game.

Shore was always community minded, and if a young fellow showed up during Bruins practices, he would take the time to teach the youngster some hockey tricks. He also managed to take a day off in the middle of the busy 1927-28 hockey season to brave a cold February boat ride out into the choppy harbour. His boat landed at Thompson's Island, home of the Farm and Trade School, where more than a hundred orphaned boys awaited him in the main hall. The boys were enraptured as Shore talked to them about the techniques of hockey playing and about his own boyhood days on his father's ranch in Canada. There was generous applause when Shore had finished, and, it now being the boys' turn to entertain their guest, the school band of thirty pieces played popular selections interspersed with class songs and cheers. Returning to the mainland, Shore must have thought his day spent out on the island a welcome diversion, if not from the hockey, than at least from the travelling.

The Bruins spent a great deal of time riding the rails. They would gather either at Boston's North Station or South Station, dressed smartly in wrinkle-proof "thousand-mile" suits. Then they boarded their special Pullman car and braced themselves for the long, hard trip to Toronto, Montreal, Ottawa, Chicago, New York, Detroit, or Pittsburgh. They passed the time with endless games of cards and plenty of hi-jinks, but overall the experience was tedious and Shore in particular found the travel difficult. The interminable rides sapped his reserve strength, and the changes in environment unsettled his system. As an antidote, he carried his own supply of pure Canadian drinking water with him and, when he could, he travelled a day or two ahead of the team. "He was a loner," Milt Schmidt remembered. "He roomed by himself on road games. He did this to get the proper rest; he needed his rest."

With a month left before the 1927–28 playoffs, the Bruins had an impressive 16–10–9 record, but it had come at a cost, and the Bruins were thoroughly beat up. The cigar-chomping Win Green, formerly the Arena bandleader, had been either promoted or demoted, depending upon one's viewpoint, to become Tommy Murray's assistant trainer. Murray and Green had a busy time of it, since there were many injuries and maladies to treat. Hitchman was one such casualty. In a game against the Maroons, Hooley Smith butt-ended him over the eye and, blood pouring down his face, "the lion-hearted Hitchman," as Art Ross called him, at first refused to leave the ice, but then agreed when the clock was stopped long enough for him to take five stitches. Wearing a patch, Hitch returned and play resumed. The teams were at a stalemate when, from outside the Montreal end, Hitch launched the disc. It gained altitude, deflected off an opponent, and Clint Benedict whirled around, only to see the rubber fly through the mouth of his cage. With forty-eight seconds to go in the game, the one-eyed Hitchman had scored the winning goal.

Soon afterwards in Ottawa, Hitchman received three more stitches above the same eye. Eddie Shore was also among the skating wounded, sporting a bandage over his chin where the stick of the Rangers' Bill Cook had carved a gash a quarter-inch into the bone. The injured list continued: Harry Connor was patched up where a slash received in Toronto was healing; Dit Clapper spent time at home in Canada recovering from a knee injury; Leland Harrington was ill; Art Ross had stomach problems and, now back in Montreal, had relinquished coaching duties to Sprague Cleghorn (whose brother Odie was coaching Pittsburgh); and Hal Winkler had a sore thumb from stopping a puck. "It felt," Winkler confessed, "as if the flesh had been ripped right from the bone."

Winkler was able to sustain his teammates while they recuperated, and by season's end he would have fifteen shut-outs in forty-four games, a Bruins record that will stand the test of time. Like all great goalies, he had a distinctive style. Although he shunned spectacular jumping and diving, he had lightning-fast reflexes and enormous hands that could snatch the speeding disc out of thin air. Winkler could also make his feet dart from side to side, and his specialty was to deflect the rubber with a dead-eye-dick bunt from the blade of his stick.

As a boy, Winkler had been saved from a soft life in southern California by his family's move to Winnipeg. There he learned the goalie's craft from his older brothers, who plunked him in net and then fired away. During the war years Winkler donned the pads to protect the 61st Canadian Battalion's citadel, and afterwards he played amateur, where the money was better than in the pros. A memorable game was when Saskatoon met Moose Jaw in the playoffs. At a break in overtime, the fans, he recalled, "were so excited that they walked from the building to stand outside to rest their nerves."

Before the Bruins' regular season was over, Billy Coutu, like a bad penny, showed up at the Arena. Frank Calder had granted Coutu an absolution of sorts, letting him play with the New Haven Eagles of the Can-Am league, and predict-ably, Coutu had left a trail of gore. In a recent game against Philadelphia, for example, he had managed to extract Dave Campbell's seven front teeth with an instrument no more precise than his own well-aimed body. The Can-Am would soon suspend Coutu for one atrocity or another, but tonight the Eagle was on his best behaviour in the match against the Boston Tigers, restraining himself from sinking his talons into anybody beyond a justifiable extent. The Tigers devoured the Eagles 3–0, and afterwards Arena fans were invited to remain for some more fun. An hour of Tigers–Eagles hockey had by this time shaved up the ice so completely that it was covered entirely by snow. Never, in reporter A. Linde Fowler's opinion, had the surface looked whiter, particularly "by contrast with the appearance of the first negro hockey team that ever played in the Boston Arena."

Thousands stayed to watch as the Black Panthers sparred with the St. Joseph's club of East Boston. This was just local amateur (very amateur) action, but even so, Fowler explained of the hockey players, "their very earnestness, the spirit which they injected into the game, the way they tossed each other around, climbed on each other's backs, fell down from the very excitement helped to swell the ha-ha's that never died away from start to finish." The East Boston goalie, a Mr. Campagna, declined to prove that he was "the great white hope" when nearly ground into the ice from a "catapultic" Panther assault, and instead of leaping up again, Campagna took his time rubbing the sore spots and replacing his battered cap. The Black Panthers had a slight edge on team play compared to their opponents, although the game ended in a tie. The fans, though, seemed satisfied enough, all having, Fowler reported, "the broadest smiles on their faces that the most cheerful optimist in the world would ask to see."

Hal Winkler had earned his historic fifteenth shutout in a game against the Cougars on March 13, and for Boston all was as it should be. During that contest, a disgruntled Arena spectator had whipped a red apple at Mickey Ion and, later, Shore had skated straight down centre ice, poked the puck through the defensive points, picked it up inside Chicago territory, and blazed a fiery drive into the left side of the net. Next morning, the Boston *Herald*'s Stanley Woodward wrote, "The rosy path ahead for our heroes, coupled with the classy performance which they displayed against the outraged Cougars last night, leads to pipedreams of the Stanley Cup."

The New York Rangers and Boston Bruins met for the first of their two-game, total-goals playoff series at Madison Square Garden two weeks later. Waiting for its turn to perform at the Garden was the Ringling Brothers circus. As the clash of the blue and brown armies on the rink above commenced, the circus lions in their basement cages were "cowering in fear" and the circus "sword swallowers, fire eaters and ambassadors from Mars" sought refuge amidst "the straw under the elephants." Then, according to the New York *Herald Tribune*'s Kerr N. Petrie, "With the light of battle in his eyes the wild man of Borneo broke his fetters and dashed out of the cellar, but turned tail on the last stair and fled to the boiler room. Last night the circus press agent announced that the wild man was blabbing incoherently of Eddie Shore, Lionel Hitchman, Taffy Abel, and Ching Johnson, and because of his overwrought condition was likely to miss the circus opening Thursday."

The Rangers were well positioned for a championship run, even though Art Ross's men were favoured by the super-wise New York gambling element. Lester Patrick had taken up coaching duties for the Rangers, and he had the smallest and most sportsmanlike player of the Boucher clan playing for him, little Frank. Boucher had just won the Lady Byng

Trophy as the league's most gentlemanly player and turned out to be a breath of fresh air for those who respected sportsmanship and liked their hockey hard but fair. On Boucher's left and right were the talented Cook brothers, Bill and Bun. The brothers had played superb amateur hockey in Sault Ste. Marie, Ontario, and were farming 640 acres northwest of Edmonton when they got the urge to play hockey again. The duo caught on with Saskatoon of the WHL and later followed Patrick to New York.

With Boucher and the Cooks, Patrick could count on a high-scoring offence up front. "New York's Cook-Boucher line," Toronto's Conn Smythe once said, "never seemed to make a frontal attack. They skated in circles, dropping the puck here and there." Myles Lane, who in the winter of 1928 was still at Dartmouth College and had yet to become a Bruin, was another admirer. "I haven't seen their equal yet," he marvelled of the Cook-Boucher combination. "They played together so much and knew each other's moves so perfectly that watching them move the puck was like observing how a clock works."

To protect his splendid goalie, Lorne Chabot, Patrick counted on a granite wall comprising the "big fellow" Taffy Abel, the fattest man in hockey, and the formidable Ivan "Ching" Johnson. Abel was a former hockey Olympian and the first American-born player in the NHL. Abel was good-natured, he liked his ale, and despite his outsized body, he was, as Frank Boucher recalled, "quick and light as a feather on his feet, something like Jackie Gleason." Abel could certainly throw a check, but, Boucher said, usually "Taffy simply placed his body in people's way and bunted. When he hit a man there was no damage; it was like being hit with a pillow." Abel's girth was cause for endless ribbing, which he seems to have taken fully in stride, and once, when asked by Patrick what he would do if all alone and a three-man rush came down upon him, he replied, "Why, I'd *spread* out, of course."

Abel's defensive linemate was the ever-smiling Ching Johnson. "He was one of those rare warm people who'd break into a smile just saying hello or telling you the time," Boucher remembered. "He always wore a grin, even when heaving some poor soul six feet in the air." Punch Broadbent and Ching Johnson once exchanged pleasantries just before the start of a Rangers–Americans game. "He says to me," Broadbent recalled, "'How are the wife and kids?' 'Fine,' I says. 'And yours?' 'Fine, too, thanks,' he says. Then the game starts and just because I am going for the puck he hits me over the head."

Ching Johnson was from Winnipeg, where, it was said, as a child he had been caught in an Indian raid and scalped—a story that, to gullible New Yorkers, explained his totally bald head. Another thing said about Johnson, and something that had more truth to it, was that he was a dirty player who had never made a fair check in his life.

"Ching loved to deliver a good hoist early in a game," Boucher explained, "because he knew his victim would likely retaliate, and Ching loved body contact. I remember once against the Maroons, Ching caught Hooley Smith with a terrific check right at the start of the game. Hooley's stick flew from his hands and disappeared above the rink lights. He was lifted clean off the ice, and seemed to stay suspended five or six feet above the surface for seconds before finally crashing down on his back. No one could accuse Hooley of lacking guts.

From then on, whenever he got the puck, he dove straight for Ching, trying to outmatch him, but each time Ching flattened poor Hooley. Afterwards, grinning in the shower, Ching said he couldn't remember a game he'd enjoyed more."

Bruins president Charles F. Adams was absent from Madison Square Garden for that first game against the Rangers. Always wary of being a jinx, and especially because it was April 1, the superstitious owner was at home working on crossword puzzles, hoping to find a way for his team to win. Driven to distraction with worry, however, Adams could stand it no longer and sped to the office of radio station WEEI, where Bruins publicity man Frank Ryan was receiving telegraphed updates from New York in preparation for his 10:45 p.m. rebroadcast of the action.

There was plenty of action occurring down in New York by the time Adams joined Ryan at the radio station, but little hockey. Throughout the contest, players tossed each other to the ice, and referee Cooper Smeaton whistled until he had whistler's cramp. By the time the contest was over, twenty-one penalties had been handed out. Shore was sent off for committing, it was reported, a "somewhat severe job" on Taffy Abel, was sent off again for pulling Frank Boucher's feet out from under him, and then once more for tackling Bun Cook. Late in the first period, however, Shore managed to avoid a "vacation" in the box long enough to put on the most spectacular display of showmanship of the entire game.

The act started when Shore gained possession of the puck in his own end, worked up speed, and then rushed the ice deep into Rangers territory, where waiting for him was Ching Johnson. Forced to think quickly, Eddie chose to entertain the spectators. He took a flying leap that carried him high in the air and over Ching. Upon landing on the other side, Shore was sent tumbling, almost falling, still catapulting ahead, half catching himself, almost recovering his feet, going half down again, and finally, for the finale, sailing his bulky frame into the end boards with enough speed to put both doctors and carpenters to work.

This Boston excursion into enemy territory was the exception rather than the rule that night. During the greater part of the contest, the Rangers forced the pace, while Shore and the Bruins seemed fearful of leaving their own zone. To observers, the game was hard fought rather than brilliant, and with both teams covering each other so closely, there were few scoring chances. At the opening of the third period, Frank Boucher and Harry Oliver did manage to cage the puck within minutes of each other, but that was it, and the match ended as a 1–1 draw.

Combat resumed at the Boston Arena two nights later. Tickets had sold out six weeks in advance, and the crowd was in early—and ready for the fireworks—long before starting time. A hubbub broke loose in the stands when the puck was finally dropped and the Bruins, in four-man rushes, worked feverishly for a goal. Shore went around flattening opponents per usual, although the astute rooter may have noticed that something was missing from his play that night. The fact that Shore got not one penalty all evening, and made not one cyclonic rush worth reporting, was something of a hint.

During the first period, poetic justice was afforded Ching Johnson when the smiling defenceman heaved poor Harry Oliver six feet up and then, on the way down, Oliver's skate sliced deeply into Johnson's nose. Oliver landed badly on his knee and was done for the period. Johnson, his face all bloody, had to be assisted off the ice. Someone in the Boston crowd threw a bottle at him. When play resumed, the Rossmen became fighting furious, and a roar went up when Harry Connor passed the disc past Lorne Chabot, only to have the play called back for an offside (that rule, so vexing to the novice hockey fan, had just been introduced that season).

Connor, Dit Clapper, and Norm Gainor, second-stringers to the Bruins' first line of Oliver, Fredrickson, and Galbraith, came on for Boston during the third period, and the trio had some good scoring chances. Gainor, to his credit, sparked a crowd-thrilling fight in front of the Rangers net while New York goalie Lorne Chabot was down on the ice with the puck under his belly. Injuries were plentiful, and at one point it seemed as if all the Rangers were playing with a plaster on their faces. The Bruins charged in bravely time and again, but an earlier goal by Bill Cook late in the second period made it 1–0, and then three unanswered New York goals in the third made it 4–0. This sealed Boston's fate. Gainor, with just two minutes to go, passed the disc to Harry Oliver, who scored, but it was far too late for a Bruins rally, and the Rangers were, by total goals, the American Division champions, 5–2.

"It was," New York correspondent Seabury Lawrence reported, "a great surprise for Back Bay, Bunker Hill, and contingent points, as the local fanatics expected the great combination of Fredrickson, Oliver and Galbraith, supported by the mighty Shore, to run roughshod over the Ranger defense for an easy victory."

The mighty Shore, it transpired, had all along been suffering from what was described as a case of "neuralgia" that had him tossing about in sleepless nights and worn out physically and mentally. "A player gets trained down so fine that he is under a nervous tension," Shore once said about late-season hockey. "The continual playing, the sleeping on trains, and the general excitement gets pretty tough. You are trained to such a point that your body loses its moisture and sometimes your skin becomes dry and scaly, no matter how fast and hard you are playing, you don't perspire at all."

One reporter tried to console morose Boston fans by telling them that Shore had been "an inspiration to his mates, a driving power" all season, and that his illness "was another of the bad breaks for the Bruins, to have his troubles crop up at such an important time." Indeed, the man from Saskatchewan had given his all that year, missing just one game, scoring eleven goals (second on the Bruins only to Oliver, who had thirteen), making six direct assists, and leading (one place ahead of Ching Johnson) the NHL in penalty minutes with a tremendous 165 of them.

The Bruins quietly gathered up their odds and ends in the Arena dressing room. A few diehard fans were present to see them off and, thankful for their loyalty, the players auto-graphed programs and gave away hockey sticks, jerseys, and whatever else was at hand before Art Ross stepped in and put a stop to their generosity. The dejected Bruins then headed north and scattered across Canada's vast expanse.

With still more hockey in front of them, Lester Patrick and his Rangers took the ten-hour train ride to Montreal to meet the Maroons in the Stanley Cup final. Remarkably, the Maroons had just vanquished their French foes in the playoffs, even though the Canadiens that year had gone unbeaten for nineteen straight games, had scored 116 times, and had the cool, forever-yawning, George Hainsworth in net with his astonishingly low 1.09 goals-against average.

In the first match of the final, the Rangers were beaten soundly by the Maroons, and in the second match, which was again played at the Forum (the circus having refused to leave Madison Square Garden), the Rangers, as Frank Boucher recalled, "Were making small headway against the Maroons defense when we ran into real calamity."

The trouble occurred when, in the first period, Lorne Chabot was struck in the left eye by a puck driven in hard by the lethargic yet lethal Nels Stewart. Chabot was examined by a doctor, who diagnosed a hemorrhage and prohibited him from resuming play. Soon the goaltender was in an ambulance on his way to the Royal Victoria Hospital, where he would spend the next month in a darkened room while doctors hoped his eyesight would return (it would). Meanwhile, the Rangers were left with an empty net because, amazingly, they had failed to plan for such an eventuality. Seated in the Forum stands, however, were enough NHL greats to form an all-star team of their own; next to Ottawa's incomparable King Clancy was his fellow Senator and childhood friend, the ace goalie Alex Connell, who that season had gone 446 minutes and 9 seconds without being scored upon.

Willing to offer his services, Connell left his seat, went to the visitors' dressing room, and knocked on the door. The Rangers, needless to say, were glad to see him, but first NHL president Frank Calder had to be asked whether the substitution was permissible. The mild-mannered Calder, a former schoolteacher, did not answer directly, saying only, "I will put nothing in the way if the Maroons care to consent to the Rangers using a borrowed goaltender."

The game was delayed indefinitely, and it looked as if the crowd would have to sit up all night while a hockey council of war was held behind the scenes. The possibility of bringing Connell in for Chabot was put to Maroons coach Eddie Gerard. (Connell's boss, Ottawa manager Dave Gill, said that the proposal was perfectly all right with him.) Gerard left to consult his players, and came back with the news that they could not agree to this. The Maroons' position was that the team had paid good money—five thousand dollars—to carry a spare goalie all season, and if the Rangers had chosen to skimp on this expense, well, too bad for them. Referee Cooper Smeaton gave the Rangers ten minutes to figure something out, or else, he warned, New York would forfeit the game. Lester Patrick and his Blueshirts were in a quandary.

Frank Boucher described the Ranger dressing room at this juncture as being "in an uproar. About a dozen well-wishers, among them the Toronto manager Conn Smythe and the Pittsburgh coach Odie Cleghorn, added to the din with suggestions and advice, waving their arms and shouting at anybody who would listen." Boucher and Bill Cook discussed the situation in a corner by themselves. Suiting up a Ranger in goalie garb, both agreed, would be too dangerous because it would put the team down a man. "My eye caught Lester," Boucher said of the one-time west coast hockey baron, age forty-four and immaculately dressed, silver-haired, and with an elegant bearing, who was "standing in the middle of the room trying to restore some semblance of order, and I suggested to Bill that perhaps he was our solution." Patrick sat down to hear what Boucher and Cook had to say. The coach thought for a moment, and then, according to Boucher, "Suddenly, and dramatically, he rose to his feet and called to our trainer Harry Westerby." Patrick instructed Westerby to collect Chabot's equipment. "I will," Patrick said calmly, "go into the goaltender's position myself."

Even though Lester Patrick's name has become linked inextricably with NHL history, this was, remarkably, only his second appearance in a league game—he had made his debut, as a defenceman, the year before—and his first between the pipes. Patrick came "sauntering out," Montreal columnist Baz O'Meara wrote the following day, "with a little black cap askew over his whitening thatch" and "his lanky legs upholstered by brown pads that seemed to fit him like father's old trousers." Patrick took his place in goal, play resumed, and when the Maroons rushed his way, he cried, "Let them shoot!" The Montreal fans, it was reported, gave their native son "a great reception as he swung into action," while Pittsburgh's Odie Cleghorn, over the vociferous objections of the Maroons' portly captain, Dunc Munro, stood gamely behind the New York bench to coach in Patrick's absence.

Patrick's first test came from a Hooley Smith shot that he poked away. The Maroon shots continued, and soon Patrick was displaying a fair amount of craft and artistry. Taffy Abel was sent off by Smeaton, and during the penalty, Boucher lay back to let the two Cook brothers carry the Ranger offence. The situation reversed itself quickly when Abel was sprung. The Maroons were now down by one, and then by two, men. Only through hard play did the Maroons hold the eager Rangers at bay. A few seconds from the end of the period, a beautiful shot by Bun Cook almost beat Clint Benedict when the puck hit between Benedict's skates. It was Patrick, though, who made the last stop of the second period, which closed without a score.

Less than a minute into the third session, Bill Cook was fouled by Munro. Just as Munro reached the penalty box, Cook swooped in to beat Benedict for the first goal of the night. Immediately after New York scored, Smeaton caught Abel doing something wrong and banished him. In Abel's absence, the Maroons started a smashing attack in which Patrick turned in a clever exhibition. With Abel back on the ice once more, the Rangers almost immediately lost Ching Johnson, sent off for boarding a Maroon, and then Hooley Smith sent in a tricky shot and Patrick threw himself along the ice to smother the puck. Patrick executed yet another spectacular save a few minutes later, when Nels Stewart, carrying the puck and lumbering down the left side dasher, sent in a corking drive. Stewart quickly recovered the disc and drove in a slanting shot to tie the game, 1–1.

"The shot that beat Patrick," it was apologetically explained by a New York reporter, "represented the hardest kind of a break, as the puck landed no more than inside the far upright." Five minutes, forty seconds remained in the third, and both teams worked feverishly for the winning goal, but were forced into extra time as the period closed.

The spectators were not kept up much longer. Minutes into the fourth frame, Ching Johnson, with pursuing Maroons on his flanks and heels, was pushed into a corner behind the Montreal citadel. Johnson fought his way out, and with the crowd shrieking like mad, he passed to Frank

Boucher. Boucher knew exactly what to do with the rubber, smashing it into the back of the Maroons net. Immediately, the "exhausted Patrick," as the sportscaster Brian McFarlane recounted decades later, "dripping with perspiration, was mobbed by his players. It was one of hockey's most electrifying occasions."

The Maroons were always an arrogant lot, the spoilt children of rich guardians, the wealthy English Montrealers who owned the franchise and who lavished everything on it. Their refusal to grant Alex Connell's selfless offer to play in place of Chabot should not have been unexpected, although it was for some. When the facts became known, a cascade of criticism fell the Maroons' way. They were called unsportsmanlike, accused of having given in to "sordid commercialism," and many a hockey fan vowed never to support the team again. True to character, the Maroons were entirely unbowed and refused Lester Patrick's request for a real goalie to replace the hospitalized Chabot for the remainder of the series.

Because of the Maroons' intransigence, the Stanley Cup championship that year was endangered. Furious negotiations ensued, with president Calder doing his best to bring the two sides together. The Maroons offered Patrick the use of their spare goalie, Flat Walsh. Patrick rejected this preposterous suggestion, and finally an exasperated Calder, out of character, stepped in and settled the dispute by appointing Joe Miller as the Rangers' substitute goaltender. Miller was an acceptable choice to the Maroons; as the sometime goalie for the New York Americans—but more recently for the Niagara Falls Cataracts of the Can-Am league—he had earned the nickname "Red Light Miller" in honour of the number of times he let the puck into the net, illuminating the red light above his cage.

The lowly Miller, who had been home in Ottawa when he got Calder's call, took the next train to Montreal, where the NHL had reserved a prime spot for him at the Forum to see the next Stanley Cup game.

If indeed Miller had something to prove, he did so on the night of April 10. Staying as cool as a cucumber, even as wild scuffles broke out all over the ice, he faced a barrage of savage shots, yet after three periods had been beaten only twice. The brilliant Benedict, however, let in not one shot, and the Maroons won the raucous game, 2–0. Both goalies performed superbly again two nights later, and this time it was Miller who had the shutout and New York, on the strength of Frank Boucher's lone goal, the win. The series was tied at two games apiece. Pleased with his Rangers, Colonel Hammond gave each player a hundred dollars. However, two nights after New York's hopes had risen, Hooley Smith, in a shameless imitation of Nels Stewart, opened the fifth and deciding match by shooting the disc squarely into Miller's right eye.

Miller was badly cut, he dropped down in pain, his new teammates rushed to his aid, and he was taken away to see a doctor. Ten minutes later, to the cheers of the Montreal crowd, Miller reappeared with his eye so swollen it was practically shut. The injury, though, did nothing to dampen his fearless defence of the Rangers citadel, and after sixty minutes of enormously entertaining hockey had passed, only the Maroons' Russell Oatman had managed to sneak the puck in behind him. But the Rangers' Frank Boucher had, meanwhile, caged the disc twice. This meant the dinged-up old rose bowl and the cause of all this fuss, the Stanley Cup, was destined for proud display at the following address: The Mayor's Office, City Hall, New York City, New York.

More than two thousand miles from the skyscrapers of New York, Eddie Shore was hard at work, having paid $16,400 for 480 fertile acres just over the Edmonton city limits. With the acreage came the stock, equipment, and buildings of the Albert Elliot farm, one of the finest in the district. With grain prices at an all-time high, the brawny Bruin wasted not a day before he was in the fields, toiling eighteen hours straight to plant the seeds on time.

FIVE

===

EDDIE SHORE WAS PRESSED IN from all sides, and teammates George Owen, Mickey MacKay, and Lionel Hitchman, cowering in the distance, were powerless to help. With his enormous right hand, huge wrist, and muscular forearm, the toughest of the "Bruising Bruins" fought furiously to attach as many autographs as he could to the reams of paper thrust at him by the screaming youngsters. The children pushed and pulled and carried their beloved Eddie almost off his feet. Also in the sporting-goods section of the Jordan Marsh department store in downtown Boston was the equally popular Percy Galbraith, under similar assault and attempting to sign papers while the kids were crawling up his back until they were practically standing on his head. From the crush created by their diminutive fans, it was a wonder that the Bruins had air enough to breathe. Art Ross, desperate to save his team, yelled at his men to stop their signing and make their getaway. With great effort, Shore inched over to one of the elevators and then, according the press reports, "finally had to exert his strength, convert himself into a full-back and literally hurl himself into the lift. Even then a dozen of the kids squeezed in with him before the door could be shut."

In 1928, you could buy anything you wanted at Jordan Marsh, and Boston, which only half-jokingly referred to itself as the "Hub of the Universe," was the economic epicentre, not only of the smaller cities that crowded each other outside its borders, but of all New England. Fifty cents of every whole-sale dollar spent in those six states was spent in Boston, and fifty thousand workers were employed by the city's four thousand firms, and these firms enjoyed sales that placed them third in the nation, behind only New York and Chicago. Boston had textile mills, shoe factories, foundries, sugar refineries, machine shops, and the massive sheds on Summer Street, through which more wool passed than anywhere else on earth. A fleet of five hundred fishing vessels made Boston the number one fishing port in the whole of the western hemisphere, and to handle the massive catches of cod, flounder, and mackerel that were landed daily, the city also had the world's largest fish-freezing and storage plant. A few blocks from the screaming gulls and the docks teeming with sweaty labourers were the marble floors and oak-panelled offices of Boston's many esteemed financial institutions. These were investment houses, banks, and insurance concerns that were the equal of any other anywhere.

At the close of the decade, however, many a "proper" Bostonian had the ominous feeling that their best days were behind them. The New England economy, on which Boston was so dependent, was not merely stagnant but, alarmingly, showing signs of decline. Industrially, Massachusetts had lost valuable ground to other states since the turn of the century, and Boston was by no means the international port it had once been. While the harbour was still bustling with cargo vessels, half the ships entering and leaving the city's waters were devoted to the lesser coastal trade. "The decaying grain elevators and crumbling wharves of East Boston and the abandoned hulks of once noble ships," the historian Charles H. Trout wrote hauntingly, "gave the harbor a sepulchral appearance."

The most proper of the proper Bostonians at the time was Charles Francis Adams, great-great-grandson of John Adams, the second American president, and the great-grandson of John Quincy Adams, the sixth American president. In 1929, Charles F. would be appointed by the current occupant of the White House, Herbert Hoover, as Secretary of the United States Navy. Adams had graduated from Harvard College as president of his class, gone to Harvard Law School, travelled throughout Europe for a year, entered politics, and, ultimately, become one of the pre-eminent financiers in the country. Adams controlled several New England banks, was a director of many of the nation's largest companies, and held the prestigious position of treasurer of the Corporation of Harvard College. Adams was a man who garnered nothing but respect, and for sport he preferred the one fit for a gentleman, yachting—at the helm of his boat, he had successfully defended the America's Cup in 1920.

One evening around midnight, the telephone rang at his elegant home and was answered by his wife. She listened for a moment and then, putting the receiver down, dryly informed her surprised husband, "The Bruins' goal guard is in jail."

In Boston there lived another Charles Francis Adams, for whom the misdirected call was, of course, intended. This man, who was the head of a grocery chain numbering over two thousand stores, was, according to Boston high society, the "wrong" Charles Francis; the "right" one would have had nothing whatsoever to do with ice hockey.

The "wrong" Charles F. Adams was the product of a modest upbringing in northernmost New England, where he had learned the grocery business at age eighteen from his uncle. The work, for which Adams was paid three dollars a week, was from 7 a.m. until 8 p.m., Monday to Saturday, with a day off on Sunday so that he could go out and collect overdue accounts. From that job with his uncle, the ambitious and competitive Adams went on to become a grocery magnate selling to the common man. "Every week," ran the slogan for his First National Stores, "is thrift week here!"

Because of a life devoted to hard work, Adams had never had time for athletics, and he discovered the game of hockey only in his later years. Visiting Montreal in 1924, Adams witnessed the Stanley Cup final, fell for the sport, and was introduced to a dour Scot named Art Ross, who knew a wee bit about the game. Adams returned to Boston, and by the start of the 1924–25 season had shrewdly outmanoeuvred several American syndicates to purchase and establish the first active NHL franchise outside of Canada. That inaugural season was a challenge, and Ross, in a frenetic search for hockey talent, any hockey talent, hired and fired at a mad rate. "We had three teams that year," Adams would later quip. "One coming, one going, and one playing." The new Bruins were a collection of hockey nobodies, as Walter Brown, manager of the Boston Garden in the 1930s, recalled:

> Wilf Schnarr, he didn't last any time. George Redding, who played goal the night they had to take Hec Fowler off the ice at the Arena when Toronto won 11–0. Cook— I've forgotten his first name, but he wasn't related to the famous Cooks—a forward. Carson Cooper, who broke his leg that year and didn't play much. Bobby Rowe, a forward. Jim Herberts, who was a defense man then. Alfie Skinner, another defense man. Smokey Harris, the original Smokey, who had only one eye. Curly Headley, who just wasn't good enough. Herb Mitchell, Art Ross's brother-in-law, who is now managing Hershey. Redding, who is now coaching amateurs in Harringay, England. He was a smooth-faced young fellow; now he wears a mustache and has little hair on his head. That first team had eleven players to start with. Three of them lasted the season—Herberts, Skinner (almost all the season), and Cooper, who they had to keep when he broke his leg. They won six games and lost twenty-four.

To make matters worse, the Bruins were forced to play all their home games on Monday nights that first year, because that was the only slot the Arena management would give them, and by the end of the season, Adams was seventy-five thousand dollars poorer. However, the man who would become the cornerstone of the young franchise, Lionel Hitchman, had arrived in

January in a trade with the Senators, and in the Bruins' second year, he and Jimmy Herberts, Carson Cooper, and Bill Stuart propelled the team almost to the point of making the playoffs. As importantly, the Arena was packed tight game after game with screaming fans and with many new converts to hockey having to be turned away at the door.

An audacious venture like Adams's hockey enterprise was a seldom-seen occurrence in staid old "Beantown," and Tex Rickard, president of Madison Square Garden, took note. Rickard at the time had the fantastical idea of building mammoth amphitheatres all across the country to mimic the success of his building in New York, and Boston was on his list of possible locations. Rickard knew the right people, and the wrong ones, to approach in Boston about such an outlandish scheme, and so he went to see the owner of the Bruins. Adams immediately realized that this was what his city needed, figuring that Rickard's new garden would be a modern palace for Boston's masses and, for Boston commerce, a sport, entertainment, and convention magnet. The Bruins owner, a man whose astute business sense was rivalled only by his love for hockey, gave his word that if Rickard were to build it, then he would rent it, at a hundred thousand dollars a season, for five seasons. This was the guarantee Rickard's bankers needed, and they agreed to finance the project.

The Boston & Maine building over the North Station railway tracks was demolished, and in its place the Boston Garden rose rapidly. Construction began on December 5, 1927, and the enormous edifice was ready for its hockey baptism on November 20, 1928. The building had a central public-address apparatus, five fresh-air fans, eight exhaust fans, and thirteen miles of pipes buried within a concrete slab, which was topped by a terrazzo surface, which in turn was topped with water. Cooled brine was forced through the pipes to make ice. When the venue had to be quickly readied for another event, steam was forced through instead. White pigment was added to the surface water before it froze, and this meant that the days in Boston of playing hockey on a black surface were over, because the Garden surface was as white as snow.

The giant structure was designed to accommodate 14,800 for hockey, and it had multiple entrances. Those who could afford the expensive, reserved seats used specially-marked doorways and were politely ushered by uniformed attendants to their spots on the main floor or the first balcony. Nothing stood between the front-row seats and the action, and a first-row seat on the first balcony perched the customer practically over the ice; an experience not to be forgotten. Less prosperous patrons, the ones with the cheap passes for open seats, had their own entryways, which led them via a labyrinth of ramps and stairwells to a pair of second balconies situated almost within touching distance of the rafters. It was here, a mile up, where Boston Garden's own "gallery gods" were destined to reign for decades to come. These blue-collared deities, thundering and roaring for their Bruins in the heavens above, would not trade places with the better dressed in the seats below for all the money in the world.

The Montreal Canadiens were the first to invade the brand new building, and public interest in the inaugural game was considerable. Long before showtime, the elevated trains over Causeway Street began to deposit passengers by the carload, and the multitudes flowed down from the trolley platforms

Shore posing with a radio, a gift from the gallery gods.
(The "Ross-net" is in the background.) *(Courtesy of Edward W. Shore Jr.)*

and surged towards the Garden gates, which were closed tight. "Everybody who ever saw a hockey game in Boston," it was reported, "seemingly decided to go last night, along with a lot of others to whom the experience was new."

At around eight o'clock, the entranceways still had not been opened and the crowd's patience was at an end. Lunging forward, the hockey-mad throng broke down the doors, pushed in the windows, and pried open the fire escapes. "It was a riot, a mob scene, a re-enaction of the assault on the Bastille," the Boston *Herald*'s Stanley Woodward wrote. To relieve the human pressure so that it would not collapse the sides of his untested vessel, Adams quickly ordered internal passageways opened. "It looked like the Oklahoma land rush," Clif Keane, age sixteen at the time, later remembered. "Guys were kicking and clawing and climbing over each other trying to reach the first row of the second balcony, which were choice seats for half a buck. You would have thought there was a fire. It was 10 stories to the top; 10 flights of stairs; 13 steps to a flight, a total of 130 steps. I counted them one time. And you ran all the way up, taking four steps at a time all the way to the top of the building. But it was always worth it. Especially that first night."

Thirty seconds into that first night, Eddie Shore, the Alberta farmer, suffered a severe charley horse in the leg, and although he played for the rest of the game, his dashes and crashes, so necessary to pep up his teammates, were not there. The red shirts won, yet Bruins fans seemed not to notice, so in love were they with the new Garden.

Shore had been in prime form before the first Garden game; after the game and the charley horse, less so. His injured leg worsened, he had to undergo an operation to drain the fluid, and, as if that were not enough, he came down with a stomach disorder from which it took him a couple of weeks to recover. Shore, though, was better in time for an early-December bout against New York, and shortly into the game, he started down ice on one of his flashy jaunts. As was frequently the case, the speedster sped well ahead of his teammates and, unable to take a clean shot, had no one to pass to as he neared the enemy net. With his options limited, Shore chose to execute perhaps the most classic of his many most classic moves, which was to leverage all the strength that his charging body could muster, let loose a wicked drive at the back dasher, collect the rebound, and then shoot it into the goal.

Over the summer, Art Ross had gotten rid of some Bruins, including that old warrior Sprague Cleghorn, now in the Can-Am league, where he was happily reunited with Billy Coutu on the New Haven Eagles' blue line. The Garden continued to sell out every game, but by mid-December the Bruins were the third-worst team in the league, and Ross intended to make more changes. In New York, the former Dartmouth football star Myles Lane was unhappily wearing a Rangers uniform, and owner John S. Hammond saw that the Bruins were struggling. Hammond sent Ross's boss a telegram: "Myles Lane has given us all publicity we hoped. His heart and public are in Boston. Would you consider his trade for Shore?" Came the reply: "You are so far from Shore you need a life preserver. Best regards, C.F. Adams."

The Bruins left 1928 behind them with an unimpressive record of 5–6–2, but found their old aggressiveness just in time for a New Year's Day shutout over Ottawa at the Garden. The next Bruins contest, a January 3 engagement with the Maroons in Montreal, was an important one if the team was to turn itself around. Shore was dining with a friend just outside Boston before heading to the train station for the overnight trip north. On the way to the station, with no time to spare, his friend's car broke down; refusing to grab a taxi and abandon his friend, Shore insisted on fixing the engine himself. He tinkered around under the hood as precious minutes passed by, and "I got to the station late," Shore recalled. "The team's train had already left. I knew I'd be in a jam if I blew that game."

Shore placed a call to the Boston airport about hiring an airplane, but was told that the runway in Montreal was closed due to snow. "There was a cab line outside the station," Shore explained in a 1960 interview. "I talked one cab driver into driving me the 340 miles for $100. It was a lot of money but I figured it would cost me twice as much if I didn't show." Shore jumped into the cab, which roared out of the city. Bill Grimes of the Boston *Evening American* learned of this feat, and in the paper the next afternoon, he observed, "Unless it snows, Shore should have no trouble getting through." The optimism turned out to be unfounded. "Well," Shore recalled, "what started out to be a rain froze over. I drove, the cabbie drove."

Thus begins the quintessential Eddie Shore story, a tale that has rightly become legend in Boston because its elements embody his loyalty to the Bruins, his Canadian mastery of the elements, his superhuman energy, his athlete's dedication, and his enormous heart.

As the taxi inched its way north through rain mixed with sleet, Shore tried to rest in the back seat. Meanwhile, on the train to Montreal, Ross was distraught over the absence of his star (and would become more distraught the next morning when there was still no word from the missing athlete). After nightfall, the taxi approached the hills and treacherous slopes of the White Mountains that lie directly in the way between Boston and Montreal. Anticipating the worst, Shore had the cabbie flag down a passing truck. Shore bought a snow shovel and ice axe from the truck driver, and the taxi moved north-ward again on its long ascent into the mountains. The going was slippery, and Shore suggested that the driver stop to put on the tire chains. There were no tire chains. The cabbie, who had no experience with country roads, suggested they turn back. Shore refused and took over the driving himself, stop-ping at an all-night gas station to get chains. They quickly wore out, and the taxi slid off the road. Shore leapt out and used the axe to cut down tree branches and shrubs to put under the tires for traction, and with the shovel cleared away the snow. The cabbie gunned the engine, Shore pushed, and the taxi was on its way.

The temperature dropped ever lower, and the windshield froze over. The windshield was an old-fashioned split-glass type, and Shore folded it down, letting in the bitter cold and wind. In the distance, he could make out some lights, which turned out to be the camp of a construction crew. The camp had a little store, and there Shore bought a second set of tire chains; they, too, soon wore out. "We wound up in a ditch," Shore recalled. "The cabbie quit right there. I found a farm house a mile or two up the road. The farmer hitched up a sleigh and drove me to a connecting train line. I made it to Montreal in 22 hours and so I was there at 6 o'clock the night of the game."

Ross fined Shore heavily (two hundred dollars) for missing the train in Boston, but not before getting him ready for the game. "Both his eyes were practically closed," Ross remem-bered. "His face was all raw and almost bleeding from the bliz-zard. We actually had to put raw steaks on his face all the next day. But that was the next day. He ate a couple of steaks, took about a half hour's rest and then played one of the greatest all-around games I've ever seen."

The next day, Montreal hockey writer Elmer W. Ferguson described the game in his newspaper column. "Mr. Bam! Bam! Bammy Shore," Ferguson wrote, "the blonde tiger of the Boston Bruin defence, furnished more than the orthodox thrills in the season's most colorful hockey battle, when the Boston club out-fought Maroons in a tough, bustling, devil-take-the-hindmost hockey tussle at the Forum last night. Bam, Bam, Bammy scored the only goal, when with Maroons two men short, he twice went plunging through the remaining forces, circled the nets and, on the second occasion, whipped home a thudding drive."

Detroit's Bill Brydge, in a Boston Garden game two weeks later, tossed "Mr. Bam! Bam! Bammy Shore" hard into the boards. "Cry baby Shore," as Shore was known by his critics, instantly fell to the ice and writhed around as if in great pain. Normally, Shore would have quit the act after seeing that no penalties were being called and be back wreaking mayhem in no time, but it was the real thing. The bruised Bruin was carried from the field of battle by his teammates, and the usually bois-terous Garden crowd grew unnaturally silent as it became clear the situation was dire. Shore was laid out on the trainer's bench, and the Bruins' physician, Dr. Joe Shortell, began to feel around for the injured spot. "The beads of perspiration came out on Shore's forehead," it was reported, "bigger and faster than from the outmost physical exertion out on the ice, and Shore nearly turned inside out when the doctor touched the spot that was most affected."

The pain was incredible, and Ross had to keep his star out

of the entire second period before setting him loose again in the third. It was obvious to the Garden crowd, now vastly restrained, that their man at right defence was suffering terribly (and indeed, after the game Shore's ankle would puff out like a toy balloon). Shore did very little rushing and appeared to have been tamed, but looks can be deceiving, and a hurt bear is an exceptionally dangerous animal—a fact of which Bill Brydge had to be reminded. Brydge was carrying the puck down the left lane when he got too close to the wounded Bruin. When all was over and done with, Shore had a five-minute major to serve, while Brydge was last seen holding his hand over his badly lacerated mouth, missing four teeth.

Hockey had an unfortunate reputation for violence, and a campaign waged by A. Linde Fowler, hockey man for the Boston *Evening Transcript,* the city's society newspaper, to bring Ivy League cachet to the professional game had the backing of Weston Adams, the owner's son. Weston had been some years behind George Owen, Class of '23, at Harvard, but he knew him and, like everyone else in Boston, knew of Owen's athletic prowess. In a day when a collegian could letter in more than one sport at a time, Owen did so in nine of them. Owen had been a star for Harvard's football, baseball, and hockey teams, and of the three, hockey was his favourite. "There are some things you think you can do fairly well," Owen once explained modestly, "and hockey is one of them for me." And so, Fowler and Adams wondered, how about making Owen a Bruin?

Weston's father had no problem with the idea, but while Owen was tempted to join the Bruins, he was now a reputable stocks-and-bonds associate at Coffin & Burr. "Playing professional sports, especially hockey," Owen explained decades later, "wasn't fashionable at the time." As a proper Bostonian who'd grown up in the leafy suburb of Newton (although born in Hamilton, Ontario), Owen, like others of his ilk, had been led to believe that to be paid for playing sport was somehow "smelly," and he probably cringed at the thought of playing, say, the Black Hawks and having the entire Harvard Club of Chicago present to witness his debasement. Owen rejected Adams's initial offer, but, with Fowler cheerleading in the pages of the *Transcript* and Weston pleading behind the scenes, he agreed (but not before Conn Smythe of Toronto nearly stole him out from under Ross's nose). The exorbitant salary that the elder Adams told the press he would pay Owen—twelve thousand dollars for one year plus an eight-thousand-dollar bonus if they won the Cup—was perhaps a publicity stunt in a league where the very best players were probably not paid that. This sort of talk helped, though, since it put everything in attractive business terms that any of Owen's Ivy League friends could readily appreciate.

The Owen acquisition was, Fowler gushed, "The most sensational bit of hockey news that has developed since pro hockey was introduced into Boston." Fowler continued, "It is an angle of the developing tendency among high-class amateurs to enter a field which is lucrative, which keeps them in a game which they love to play and a game which, through the acquisition of such men as Owen, ought to move along a higher plane of sportsmanship."

Uncomfortable in a new pair of skates, George Owen took his place on the Bruins blue line before the start of an early-January game against Toronto. "I was," Owen admitted, "scared stiff." In the dressing room beforehand, his new teammates warned him about Toronto, telling him that the Leafs would try to knock the stuffing out of him. The only thing Owen, who was recovering from a recent illness, had done to ready himself for the NHL was to skate some at the University Club, and the only thing he could think about while standing exposed on the Garden ice was all the family and friends sitting up in the stands, watching his every move. At that tense moment, up slid Owen's defensive partner, Mr. Edward William Shore of Daugh, Alberta. Those in the Garden press box thought "Owen looked a trifle ill at ease" standing next to Boston's bad man. The veteran Bruin, however, sought to reassure the new guy.

"Don't worry boy," Shore said calmly. "We'll get these babies. This is easy for you. We're all with you."

Owen's mother and sister, perhaps never having seen a Bruins game before, complained afterward that they had to keep getting up from their seats because every time Shore got the puck, the crowd stood and they could not see a thing. Shore was at his best that night. "A veritable whirling dervish," Fowler reported. "Where he gets the energy to put so much physical effort into game after game, without ever looking or acting tired, is a mystery." Shore's rushes were spectacular, and he was a real threat to the opposition. His speed and his sweeping strokes baffled the Leafs, and he used smart headwork to position himself for testing shots.

Playing spectacularly, Shore covered for Owen, but more important, he coached Owen the entire time. The astute hockey observer could see that the Bruins star was helping the Harvard guy shine, and with his help, shine Owen did. The rookie was considered to be the hero of the game, scoring his first NHL goal, to the delight of family, friends, and perfect strangers, in a match in which the Bruins beat Toronto 5–2. Owen would never have a bad thing to say about Shore, and Owen's presence in a Bruins uniform, according to a 1971 article in *Hockey Pictorial*, "Enticed a new type of fan to the Boston Garden. Because of him, prominent businessmen and officials brought their wives and children to the Garden, and a Bruins home game became as important an event on their social calendar as the Friday afternoon symphony." Indeed, for couples smartly dressed to the nines, a Bruins game became *de rigueur* after a meal at Locke-Obers or the Ritz-Carlton, and gentlemen who, on Sunday afternoons, were on their best behaviour at the Country Club or Brae Burn, had, only the night before, been screaming for blood at the Garden.

Charles F. Adams, as always, was willing to spend whatever it took to win the Cup, and the grocery tycoon dug deep into his wallet. The Bruins' collegiate trend continued first with the acquisition of Myles Lane, a Dartmouth man and Melrose, Massachusetts, native who had been unhappy in New York, and then Dr. Bill Carson, a University of Toronto–trained dentist. Lane played left defence and Carson centre. To get the players, Adams had to write cheques, payable to the New York Rangers and Toronto Maple Leafs respectively, for $7,500 and $25,000, but Adams would do anything that Art Ross asked if it meant possession of that silver trophy. Ross also had Adams acquire Ralph "Cooney" Weiland as a spare centreman and dispose of Hal Winkler, who, so good in goal last year, had not been as good as his challenger, Cecil "Tiny" Thompson, this year. Adams, as instructed, also dumped the popular Freddie Fredrickson. According to an unsubstantiated Boston *Herald* story, Fredrickson was to become manager of the Bruins, and while the story had no truth to it, Ross failed to see the humour; he insisted that Fredrickson be traded to Pittsburgh for Mickey MacKay. Adams, embarrassed, slipped Fredrickson a thousand dollars as he showed him the door.

"I will always cherish," the classy Freddie, who would later coach Princeton University, wrote to his fans, "the privilege of having the opportunity of knowing something about Boston and Bostonians."

Eddie's fame and popularity grew stronger, if that were possible, as the 1928–29 season progressed, and the Bruins figured that the only thing better than one Shore was two. In Melville, Saskatchewan, Aubrey Shore had taken his younger brother's place as the local hockey star, and Ross summoned the Millionaire to Boston, promising him $2,400 if he would play for the rest of the season. Eddie showed his big brother the sights along Commonwealth Avenue, and Aubrey did some skating with the Bruins, but he never dressed for a single game and soon went back to Canada. No explanation was given until the *Toronto Star* revealed that Aubrey had a previously unannounced "commitment" to Kitchener of the Can-Pro league. The truth was that things had not worked out for the older Shore brother in Boston. Aubrey had been devastated by his father's death in a way that Eddie never had, and he drank—a fact that had likely become obvious to Ross.

Aubrey went home and Eddie continued to be a veritable whirling wizard with the puck. In most games, he played the full sixty minutes. He remained the target of more shocks, bumps, and outright attacks than any other man in the league; eventually, every part of Shore's body would be injured in one manner or another. "I recall trying at one time," the

Shore, at left, with older brother, Aubrey, during Aubrey's unsuccessful try-out
with the Bruins. *(Courtesy of Edward W. Shore Jr.)*

sportswriter Austen Lake said, "to catalogue his scars and
fractures preparatory to having a news artist make a diagram.
Only there were so many conflicting scars where his skin had
been torn many times in the same area that the idea was hope-
lessly involved. In a rough sum up, he had more stitches in his
flesh than a tailor needs to make an overcoat."

Shore's face, remarkably enough, showed only hints of
damage, and except for nicks chipped out here and there, small
dents in the jaw, a synthetic dimple on the left cheek, slight
scratches under the eyes, and faint scar tissue under the lips,

there was little evidence of all it had been through. Nearly all of Shore's gleaming white teeth were store-bought, the originals having been ejected from his mouth, and his nose, despite having been broken countless times, was straight. Shore had light hazel eyes that crinkled when he laughed, and when he spoke, his voice was disarmingly soft, lowering almost to a whisper. "Oh," he once confided quietly of how he had kept his nose in line, "if you grab it quick just after it is busted and fit the edges together, it will grow as good as new. I always set my own nose. I twist it around until I feel the edges grit and then put a plaster across it to hold it flush."

Shore was playing some of the best hockey of his career, and to meet up with him on the ice was something to remember. "I'll never forget the first time I played against him," the Canadiens' Johnny Gagnon recalled. "He knocked me cold. When I got up, he said, 'Kid, next time you keep your head up!' That turned out to be good advice."

Rugged as always, and never subtle, Shore in the latter part of the 1928–29 season was maturing as a player, and for the next several years would be at the zenith of his career. He had made a significant about-face in tactics. Still giving the fans the spills and thrills they so longed for, he was now using increased headwork in his play. His shots had more of a tricky sweep to them, he was using his amazing skating ability to outwit opponents and not just run them over, and, in perhaps the biggest change of all, the "Lone Wolf" who had travelled to the Château Laurier in Ottawa back in 1927 before the rest of his mates had even left Boston was now regularly passing to his fellow Bruins as he rushed down ice. With an uncanny ability to perfectly place the puck onto the tape of other Bruins' sticks, Shore was now giving his colleagues every opportunity for easy goals.

The 1928–29 edition of the Boston Bruins was, according to Fowler, "made up of a bunch of fighters, the never-say-die kind who once they set their minds to it are almost unstoppable on the ice." The Bruins were well poised for the upcoming "moneyed game," as it was called, and they relished the thought of the extra pay and fat bonuses that a championship run would net them. Manager Ross, who would also share in the riches if the Stanley Cup could be won, was lucky because he not only had the hockey stalwarts of Percy Galbraith, Henry Oliver, and Bill Carson as his first line of offensive thoroughbreds, he also had Dutch Gainor, Cooney Weiland, and Dit Clapper as his very able ponies. Immensely popular with the press and the public, these three second-stringers were collectively dubbed the Dynamite Line.

At left wing on the Dynamite Line was the man who carved a deadly serpentine S down the ice, Dutch Gainor, who (it could now be revealed) had suffered terribly from ulcers of the teeth during that disastrous series against New York last spring, but was now in the pink of health, and his baffling style could be counted on to tie opposing players up in knots. Gainor's trick was to keep the other team puzzling over what he was about to do next with the puck—only to realize that he had already caged it. Gainor's tricks would earn him fourteen goals during the regular season, placing him second on the Bruins only to Harry Oliver, who would score seventeen.

The Dynamite Line was centred by Cooney Weiland. As a youth, Weiland had honed his hockey skills on the frozen ponds of Seaforth, Ontario, using cow pats as pucks. At only

150 pounds, Weiland was a giant in action, if not in size, using his extra-long hockey stick to poke or hook the puck away from opposing players. "Little" Cooney Weiland was not only a defensive wonder, but shifty on the attack, baffling to the enemy, and great at making pretty dashes. It was not unusual for him to score a couple of goals in a game. Off the ice, however, he was an odd sort.

Weiland had a raspy voice, and he purposefully set himself apart from his teammates. They saw nothing of him outside of practices and games, he lived alone, and even when he got married, he kept it a secret. Weiland leaned towards studying art, and if not for hockey, he said, he would have happily been a drugstore clerk. In 1962, he made headlines by barricading himself in front of beautiful maple and elm trees that were going to be cut down in the suburban Massachusetts town where he lived. By this time, Weiland was very well known, not only for having once played for the Bruins, but also for having coached the Bruins to the Stanley Cup championship in 1941 and for currently coaching the Harvard College hockey team (a position he would hold for twenty-one years). Weiland made his point with the barricade, and the trees were saved.

Aubrey "Dit" Clapper was the Dynamite Line's potent man on the right wing and was just barely into what would become a twenty-year career with the Bruins, after which, like Weiland, he would one day coach the team. Clapper was universally adored, and what was there not to say in praise of the man? An outstanding player, the amiable Clapper was friendly to reporters, shook hands with new referees before their first game, and had the trust of his fellow Bruins. He was a caring big brother to younger Bruins, and was always ready to pull a solid punch out of his pocket if any of them needed protection. Dit (a name he had given himself as a tot since he could not pronounce his middle name, Victor) was also great-looking. He had slick black hair parted knife-like in the centre, a movie star's face, what would have been described in those days as a "toothpaste smile," and a massive and muscular six-foot, two-inch frame.

Clapper was amazingly fast on skates and had the swiftest, most bullet-like shot in hockey; a shot so blindingly fast that the puck was in the net long before goalies knew what had happened. The strongest man in the league, Clapper could toss the toughest men around the rink, and he once checked Ching Johnson so hard that the Ranger defenceman's jaw broke in four places. Clapper was stronger even than the almighty Eddie Shore, and the only person on the team, if not the entire planet, who would dare josh him. Once, Dit partially sawed through Shore's new hockey stick and covered the gash with adhesive tape; whatever Shore's reaction was after he attempted to take a shot, Clapper lived to laugh about it.

For the defence, Ross had, of course, Shore and his twin titan, the steady and reliable Lionel Hitchman. "Shore may be the dynamo of the Boston club," a sports columnist once observed, "but Hitchman is the balancing wheel." Hitchman was cool-eyed, fearless, and had all the polish of the ex-mounted police officer that he was. With his long and angular body, Hitchman was a ferocious bodychecker who could, and would, give back better than he got.

Should either Hitchman or Shore ever falter, George "Harvard" Owen was there to jump into the breach. Owen must have learned something at his alma mater, because he was the only Bruin intelligent enough to wear a helmet (the leather football type), and he had nothing to do with fighting, content to sit alone on the bench while his teammates and the opposition whaled the tar out of each other. Owen, though, was a fine, gritty hockey player who was as tough as nails and always at his best when the stakes were at their highest.

Behind all of these never-say-die sorts was Tiny Thompson, the quiet young man in net. Tiny had been an outstanding semi-pro basketball player in Calgary, and, like a basketball player should be, he was tall, lanky, and a devil with his hands, which were apparently made of steel. He also played first base in baseball, where he used his left mitt to great advantage, as he did in hockey. "When Tiny gets that big glove of his there," Nels Stewart once said, "you might as well give up."

The young Tiny had absolutely no fear, risked life and limb to shut off a score, and, in an age before face masks, enjoyed nothing more than to dive at the pointy ends of hockey blades. He was on a nervy crusade to show that fear was a useless emotion, and did not bother to blink at blistering drives of the type that would have beaten nine-tenths of the world's best goalers. He calmly faced down pucks that ripped in at him like high-velocity shells, ones that no other mortal could possibly have saved. Yet save these shots Thompson did, being simply the most courageous goal guardian in the game.

The Bruins completed the regular season with 57 points, on top of the American Division and second in the league only to the Canadiens, who led the Canadian Division with 59 points. To boost profits and sidestep the possibility that the division champions might not be matched up in the Stanley Cup final, the NHL decided to pit two best teams against each other in the first round of the playoffs. Howie Morenz, slowed of late by extra weight and a bothersome knee injury, was an exception rather than the rule when it came to how prepared the Canadiens were for the upcoming series, and the clash of the two best teams in the league was eagerly anticipated on both sides of the border. Twelve mounted police officers maintained order outside Boston Garden, while inside, three hundred foot police and one hundred railroad officers kept a wary eye on the throbbing mob. Seats were scarce and standing room limited, and as the Canadiens made their way along the wooden planks to the ice, a swarm of Boston fans gleefully taunted and insulted them.

In the first period, Cooney Weiland scored the game's only goal. When this happened, the gigantic crowd rocked the Garden, shouting and roaring with such tremendous volume that the referee's whistle could not be heard for several minutes. For the remainder of the evening, the Canadiens found themselves smothered. From the first whistle to the final bell, the Bruins had simply shut the Frenchmen down.

"Forget that one," Morenz yelled from the steamy showers after the contest, "tomorrow's another day!"

The next night was a repeat of the first game, as Weiland again scored the game's only goal, again driving the Garden crowd plumb daffy. There were cowbells clattering, horns blaring, and whoops of joy all around, and from the upper regions, the gods, to show their great pleasure, threw down gifts that, upon later examination, turned out to be torn newspapers, train transfers, Jordan Marsh rain checks, cigarette butts, shredded programs, and one neatly wrapped two-pound package of steak. The contest resumed at a mad clip, and

Morenz was tireless throughout, blaming no one but himself for Weiland's goal because he had been playing opposite him and had failed to block his drive.

Despite the lack of further scoring, the hockey action was terrific—and terrifically entertaining. In a thrilling sideshow, Boston's Bill Carson and Montreal's George Patterson engaged in a sensational butting match at the south boards. Patterson got the better of Carson and had "Dr. Bill" over his shoulder with one hand; he was making ready to throw him headlong onto the ice when George Owen skated up and seized Patterson in an attempt to rescue the dentist. With his free hand, Patterson retaliated by grabbing Owen's face in a vice-like grip and clawing for his eyes. The fans were all agog over how it would turn out when referee Cooper Smeaton, who had no appreciation for drama, ruined everything by stepping in and promptly showing Patterson the gate.

The game carried on like this at an unprecedented rate. The gallery gods yelled down instructions to the Bruins and threats to the Canadiens, while the rest of the fans were in a state of overexcitement. "One pop-eyed individual," sports columnist Jack Conway complained, "leaped from his seat and crashed his hands down on my imported headgear every time one of the Bruins carried the puck a few yards."

Elmer W. Ferguson was in Boston to cover the game, and after the Canadiens' second, heartbreaking, loss, returned to his hotel room and later wrote:

At six o'clock the next morning there came a knock on my door. I opened the portal and there stood Morenz, dressed in his street clothes. It was still dark and a surprised host said a bit testily, "What's the idea? Where are you going so early?" "To bed," said Morenz wearily. "I've been walking the streets all night, trying to forget that goal. We lost and it was my fault." And the kid was sobbing.

Following the two contests at the Garden, there was, for the elated Bruins and the frustrated Canadiens, the familiar train ride to Montreal, with each team aboard its own Pullman car. At the Forum, the extra-wide ice surface was perfectly smooth and hard—too wide and too slick for the Bruins. The Canadiens, comfortable in the open space and gliding along at great speed, were enlivened by the vocal enthusiasm of fans banking the Forum floor to the Forum roof and skated freely into the Boston zone as if no Bruins were present to stop them.

Aurèle Joliat quickly scored, and nine seconds later the excitable Albert "Battleship" Leduc made it 2–0. Shore happened to be off the ice at the time for high-sticking. He had only to raise the hickory ever so slightly and Cooper Smeaton would chase him to the "stout house," where he spent six of the first ten minutes of the game. In the second period, Shore managed to keep his artillery low enough for Smeaton's liking and launched a phenomenal offensive. He was, according to reporter Stanley Woodward, "The life, mainspring and keystone of that Boston attack."

Sparked by Shore, within less than six minutes the Bruins had scored twice (first Carson and then Gainor), and, according to A. Linde Fowler, "the crazy French populace of this metropolis saw the chances of prolonging this series lost."

What chance Montreal might have had to reverse the situation was further lost when Shore got into a race for the disc with Leduc in the Boston zone. Shore won, and then, Fowler reported, "stopped with a suddenness that started a tiny snow storm of vivisected ice." Shore wheeled a half-turn, started back, was bottled up at the Canadiens' blue line, and drilled in a fierce one that fooled George Hainsworth into flopping one way while the puck whizzed the other way and into the net. With that amazing play, Shore proved beyond any reasonable doubt that he was the money player of all money players.

Shore's goal, which put the Bruins ahead, 3–2, was the winning one, although the Canadiens' fans, many having earlier stood in a driving rain for six or seven hours to buy tickets, did not know this as yet. In the last part of the game, with the once-pristine Forum ice badly deteriorating, the Flying French poured it on, but Tiny Thompson was dazzling. With less than two minutes remaining, Morenz broke away and, at the Boston blue line, cut loose a fierce one for the right side of the net. Tiny coolly blocked the rubber with his foot. There were only seconds remaining, and the Canadiens rushed in with five-man attacks; this impressed Thompson not in the least. The pucks flew and the Bruins goaltender stopped them all. Howie Morenz later declared that Thompson was "a highway-robber."

The next day, Sunday, March 24, three thousand fans greeted the Bruins' train as it entered Boston's North Station, located beneath Boston Garden. It was the largest homecoming reception ever afforded the team, and the crowd threw up a cheer as each Bruin disembarked. Captain Lionel Hitchman, plastered from the top of his forehead to the tip of his nose, was a little hard to make out at first, but when the crowd realized who it was, he got a rousing welcome. But it was, according to the Boston *Globe*'s John J. Hallahan, "Eddie Shore, the hero of Saturday night's game at Montreal, who was the man most sought. He was wearing a patch over one eye, but was recognized at once. The rafters of the station fairly shook with the reception he received."

Hockey history was about to be made the next night with the first-ever Stanley Cup final game played between two American clubs. The Canadians of the Boston Bruins were set to challenge the Canadians of the New York Rangers (Taffy Abel and Myles Lane being the only American-born players on either team), and Charles F. Adams, having agreed to certain financial terms with Rangers owner Colonel Hammond, had secured the first game for the Boston Garden.

Lester Patrick was en route from Toronto, having just coached his Rangers to victory over the Maple Leafs in four games. Patrick had with him the smooth working combination of Frank Boucher and the Cook brothers, Bill and Bun. He also had with him Butch Keeling, Tiny Thompson's little brother Paul, Murray Murdoch, and the two huskies, Ching Johnson and Taffy Abel. Ching had almost not lasted the season. During a game in Montreal, he had broken an ankle; they lugged him to the hospital, the hospital burned down, and Ching escaped to the street, where the temperature was ten degrees below zero Fahrenheit. Patrick was also travelling south with his new goaltender, a man named John Ross Roach, who was, according to Frank Boucher, "a moody little fellow." Patrick would end up liking the moody little fellow well enough to use him in goal for every single Rangers game for the next four years.

In Boston Garden on the evening of March 28, 1929, clouds of blue and grey smoke wafted up from the stands as fans nervously pulled on their cigarettes, trying to calm themselves before the contest started. It promised to be a corker. Vendors did a brisk business selling ice cream cones and hot dogs; hawkers yelled, "Offishul programs that you can't tell 'em without!"; and from silver flasks, bootleg gin and home-brewed moonshine were furtively gulped. Johnson and Abel could be seen warming up down on the ice, and Garden fans joked about Ching's bald head and the fact that it looked as if the fat Taffy parted his hair with a wet sponge. On the electric board, the coming Garden attractions were being advertised: "Royal Belgium Guards . . . Otto Von Porat and Johnny Risko . . . Cantor Rosenblatt . . ." Hitchman was also warming up, and the sizable cocoon over his left eye, a souvenir of the games in Montreal, was visible even from the second balcony. In a surprising development, Hal Winkler, who had been playing for a minor-league club in Minneapolis, was also warming up, there as a replacement in case Thompson was injured. Then the dignified voice of Frank Ryan came over the public-address system asking all to stand for the American national anthem (there being, of course, no need to sing Canada's song, "God Save the King," this year). The puck was dropped.

Ross, sporting his trademark iron-kelly derby, assumed his normal posture on the Bruins bench, resting his chin on the rail and, dangling both arms down over the sides, thumping the boards like a worried beaver. As agitated as Ross was, all of his men played flawlessly that night, with not a weak link in the chain. The Boston aggregation was as strong as it would ever be, and all to the detriment of the Rangers.

With his poke check and hook check, Weiland was a pest, and Shore and Hitchman were both stone walls. Never did Clapper skate so fast or take so many blasts at the enemy net, and every one of his fiercely drilled shots gave Roach the quivers. Dit also played like a man possessed, but five minutes into the second period, he stopped to take pity upon a hockey puck abandoned in the middle of the ice. He scooped it onto the blade of his stick, skated over to the mouth of the Ranger's cage, lofted it over Roach's shoulder, and there was bedlam at the Garden.

Five minutes after Clapper's goal, which did not improve John Ross Roach's mood any, Dutch Gainor took a shot from a distance that hit Taffy's leg, and then, reclaiming the puck, he let go with all his power, aiming for the smallest of openings between Roach and the inside of the far post. The red light behind Roach blazed brightly once again, and announcer Frank Ryan lost all composure, his shrieks blaring from loudspeakers while the crowd dissolved into happy chaos with cowbells ringing, tin horns piping, and trash strewn all over the ice. The seventeen thousand spectators were once more plunged into ecstasy minutes later, when Hitchman accidentally sent referee Bobby Hewitson head-on into the boards. "He plainly was knocked out," Stanley Woodward reported, "and it took several minutes to revive him to such an extent that he could continue with his thankless duties. The crowd, which had seemed tickled to death when he was hurt, was gracious enough to applaud him when he got back on his feet."

The Rangers had their scoring chances, and Thompson was not idle, saving half a dozen lightning shots in the first period alone. Paul Thompson, for one, had a good chance but could not beat his big brother, and so it went for the rest of the contest, with Tiny remaining as cool as a cucumber and as steady as a chronometer. Like a hardy helmsman, he stood upright as the Rangers storm gathered strength in front of him. Then, from out of the maelstrom, the disc would come hurtling in like hail, and, utterly emotionless, Thompson would smother the shot. He let not one in all night. The Bruins won, 2–0.

President Adams was in a rush to finish up the Bruins' season before baseball started (an investor in the Boston Braves, he saw no profit in having the two teams compete for the same fan dollar). Directly following the Bruins' domination of the Rangers, therefore, both teams quickly boarded their respective trains and the Rangers arrived in New York, bleary-eyed, at seven in the morning. Not so the Bruins. "Uncle Art" had learned a trick or two over the years, and as the Rangers' train roared on throughout the night to reach its destination at an early hour, Ross arranged for the Bruins' Pullman to lie over in New Haven so that his boys, cozy in their berths and dreaming sweet dreams of bonus money, could get their beauty rest.

It was not twenty-four hours since their last meeting when the hockey foes gathered at Madison Square Garden. The place was virtually empty. Everyone in Manhattan had apparently been stuck with theatre tickets, or perhaps, knowing that the Boston club would skate away with the Cup, was not bothering to show. In either case, it was a shame, because they missed a great game.

Lester Patrick's men ignored the thousands of vacant seats and, throwing off the lethargy caused by too much travel and too much hockey in too few days, skated like mad over the dirty white ice. The Rangers checked desperately, pressed constantly, dangerously, into Boston territory, although the Bruins were meteors themselves and dashed into the Rangers end repeatedly. "It was a battle all the way," Woodward, doubled over in pain from an attack of the grippe, reported from the press box, "but a result that was shaded in a different way would have been unjust before the fates."

Percy Galbraith in the first minutes got off a haymaker from the right boards that severely tested Roach, and moments later, Eddie Shore bolted from the Bruins defence and charged in on the Rangers net before being stopped by Ching Johnson and Taffy Abel. The brothers Cook attempted to breach the Boston defence, but instead were turned back by Oliver and Galbraith. Johnson tried his luck with a solo dash, and Eddie Shore smashed him to the ice. Dit Clapper took some gratuitous shots well outside of the Rangers blue line, and then the trickster Gainor, moving in closer, blasted one from the left side that Roach had some difficulty saving. Gainor and Clapper decided to team up for another go, but the two together had no better luck beating Roach than they had had alone. Mickey MacKay, who had been in for only a brief whirl early in the period, decided to give it a try and, skating into New York territory, was rewarded with a stiff bump by Ching Johnson. Then Lester Patrick's spare man, Sparky Vail, took a poorly planned route up ice that led him between Shore and Hitchman, and that was the end of that. Carson, Oliver, and Galbraith were all up to no good in front of Roach's net, yet Roach continued to hold on when Butch Keeling, all by himself, split the Boston points and likely would have scored, had he not first been ground into the ice by Hitchman. Hitch, for this offence, was serving time in the hoosegow when the period ended.

With Hitchman still in jail at the start of the second frame, Galbraith dropped back to defence alongside Shore, and as the two tried to hold off the Rangers, the New Yorkers enjoyed some open-and-shut chances on Tiny Thompson. A minute later, Hitchman's sentence was up and, to celebrate, he got away on a whooping rush with the Bruins forwards lagging far behind. Hitchman's poke from the Rangers' defensive zone, though, was slightly wide, and as he made the shot, a Ching Johnson check sent him kicking.

Both teams took turns rushing, and, at one point, a Cook brother was sent clean over the boards and into the expensive ($4.40) seats. This time, it was Oliver who was told to "take the outer air," although the crowd screamed for Shore's head, yelling to the referee that Eddie was the one to blame. Lots of players were tossed into the penalty box for various crimes, and in the midst of all this, Murray Murdoch drilled in a lulu from ten feet out that Thompson deflected with one skate. Clapper and Weiland, in retaliation, gave Roach a rough time by sending in long ones until all penitents had returned to the ice. Play continued at a fearful pace, with Galbriath barely missing a rebound and Oliver barely missing Galbriath's rebound.

Suddenly, at 14:01 of the second period, Harry Oliver scored.

"Oliver," as Woodward's dispatch the next day read, "put on the dizziest piece of stick handling of the season, fooled Abel and Johnson, and shot high and to the left, from between them. The puck went in and came out like a shuttle, but everyone in the rink saw it score, and the red light went on."

Playing defensively at the start of the third frame, the Bruins held back and let the Rangers carry the attack. Patrick's men, swooping in on Thompson with four-man sorties, got nowhere until that sharpshooter Butch Keeling unexpectedly (to Thompson, anyway) let fly from the blue line and scored. The score was now 1–1.

Shortly after the faceoff, Shore was chased to the box by the referee for a knee check, and in his absence, the Rangers stormed the Boston net in hopes of gaining the lead. The Bruins, stalling until Eddie could come to their rescue, fired the puck up ice to mark time, and Shore was back soon enough, which only convinced the Rangers to redouble their speed. Butch Keeling and Tiny's brother Paul were continuous threats as the Rangers, now with five forwards on the ice, attacked relentlessly. Time was running out when, jumping on a loose puck, Hitchman launched a one-man counterattack and skated between Keeling and Murdoch, who tried to mash him but succeeded only in squashing themselves. Hitchman caromed through the rest of the Rangers team and tried to cram the puck past Roach, but Roach somehow kicked it out and cleared to the middle zone. Bill Cook was there and had a clear channel to Thompson, but Eddie got to the disc first; for the Bruins, it was real lifesaver.

With no time left in the third period, as Woodward tells it, "Another Ranger rush met defeat at the Boston defense and Harry Oliver jumped back with Carson on his left. The twin pachyderms of the Ranger defense edged toward Harry. His pass to Dr. Bill was perfect, however, and the Doc blazed it into the far side with the hoist that meant the Stanley Cup."

Dr. Joe Shortell sailed his bowler out onto the ice, and Lionel Hitchman, the only Bruin left from the pioneering days of 1924–25, playfully batted it around with his stick.

Ross's plan had always been to win the championship within five years, and he accomplished the goal with not a year to spare. Charles F. Adams, well pleased with tonight's proceedings, announced to the press that, after his men had finished celebrating, he would take possession of the Stanley Cup and have it shipped to Boston with his personal effects in a day or two.

The conquering heroes arrived in South Station the next morning, and awaiting them was a completely deserted train platform. Not realizing that the champions would depart from New York so soon, no fans were on hand to greet them. The celebratory dinner at Boston's Copley Plaza Hotel, however, was well attended, and the dining room was adorned with two hockey nets trimmed with flowers. Charles F. Adams complained good-naturedly that he had probably lost sixty thousand dollars in ticket sales due to the expediency with which his team had completed the playoffs, and then, in the moment all had been waiting for, he gave each Bruin a package containing a pile of gold coins worth five hundred dollars, which was apart from the thirty-five-thousand-dollar bonus pool that was to be divided into various sums. There were other presents to be handed out, and Cooney Weiland, his secret revealed and his new bride at his side, was presented with a silver cutlery set as a wedding gift. The players gave Adams a bronze statue of a bear, and Ross a new set of golf clubs. Ross told the dinner guests that he considered Tiny Thompson, with his minuscule 0.60 goals-against average in the playoffs, to be the most valuable man on the team, and Eddie Shore the second most valuable. Shore may well have just then been lost in thoughts of Daugh, Alberta, where, he told the Boston *Herald* on the train

Shore riding his grain binder on his farm in Daugh, Alberta.
(Courtesy of Edward W. Shore Jr.)

ride up from New York, he reckoned he could raise fifty-four bushels of red wheat to the acre this summer. "Holy smoke," Shore had exclaimed of his own calculations, "I've got to get back to my plowing."

SIX

===

THE CHAMPIONSHIP BRUINS expected the reception awaiting them at the Forum, the night of their third game of the 1929–30 season. Eddie Shore knew what was in store for him personally: that he would be, in a manner of speaking, the Maroons' "guest of honour." This was the game in which Hooley Smith, Dave Trottier, and Babe Siebert had done their best to do in Eddie, and had nearly succeeded.

The Boston press got a glimpse of "Edward Saskatchewan Shore" as he disembarked from the train at North Station. To them, "He had all the appearance of a man who had exploded a charge of dynamite with a hammer." Shore's nose looked "like a crushed egg," and he had teeth missing and others broken, two black eyes, a fractured jaw, and a cut and swollen face. Shore remembered little of what had happened, except for being shoved into a cold shower before going out to play again. Speculation in Boston was that this was payment for Shore's attack on Nels Stewart back on January 7, 1928, the night Eddie mercilessly pounded the sizable Nellie while the rest of Art Ross's men held him to the ice. According to the Maroons, Eddie had used his stick on that occasion, but the accusation is nonsense because the referee for that game, Dr. Eddie O'Leary, clearly stated at the time, according to the Boston *Evening Transcript,* that Shore only hit Nels "with his fists."

Art Ross was incensed with the reception his team got in Montreal, and told the press, "The hockey displayed by the Maroons was a crime. It was brutal. Eddie Shore was knocked out four times." Charles Adams complained to NHL president Frank Calder, but expected nothing from the ineffectual Calder; and when, as anticipated, Calder did nothing, Adams made amends himself by giving Shore five hundred dollars for the "game way he took his punishment" at the hands of the Maroons. Shore, though, insisted that the money be shared equally with the rest of his brave teammates—men like Lionel Hitchman, recipient of five stitches after a Maroon skate found its way into his leg.

The bloody affair at the Forum had no repercussions in the world of hockey other than to bring Boston and Montreal together in agreement that, in the words of the Montreal *Herald,* Eddie Shore had given a "robust display of great hockey class and an even greater display of sheer courage in the raw." The episode would have no effect on the Bruins other than to send them off to a record-breaking year.

Shore missed just one game due to his injuries and returned to duty to meet the Canadiens at the Garden, where he and Howie Morenz did their best to annihilate each other. Next up on the Bruins schedule was a match against the Senators, which was good news for Boston fans because, it was said, "Playing against Ottawa always has a stimulating effect upon Shore, who delights in his rivalry with King Clancy."

Francis Michael "King" Clancy was the nearest thing the NHL had to Shore in terms of showmanship, lightning dashes, great breaks, fighting qualities, and overall colour. Ottawa's native-born King was an irrepressible Irishman and a chatter-box who fascinated sportswriters with his gift of the gab. Andy Lytle of the *Toronto Star* once imitated Clancy's storytelling: "I'm doin' one of my summer visits, see and I get into this little hamlet shortly before four in the ayem. It's darker than the inside of a hitch-hiker's mind when they dump me off the train. I'm all dolled up. I'm wearin' white pants, white shoes and a white shirt. I'm hot see. I see a light shinin' about a quarter mile off and I make for it . . ." and on and on.

King Clancy could tell stories by the hour, acting out the drama as he told them and keeping his audience laughing. In stark contrast to the quiet Eddie Shore (whose voice when interviewed by Frank Ryan on the radio was barely audible), the jolly Clancy just loved to talk. He became known around the league as 135 pounds of muscle and conversation, and from the press box, reporters watched in amusement as Clancy, down on the bench, yapped away nonstop to anybody and everybody. In the dressing room, Clancy would climb atop a chair, wave a handkerchief in the air for emphasis, and deliver a stirring speech to his teammates—all while totally naked. The King once switched on the blarney while sitting in a meat cooler, and by the time he switched it off two hours later, he had, according to legend, caught pneumonia.

As a boy, Clancy was a small and chubby-faced child who played hockey for his school team, St. Joseph's, but spent most of his time on the bench. Whenever the principal of the school, Mr. Moriarty, who was also the hockey coach, let Clancy play, the dizzy young King would run headlong into opposing players half again his size, bounce off, and be ordered back to the bench to regain his seat. After his school days were over, Clancy joined the St. Brigid's Athletic Club of the senior Ottawa City League. Sixteen years old and playing defence at 128 pounds soaking wet, Clancy again sat on the bench, watching teammates and future NHL stars Ed Gorman and Alex Connell out on the ice. By 1920–21, however, Clancy was no longer on the bench, but instead rising to stardom. He led the league in scoring during that season's playoffs, and after seeing him play in the final, Petey Green, manager of the Ottawa Senators, thought him a "Man o' War on skates." Green asked his boss, Tommy Gorman, for permission to give the boy a tryout, and Clancy, not yet of adult age, had to have his father's permission to become a Senator at eight hundred dollars a year.

"There were just four clubs in the NHL at that time," Clancy recalled. "The fans took their hockey seriously, and for the most part they were a rough-and-ready lot. Many a night in Montreal I'd get pushed in along the fence by a rival player and a fan would lean over and give me a good punch in the mouth. There were fights every night. Sometimes when a fan would give you a belt on the ear, you'd lose your temper and wade into the stands after him. Like as not you'd get belted again in there too! The secret was to keep a good hold on your stick and wade around in the stands with your skates clomping on the seats. That would make everybody scatter in a hurry."

Clancy was a teetotaller playing in a league of hard drinkers, a devout Catholic who married a non-Catholic, and a famous athlete who lent money to total strangers. He idolized his Irish-born father, Thomas Francis Clancy, an enormous man and the original King, who got his nickname, "the King of the Heelers," when he played football for Ottawa College and won the Dominion championship against the Toronto Argonauts in 1901. The elder King's presence at hockey games would inspire his son in ways that no coach ever could. Knocked down one night by a vicious knee check delivered by Sprague Cleghorn, the younger King lay stunned and motionless until a familiar voice rang out: "Get up, or you'll have to answer to me!"

On the ice, Clancy carried a heavy, handcrafted stick, and he would use it to pin his adversaries up against the wire screen. "Put the wood to him" was how Clancy termed it. Clancy was a holy terror, tearing down ice, gritting his teeth, and glaring at opponents as if about to kill them. "He always appears fierce and determined," John Kieran of the *New York Times* explained. "He seems to take great joy in shunting a rival wingman across the rink on his ear. When he charges down on the goal with his black hair standing on end he looks as though he regretted that he didn't have an axe with him. In his really wild moments the fans would hardly be surprised if he pulled a couple of guns from somewhere on his person and began shooting everybody in sight, including the referee and several innocent bystanders."

Clancy was one year younger than Shore, but by the time Shore entered the NHL, the King had already been in the league for half a decade. Clancy took umbrage at the western pretender, and from then on it was an annual contest between the two archrivals over who would get the most points for the season. Clancy was a long-striding, fast skater, and his shot from the left was hard, low, and accurate, and could be counted upon to score the key goal when his team was in trouble. Year in and year out, the race between the NHL's two best defencemen see-sawed, with Eddie beating King in points one season and the Senator surpassing the Bruin the next, and the intense competitors (who became lifelong friends) were always happy to go skate to skate whenever the opportunity arose. The smaller Clancy would bravely take a swing at the bulky Shore, and Shore, whose fists were larger than Clancy's—he also had better aim—would usually catch his rival smack in the face. Once, when a Clancy check sent Shore sailing into the boards and the Bruin got up with a raised right mitt, Clancy grabbed it in a handshake and said, "Hello Eddie, and how are you tonight?"

"I'm pretty good," Shore mumbled, "and how are you tonight?"

In early November 1929, Shore returned east just before the start of the season. Reportedly, he had held out for $17,500 before Art Ross acquiesced, making Shore the highest-paid player in hockey. As befitted his new position in life, Shore had taken to wearing a derby hat and a natty velvet-collared coat. He was also newly married to the defence star of the Commercial Grads, the former Kate Macrae. The ceremony was in Edmonton and the honeymoon in New England. Then the groom had to practise with the Bruins at the Garden.

Anchored on defence by Shore and Lionel Hitchman, the Bruins had a surplus of talent that year, the likes of which the team will never see again. Much of this talent rested in the

Dynamite Line, still intact from 1928–29, of Cooney Weiland, Dit Clapper, and Dutch Gainor, and the fantastic trio were more productive than ever. The Clapper-to-Gainor passing machine worked flawlessly, and Weiland could float in like a ghost to snatch the puck from opponents and score (he would do this forty-three times in forty-four games that season). There was also skill in both the second-string Thunderbolt Line of Harry Oliver, Percy Galbraith, and Marty Barry, and in the relief crew, nicknamed the Red Cross Line, of George Owen, Bill Carson, and Mickey MacKay. In net, there was no small talent in the person of Tiny Thompson, who was just as amazing as ever.

"If you didn't see Tiny Thompson tend goal," it was said, "then you ain't never seen a jumping jack." Thompson would dive for the puck, drop on the puck, or throw himself to one side or the other to block the puck. He could grab the puck from an impossible angle, or leap from his cage to stop one attacker, only to hop back in time to intercept another. Then, fatigued from the jumping-jack routine, he would take a little break by playing defence, fighting for the disc from behind the net, dribbling it through a horde of attackers, and shooting it far enough down the ice to give himself time to get back to his citadel.

In the past, the word around the league had been "Stop Eddie Shore and you stop the Bruins," but now, with every Bruin a star, this was no longer necessarily the case. The Bruins were playing beautifully, and they stunned the hockey world with winning streaks lasting thirteen and fourteen games. The team was practically unbeatable, and everyone in the organization, crossing their fingers and hoping for another championship, held fast to their favourite superstitions: Dit Clapper kept a rabbit's foot in his back pocket, secured by a safety pin; Mickey MacKay had a special blue handkerchief (although he denied it had any significance); Art Ross, smoking nervously, made his men enter the ice before a game and leave the ice after a game by sweater number (Tiny Thompson, 1; Eddie Shore, 2; Lionel Hitchman, 3; George Owen, 4; all the way up to Bill Hutton, 15). Charles F. Adams was never without his tattered old hat, and for good luck his son Weston kept a two-dollar bill in his back pocket when the Bruins were playing away and in his pants pocket when they were playing at home. Tiny Thompson would personally select the puck the Bruins used for the game ("Yes sir," Tiny would say, "I think this one will win for us"), and during the warm-up he always stepped aside whenever Cooney Weiland took the final shot. But no one had more superstitions than Shore, who had enough for an entire team.

Before a game, Shore would never toss a hat on a bed, and blue was the only colour of shirt he would wear. Try to get him to sign a hockey stick, or to accept a two-dollar bill, before a game, and he would refuse. He also did not care to hear any whistling before the puck was dropped, and if, while lacing up his skates, one lace broke, then—naturally—he had to replace both. A protective pad damaged at the start of a winning streak became Shore's good-luck charm. He would not dare mend it, but rather would take pains before each game to place it on his body "just so." But even when following all of his many rituals, there were still some things Shore could do nothing about. "When I go on the ice feeling full of pep and ginger and find myself skating with the music," he explained, "we are sure to lose."

The Garden was packed tight for every game, and the crowds were treated to some lovely spectacles, such as the one on February 4, 1930, that starred Boston's Eddie Shore and Detroit's Rusty Hughes. The contest was a nasty one, in no small part because the Cougars were in danger of not making the playoffs and were desperate for a win. Early on, Shore hit Hughes with a blazing shot of hard rubber, and from then on, Hughes was after Shore's scalp. After the final whistle blew and the teams were leaving the ice, Hughes unexpectedly let go with an uppercut, which, had it landed, might have obliged Shore to buy himself a new set of teeth. "Oh, that's the way of it," Shore said. "Well come right ahead." Instantly, the two were flailing away at each other in the runway before they were separated, the Cougar being held to one side and the Bruin the other. With Shore safely restrained by referee George Mallinson, Detroit's Ebbie Goodfellow launched a straight right at Shore's face and Shore, fighting mad, broke away and took a swing at Goodfellow. Shore connected solidly and followed up with a second punch, his best of the night, which somehow landed on Mallinson.

The referee had been slugged, the crowd was in a frenzy, a woman in the promenade fainted, people screamed, spectators scrambled over the rail to get a better look, papers came scaling down from the galleries, and Boston fans who had been leaving the building rushed back to jam into the runway and punch the Cougars.

Critics accused Ross of blatant showmanship by encouraging mayhem and catering to the bloodthirsty Boston crowd, but the Bruins manager could not care less about what anybody else thought. He had more important things to consider, like planning for the upcoming Stanley Cup playoffs. As part of his preparations, the canny Ross smuggled movie cameras into other NHL arenas to spy on potential opponents, and he also diligently filmed his own players so that their various flaws could be projected onto the big screen. Ross was not loved by his men, but he *was* feared. He was known to show his displeasure by walking into the dressing room before a game, throwing down a bunch of railway timetables to various places in Canada, and then walking out. This year, no such threats were necessary, and "Uncle Art," as the Boston press dubbed him, had his boys honed to such a cutting edge that, after a late-season victory in Toronto, as it was reported by the *Toronto Star,* "The crowd went home thoroughly sold on the idea that Boston would win the championship."

The Bruins concluded the regular season with an incredible record of thirty-eight wins against just five defeats and one tie. They lost only once at home, and Cooney Weiland set a new league scoring record with seventy-three points, shattering the mark of fifty-one set just two years earlier by Howie Morenz. In the first round of the playoffs, the Bruins were paired with their old friends the Maroons, and the series was, as expected, dirty. For example, in the first game, Hooley Smith, well aware that earlier in the season a misdirected Eddie Shore shot had busted Lionel Hitchman's jaw, pushed his stick against Hitch's jaw, and in the second game gave him a jolt to the head, sending him into a stupor. Hitchman played the rest of the period solely on reflex, and at the intermission remarked to a dumbfounded Art Ross, "I've just come through the most terrific snowstorm, flakes as big as golf balls."

The Bruins won their series with the Maroons, two games to one, but heading into the Stanley Cup final against the Canadiens a few days later, the once-invincible Bruins were a sorry lot. The "prohibitive favorites" to win the Cup for a second straight year, the Rossmen had so overachieved during the regular season, and had raced so far out in front of all the competition, that they forgot to save a little something for later.

The NHL changed the championship format nearly every season in those days, and for 1930 it had been decided, for reasons known only to the club owners (but which undoubtedly had to do with money), that the Stanley Cup final would be a best-of-three series. The abbreviated series made it a sudden-death affair for the team that lost the first game, and on April 1, 1930, it was the Bruins' turn to lose the first game, 3–0. For the team and its fans, it was a terrible April Fool's joke. Rather than passing to each other, the Bruins passed to the Canadiens. Shore had difficulty with the disc and once sent it neatly against the blade of Howie Morenz. The puck bounced over the Bruins' sticks. The ghostlike Cooney Weiland lost his cloak of invisibility and was landed a blow on his left cheekbone. The clever Harry Oliver was stupefied by a hit over the eye that required two stitches. Lionel Hitchman was severely bothered by his broken jaw, and it showed in his play. Tiny Thompson was beaten three times by Montreal shooters. The tricky Dutch Gainor, sidelined by injuries, watched dejectedly from the stands.

At the start of the second match, a must-win for Boston, the Bruins looked even worse. In front of a hostile Forum crowd, they wobbled through the first two periods of play, allowing the Canadiens to run loose through their ranks. Shore, in attempting to check Morenz, flopped on the ice like a frozen fish. Thompson faced a relentless barrage of flying pucks and failed to stop four of them. Yet, just when all seemed hopeless for the Ross clan, Shore made a soft-looking shot that fooled Canadiens goaltender George Hainsworth, and with this tally the Bruins rallied like wolves at bay. They summoned up their matchless fighting spirit and tore into the Canadiens. A harried Hainsworth heroically kicked the puck out countless times, but was unable stop two sent in at him, first by Galbraith and then Clapper. The Bruins were now down by just one goal, and with minutes to spare in the third period, they had a chance. They pressed in, and they pressed in hard, and then, with no time left at all, the Bruins had nothing more to show for their magnificent season than a bitter defeat.

The Shores, with Kate now very pregnant, left Montreal and headed west to their farm in Alberta. The rest of the Bruins were sorely in need of a vacation, but instead they had to pack for exhibition games in California. Hockey continued as before, but the world was changing in frightening and unforeseen ways. In April, as the Bruins were losing to the Canadiens, a man in downtown Boston had toppled to the sidewalk and died, and was found to have expired from starvation. An estimated 100,000 people in Boston, a city of 781,000, were without work. There were wage cuts, layoffs, breadlines, and so many applicants responding to City Hall's call to shovel snow at five dollars a day that the windows and doors of the Municipal Employment Bureau were broken in the ensuing crush. Factory workers saw their paycheques cut by more than half; welfare payments for families with seven or more children were capped at fifteen dollars a week; and Boston's fishing fleet was forced to dump its record catch of mackerel at sea, because collapsing prices had made the fish worthless.

This was the start of the Great Depression, and the pain was felt all around the world. In North America, habits changed, luxuries were forgone, folks stayed home, and no-cost or low-cost entertainment became the norm. "After dinner on Saturday, Mom would give me fifteen cents and I'd run down to the corner store for a pound of brown sugar," remembers Tom Gaston, a lifelong hockey fan. "I'd make fudge and my Mom would pop some corn, and the whole family would gather around the old Atwater-Kent radio. The broadcasts came at the end of first period, and we'd sit glued to the action. I had framed pictures of Clancy and Conacher, and my dad let me hang them in the front room where we had the radio."

King Clancy, Charlie Conacher, Eddie Shore, Ching Johnson, and Howie Morenz were the men who sustained the league during the decade-long economic crisis, and millions of hockey fans who had never seen an NHL game in their lives were able to intelligently discuss the differing hockey styles of each, thanks to radio announcers like Foster Hewitt. In the grimmest years of the Depression, he did more to popularize the NHL than anyone else has ever done before or since. After Toronto's Maple Leaf Gardens was built in 1931, Hewitt, perched high in his luxurious gondola almost sixty feet above the gleaming ice, broadcasted the Leafs' games to faraway Hudson Bay trading posts north of Churchill, lighthouses on the Bay of Fundy, and quaint neighbourhoods in Victoria (and even, it was reported, occasionally to listeners in Nebraska and New Zealand). Through the stratosphere could be heard Hewitt's immortal cry, *"He shoots! He scores!"*

Eddie Junior was born that June, and a summer of fatherhood and farm work under the sunny Alberta skies was good to the senior Shore. Eddie returned to the Boston Garden ice in the fall of 1930 in top form and as hungry as ever. "He's the biggest eater we have right now," Ross explained. "Lionel Hitchman also has a high average with the knife and fork. It may also interest you to know that George Owen is the lightest eater. While Eddie is disposing of a dozen raw oysters, two plates of soup, a flock of lamb chops with all the fixings, and a double portion of ice cream, George is content to have a couple of soft boiled eggs and a slice of toast for dinner."

Fuelled by all that food, Shore's speed was remarkable. His swings to the right or to the left baffled his opponents with their suddenness, and his control of the puck was spectacular. "If there is any man in hockey harder to get the puck away from before he decides to shoot or pass," the Boston *Evening Transcript*'s A. Linde Fowler mused, "I don't know who it can be." Shore, age twenty-eight, was now playing the best and most ferocious hockey of his life. He was at the apex of his athletic ability. "When he skates out on the rink," John Kieran of the *New York Times* said, "the fans can sit back and watch a one-man wrecking company in brisk operation."

Shore remained the fastest-breaking defenceman in the league, and he continued to show off every trick that he had. He could rag the puck to his heart's content at centre ice, he could effortlessly pivot on a dime, he could reverse direction to avoid opponents and then reverse himself again to avoid another, he could fake this way and that, he could swerve around players just when contact seemed imminent, he could pass and shoot with pinpoint accuracy, and he could fight.

It was Christmas night at the Garden, and the Philadelphia Quakers (this, 1930–31, being the Quakers' first—and last—NHL season) were the invited guests. Two minutes remained in the third period. For the Bruins, leading 8–0, the holiday get-together had been a relaxing one of goals and laughter; but for Quaker Hib Milks, it had been one of humiliation. Longing for revenge, Milks deliberately collided with George Owen. Owen fell to his knees, and Milks, with a firm grip on the stick, hit the man of fair Harvard fame about the shoulders and neck. In no time at all, Eddie Shore, skating up from behind like a human cyclone, grabbed Milks with both hands, turned him a little, and landed a beauty. According to boxing expert LeRoy Atkinson, in attendance that night, Shore's punch was a "right hand, barnyard wallop that started from the seat of his skivvies." The solid wallop sent Milks sprawling across Owen's prostrate body, and then, holding Milks by the neck with his left hand, Shore swung with his right fist and bore into the Quaker like a human piledriver. Instantly, the Garden ice was transformed into a blur of fists and collisions as Bruins and Quakers rushed in to bash one another.

The mighty Dit Clapper chose not to join the fray, but rather to play peacemaker, and, all smiles, he put his 194 pounds of bone and muscle to work attempting alternately to pull Shore off of Milks and Milks off of Shore. While Clapper had his hands full, Philadelphia's Wally Kilrea landed a short right hook on his jaw. Clapper's toothpaste smile vanished. As fast as lightning, he struck Kilrea with a devastating left hook and Kilrea hit the ice, but not before Clapper managed to connect again with a short right. As soon as Kilrea was down, he jumped up; Clapper's left hook sent him back down; Kilrea jumped up, Clapper's left hook sent him down again, and so on.

Not to be left out, Tiny Thompson joined the battle. He had a Quaker securely pressed into the screen like a butterfly in a collection and was cross-checking him with his big goalie stick every time the Quaker tried to fly away. Meanwhile, little Cooney Weiland was exchanging uppercuts with the 188-pound Al Shields, and the Boston Police Department was converging on the scene. The men in blue tumbled over the sideboards, and the first two officers to make it to the middle of the ice tried to help referee Micky Ion separate Milks from Shore (who by this time had Philly's D'Arcy Coulson on his back), Shore from Milks, and Milks from the now-laughing George Owen. Shore, however, refused to be taken alive.

According to Atkinson, "Shore was just beginning. He shook Coulson off his back like an enraged bull shakes off a flock of flies. He charged at Milks from around the policemen. The rest of the fighting had ceased and all hands watched Shore. The Garden rocked with noise. The officers, slipping and sliding, tried to ward off Eddie with their elbows. They grabbed one Shore arm and one Shore leg but couldn't stop the other arm and leg from trying to fight. Then, by sheer numbers, the police and the referees, managed to grab both the Shore legs and both the Shore arms and the battle royal was over. Suddenly, on one side, Cooney Weiland was seen to be swinging uppercuts, but it turned out that he was merely demonstrating to Captain Hitchman the neatness and dispatch with which he had scored a point or two in the battle-royal. In the sudden quiet the burst of Christmas carols coming through the amplifiers was heard."

A newspaper reporter paid a visit to the Shores' apartment in Boston a few days afterwards and found the "big, bald Bruin" defensive about his reputation. "Quiet or I'll sock you on the nose," Shore told a crying Eddie Junior, his pride and joy. "And now about this bad man stuff," Shore continued, "I play a wide open style of hockey. I go down the ice expecting to be body checked. I expect to body check anybody who comes my way. When you play that kind of hockey you get a bad man reputation from everybody but the fellows who play hockey. The pro player is called a 'bad man' if he plays the game and if he has his own way of playing it. Because I play a hard style which is wide open, I've been given a bad man reputation."

"On hearing this," the reporter noted, "Mrs. Shore smiled as if to say: 'You've said it, big boy.'"

Shore was penalized a month later for "handling the puck," meaning that with Thompson sprawled helplessly on the ice and a Rangers shot coming in fast, Shore had gone down to block and the rubber had smashed him in the face. For this, Shore, who was bleeding profusely, earned a trip to the cooler. Referees kept such a close eye on Shore that it was improbable that they could be watching the rest of the game. Some referees, it was suspected, had it in for the man personally—most notably, the NHL referee-in-chief, that old veteran, Cooper Smeaton, who had been blowing the whistle since 1913.

In the last minutes of a game against the Black Hawks the following season, 1931–32, one of the Hawks committed some kind of violation that went unnoticed. Shore, to draw attention to it, rapped Smeaton on the chest with the back of his glove. Smeaton ejected Shore from the game and, against NHL rules, forbade the Bruins from sending in a substitute, forcing the team to play shorthanded as if the penalty was a minor. Smeaton accused Shore of "assault," and the league fined the Bruin a hundred dollars and suspended him for a game. Shore's next involvement of any consequence with Smeaton occurred a year later, in January 1933, during a Bruins bout with the Canadiens that saw Shore engaged in some rough play. His first dust-up was with Battleship Leduc, and then Shore cross-checked Johnny Gagnon into the boards, inflicting a heavy cut on the bridge of Gagnon's nose and narrowly missing his eye. Shore next tangled with Sylvio Mantha from behind the Canadiens net, and the two were carrying sticks high as they moved to open ice, where the fans could see them better. Shore was the first to drop his stick and pull off the gloves. He let fly with a right. "Distance, force and timing were all perfect," A. Linde Fowler noted approvingly from the press box. Mantha was knocked to the ice, picked himself up, and was starting for Shore when Smeaton intervened. Cut off from his adversary, Shore figured his only option was to punch right through, so he launched a couple at Smeaton. Assistant referee Ag Smith got hold of Shore, but the Bruin, with an expert back-arm swirl and good hip leverage, tossed the larger Smith prone to the ice. Nearby lay Smeaton, whose ribs were damaged and whose mouth was in need of a dentist's attention.

President Calder meted out a major penalty to Shore along with a hundred-dollar fine for what he did to Smeaton. This was the kind of thing that drove Charles F. Adams crazy. Shore was the least selfish and hardest-working man on his team; he was the Bruins' number one star and the biggest draw in the game when many arenas around the hockey circuit were going empty; and, just for doing his job, Shore was being penalized to death. Adams was fed up with it, and he had also had enough of the NHL Board of Governors, whom he saw as a hidebound group of men who stubbornly refused to open the game up entirely and, as he and Ross had long advocated, get rid of defensive hockey once and for all. In disgust, the old Yankee trader resigned as Bruins president, harshly criticized Smeaton and Calder for their biases against Shore, and turned the club over to his son Weston.

With Weston Adams leading the organization, by late March 1933, the Bruins were tied with Detroit for first place in the American Division and in a strong position going into the playoffs. The hope in Boston was that there would not be a repeat of the previous two years, 1930–31 and 1931–32, when the one-time Stanley Cup champions never even made it to the final. (After being swept by the Canadiens in that two-game disaster in 1930, the Rossmen posted a stellar regular-season record of 28–10–6, but were sent packing by the Canadiens in the semifinals. The following season, 1931–32, the Bruins played unevenly, losing games 6–0 and winning others 5–0, and finished last in the American Division, with a record of 15–21–12.)

Economic conditions at the start of the 1932–33 season were tough, the Depression stubbornly persisted, and the once-novel sight of empty seats was now a regular occurrence at the Garden. Still, Boston sports columnist Jack Grimes observed, "The public continues to show great interest in hockey. In times such as these, the public must get recreation to retain a proper mental balance." To ensure this proper mental balance, the Bruins renegotiated the Garden lease and the crowds returned, drawn both by lower ticket prices and the teams' ten-game regular-season unbeaten streak, which started with a 10–0 slaughter of the Canadiens on February 21 and lasted until the end of the season on March 21, with a 3–2 victory over the Rangers.

The man from Alberta had, like his team, a strong season of his own—arguably the strongest of his hockey career. He beat King Clancy's old record for assists by a defenceman, twenty-three, by registering twenty-seven of them. Those assists, combined with his eight goals for a total of thirty-five points, put Shore eighth in the NHL scoring race. Shore was also named to one of the two defence slots on the NHL's First All-Star Team for the second time in the two-year history of the award. In 1931–32, Shore did more than anyone or anything to keep hockey attendance up at the Garden, because, A. Linde Fowler explained, "he has been consistently displaying the most spectacular brand of hockey that the Boston public has ever witnessed." Urged to do so by Shore's fans, Fowler recommended that a dinner at the Copley Plaza Hotel in Boston be held in his honour. An organizing committee of Brighams, Chases, Clarks, Hornblowers, Rogerses, and other Boston bluebloods was formed, but Shore the farmer begged that the dinner be a casual one. "It's too much bother," he said, "donning one of those formal 'straitjackets' for a couple of hours."

On the evening of Monday, March 6, four hundred informally dressed guests arrived at the hotel, each having paid five dollars for admission and the chance to sample "Mousseline of Duxbury Clams." The event was carried live over the radio and the guests, to the tune of "Over There," merrily sang, "Here comes Shore / Watch the gore / Hear the roar / They want gore." The festive evening was a welcome diversion from the news of the day, which was that to prevent financial panic, all banks in the United States would be temporarily closed. The Bruins and their wives entered the hotel dining room, Ross-style, in order of their sweater numbers. Shore's fans presented him with a beautiful clock, and in expressing thanks, according to an attendee, "His voice was soft, his manner subdued and his words few." Former District Attorney Robert T. Bushnell, an ardent Shore supporter who had come all the way up from Florida just for the dinner, was the main speaker, and he announced the creation of the Eddie Shore Trophy to be given annually, as was Shore's wish, to the best high-school hockey team in Boston. Bushnell sat next to his shy hero all evening long, and never had the experienced prosecutor had a harder time trying to get a witness to talk. The only personal information Shore would reveal, Bushnell said, "was that he first learned how to take care of himself in dodging a horse's hoofs after he and the horse had tumbled in a hole while riding the Saskatchewan ranch."

On the eve of the first playoff game three weeks later, with the defending Stanley Cup champions, the Maple Leafs, due into North Station at any moment, Eddie was at home in his apartment under Kate's tender care. The big Bruin had strained his back during one of the last games of the regular season and was in great pain. He was also suffering from broken ribs (crash with a goal post) and an infected foot (gash from an opponent's skate).

The deadly Toronto attack was propelled by the Kid Line of Charlie Conacher, Joe Primeau, and Busher Jackson, perhaps the most perfect scoring group ever. The aggressive second line of Harold Cotton, Andy Blair, and Ace Bailey was hardly less dangerous. On defence, the Leafs had the hard-working and dependable Happy "Hap" Day, the tough guy and team "policeman" Red Horner, and that two-way—defensive and offensive—threat, King Clancy, who had been sold by cash-strapped Ottawa to Toronto for a record thirty-five thousand dollars. In the Leafs net stood the former Ranger goalie Lorne Chabot, behind the Leafs bench stood the fabled Dick Irvin, and on top of the Leafs organization stood the hockey genius Conn Smythe.

Constantine Falkland Cary Smythe was Toronto born and bred. His mother had been a drinker, a hard woman, and the young Conn was raised by his father, who was a tender man—a writer, vegetarian, eastern mystic, and poet. In temperament, however, Conn was entirely his mother's son: cocky, witty, abrasive, excitable, sarcastic, and quick to anger.

Smythe started taking sports seriously at the age of ten. At the time, "I felt I was always the worst player on every team," he said, "but as long as I was better than the next best one who didn't make the team, the last cut, I was happy. I knew that without size or strength I had to make it on hard work. Over the next ten years or so, it was amazing how often I was a team captain without being anywhere near the best player; just because I wanted it so much." In Smythe's final year of high school, his basketball, hockey, and rugby teams all made it to their respective city finals, and his basketball and hockey teams won. At the University of Toronto, he studied engineering, excelled at hockey, and captained the junior club to the provincial championship. In 1915, the team disbanded when all the players enlisted in the army. Smythe was commissioned as an officer and led the 40th Battery through some harrowing battles in the Ontario Hockey Association. And then actual war cut the season short. "We were beaten 4–0," Smythe said of the final match, "but at the end of the game the whole crowd stood up and gave us three resounding farewell cheers."

On the battlefields of Europe, the Canadians held the strategic Ypres Salient in Belgium against the Germans, and Smythe and the 40th Battery were in position by July 1916, shortly after arriving in France. Smythe suffered only a scratch (shell fragment in the neck) and was disappointed at the slow pace of action. Conditions changed when the 40th was transferred to the Somme, where the fighting was horrific. "One of our top players," Smythe remembered, "Jack Pethick from Regina, star on that hockey team of ours only eight or nine months before, had his guts blown out. They were hanging around him in this shell hole full of mud and water, and he was moaning heart-renderingly. We couldn't do anything for him. I groaned to the sergeant—remember, I was only twenty-one then—'This is terrible! What can we do?'

"The sergeant said quietly, 'Why don't you go up to the head of the line and see if there's anybody hurt up there.'

"I went up. When I came back a few minutes later Pethick had been put out of his suffering. I always admired that sergeant for sending me out of the way, and for doing what had to be done."

Smythe was later awarded the Military Cross for killing three Germans at close range with his revolver. Then, after getting into a dispute with his major, Smythe transferred to the Royal Flying Corps. In what would turn out to be his last day at the controls, Smythe was flying over enemy territory when a burst of machine-gun fire hit his rudder and the plane spiralled down. As the plane skimmed the ground, Smythe was shot in the calf and leg. He landed in the mud. After fourteen months as a prisoner of war, and one escape attempt, he was home in Toronto. It was 1919, and, he said, "Four years of my life were gone that I would never get back. I was twenty-four and hadn't done a thing yet. But I was going to make up for it, of that I was damn sure."

His hockey playing days over, Smythe returned to the University of Toronto to complete his studies, and when not at the university he ran a contracting business. He was very busy, and, to maximize academic efficiency during exams, he answered only enough questions to pass. Apparently, no one at the university had ever done this before, and while nowhere was it said that it could not be done, his professors argued that it *should* not be done. Conn Smythe ignored their protests, because Conn Smythe did things his way.

The next few years were even busier for him. He married his high school sweetheart, Irene, and started a sand and gravel company, which grew by leaps and bounds. A son and daughter were born, and during the winters, Irene was home with the children while Conn was working the sand and gravel business by day, and by night he was back in hockey, behind the bench, coaching teams and visiting arenas to scout players.

Smythe coached more than one club at a time, and he won intercollegiate championships and Allan Cups. In the winter of 1925, he took his Toronto Grads down to Boston, where they dominated the local collegiate clubs. It was then that Smythe informed Ross that his university men could make mincemeat out of his Bruins if given the chance. Ross was insulted, and the feud between the two managers, an epic one in the annals of hockey, had started. If Ross had been offended by Smythe's candour, Charles F. Adams found the Canadian's boast believable. He told Colonel John Hammond, who was president of the newly formed New York Rangers and in need of a manager, "There's a fellow called Smythe in Toronto who brings in college teams that are just about as good as mine. Why don't you give him a try?"

The colonel acted on Adams's tip. Before taking his new job, however, Conn built Irene and the children a large house in Toronto as an assurance that the city would always be his home and that the family would never have to move. Then, in the fall of 1926, Smythe set about putting together a professional team for the colonel, man by man. Through often difficult negotiations, he managed to sign Bill and Bun Cook, Lorne Chabot, Ching Johnson, Taffy Abel, and Frank Boucher, along with several sturdy second-stringers such as Paul Thompson and Murray Murdoch. Smythe, however, refused to accede to Hammond's order that he also sign Cecil "Babe" Dye of the Toronto St. Pats.

Smythe had made it to the big time, his NHL debut at Madison Square Garden was weeks away, but before the season had even started, and before Smythe and his new Rangers had even broken training camp in Toronto, Hammond fired him. The colonel, Smythe believed, was angry over his insubordination regarding Babe Dye. With Smythe gone, Hammond brought in Lester Patrick (who would, of course, soon take the team that Smythe had built to glory), and in letting Smythe go, Hammond cheated him out of $2,500 his contract stated was due him.

Smythe went back to sand, gravel, and amateur hockey. His offer to coach the St. Pats, Toronto's hapless NHL franchise, was turned down, the owners telling him not to bother because they were just about to sell the franchise elsewhere. Smythe was alarmed. He knew that if the team left Toronto, it might be many a long year before NHL hockey returned to the city, and so, in the winter of 1927, employing his business acumen, he pulled enough local investors together to purchase the club. He immediately changed the team name to something more Canadian sounding, the Maple Leafs, and a few years later, ignoring the dire economic conditions, he built Maple Leaf Gardens in the heart of the city. Building another team would prove more difficult than constructing the arena. Hap Day and Ace Bailey were the only former St. Pats worth keeping, and it took Smythe several years of signing, trading, and developing players before the legendary Maple Leafs of Conacher, Primeau, Jackson, Cotton, Blair, Bailey, Day, Horner, Clancy, and Chabot came into being.

Conn Smythe was a passionate manager, and folks in Boston thought he was nuts. Smythe had a savage laugh. He argued with Garden spectators and once nearly came to blows with a minister in the box seats. He would jump up on the rail and balance there while shouting at the referee. He would sit in the penalty box and refuse to leave, telling those who insisted that he do so not to "ruffle my equanimity." He once got into a shouting match with referee Bill Stewart and started to grab Stewart by the arm. When Stewart ordered him not to do that again, Smythe defiantly repeated the action. Stewart then ordered Smythe to leave the game, and Smythe refused. Garden ushers got into a pulling and hauling match with the

Leafs in an attempt to get Smythe to leave, the Boston Police Department arrived, and Bruins president Adams, to avoid a riot, ruled that Smythe be allowed to stay.

At Boston Garden, it was Smythe's custom to reserve two seats, one behind his goalie, Lorne Chabot, and one behind the Bruins' Tiny Thompson, and during the game he would run back and forth between the two to monitor Chabot and to heckle Thompson. He once circled the rink eighteen times in one game. If Smythe wanted play stopped, he would chuck an extra puck onto the ice, and on one occasion when the Maple Leafs were visiting the Garden, he spent the entire game on the Toronto bench with a broom in his hand, swearing that if a penalty shot was called, he would run out on the ice and sweep away the slush. "Why?" a Boston sports reporter asked rhetorically. "No one knows. But he has all sorts of crazy ideas like that."

It was Smythe and Ross's mutual hatred that the Toronto manager was most famous for in Boston. He was always asking the league to fine Ross for various infractions; failing this, he would try to show Ross up. One night, to demonstrate to Ross who was classy and who was not, Smythe arrived at the Garden looking like a Vanderbilt, dressed in a Chesterfield coat, silk top hat, pearl-grey spats, ivory-tipped cane, chin-prickling wing collar, and cream suede gloves. On another night, during the 1932–33 season, Boston's Joe Lamb was tripped by Red Horner, and one of the referees, none other than Odie Cleghorn, gave Horner two minutes. As Horner was leaving the ice, Lamb made a "remark," and the Leaf responded by hitting the Bruin over the head with his stick. Ross had convinced Cleghorn to let Lamb's insult go, and

Clancy skated up and said, "That's kind of a lousy deal, Ross." Ross took a swing, Clancy responded in kind, and Leafs and Bruins rushed the ice, with the police following close behind. Between periods, Clancy and Ross continued their argument in the hallway, punching and pulling at each other, and Cooper Smeaton got a whack from both parties when he got in the middle. The next time the Leafs were at the Garden, Smythe ostensibly sought to smoothe things over between his star defenceman and his rival manager, and sent a smiling Clancy over to Ross with a bouquet of roses and a little note telling Ross where he could . . .

The two managers detested each other, and from behind their respective benches they shook fists and after the games would go chin-to-chin, trading insults in the lobby. Still, Smythe had a few pleasant memories of Ross. "One time I remember best of all," Smythe said, "was at a league governors' meeting in New York, in the late 1930s. Ross was very insulting, he loved to insult anybody. One night he and Red Dutton from the Americans and the senior Jim Norris from Detroit, along with Detroit's Jack Adams and a few others, had an after dinner get-together in a hotel suite. Ross started after Dutton: what a lousy hockey player he'd been; how he figured it was never satisfying to beat the Maroons when Dutton was playing for them because winning against Dutton was no credit to anybody; on and on.

"Dutton held his temper, but Ross was crowding him and crowding him until finally Jim Norris stepped in between them saying, 'Now, let's all be friends.' That's the kind of man Jim was. But just as Jim moved in Ross threw a punch. Unfortunately, he didn't hit Red but hit Jim Norris. That was what Red Dutton had been waiting for. He wouldn't have fought Ross if Ross had hit him, but when he hit Norris, whom we all greatly respected, Red wouldn't have it. I have never seen a man so completely cleaned in my life, as Ross was. I never saw a man take such a beating and say nothing.

"The next day I had a meeting scheduled with Ross, to discuss a deal. I went to his room. His nose was broken, his cheek bone was broken, he'd lost some teeth. He didn't even appear behind the bench to coach Boston's next game. That was a Red Dutton operation if I ever saw one. Couldn't have happened to a more deserving recipient."

Shortly before the 1932–33 Boston series with Toronto was to begin, Eddie Shore limped into the Garden dressing room and lay down on the trainer's table. Ross, Win Green, and teammates huddled anxiously around. The strained back and broken ribs, Shore could play with; but his cut and gashed foot, now infected, was a serious matter. With the Bruins star out of the lineup, chances of beating the Leafs were poor. Some, though, were more optimistic. "Eddie Shore is an iron man," one hockey observer noted. "If it is possible for a human suffering from such an infection to come back tomorrow night, Shore will be at his defensive berth."

The next night, March 25, was a wild contest in front of sixteen thousand roaring Boston fans. Shore was, according to the newspaper the following day, "In fine fettle, hurling his 185 pounds into every Leaf that came within striking distance and his checking of such a nature as not to be relished by the opposition." Shore got into a mix-up with Hap Day, during which an opportunistic Garden spectator stole Day's stick, and the score was tied 1–1. Then, Marty Barry, a Bruin who played six unheralded but productive seasons for Boston, scored fourteen minutes into overtime to give Boston the victory. Two nights later, the Garden crowd saw a tamer contest and a gentler Shore, and after three scoreless periods, the disappointed Boston fans were sent home by a Busher Jackson goal fifteen minutes into extra time. Heading north to Maple Leaf Gardens, the Bruins' chances, with Shore not at his best, were believed to be much diminished.

In Toronto, Shore surprised everyone by being very much in the old ball game, even though he was suffering from injuries severe enough to have kept most athletes in bed. For the third time in a row, the contest could not be decided in sixty minutes, yet it was not long into the extra session before the Bruins' Vic Ripley passed the puck out to Shore, who rifled it into the net for the winning tally. Leaf fans were so stunned that it took them a few seconds to realize the game was over and that Boston was one win away from playing in the NHL championships.

The next day, Dr. Martin Crotty, the Bruins' new physician, was busy. "The Bruins eat an apple after every game," it was said, "but the fruit does not keep Dr. Crotty away." The medical man attended to Shore's back, ribs, and foot, and urged "cautious" play; he patched up Boston's John "Red" Beattie, who had received a slash near his knee; he treated Alex Smith (just traded to Boston from Ottawa), whose bad ankle had stiffened; he saw to Nels Stewart (now, amazingly, a Bruin), whose legs were black and blue; and he tended to Barry, who was bruised all over.

With Toronto on the verge of elimination, a record number of fans, 14,511, were at Maple Leaf Gardens to watch as referee Eusèbe Daigneault let Hap Day openly tackle Shore, yet not long afterward sent Shore to the cooler for flipping Ace Bailey. The hockey was exciting, and the game could have gone either way, but Busher Jackson scored twice for the home team, and the evening ended in Toronto's favour, 5–3. For some reason, Shore blamed himself for the loss and was, by reports, "a very much subdued, disconsolate mortal wandering around the hotel corridors after the game."

In the fifth and final match, Daigneault let the Bruins and Leafs do whatever they wanted, and fellow referee Cleghorn wrongly (as he later admitted) disallowed a Barry goal that would have sealed the win for the Bruins. As it was, after sixty minutes the count was 0–0, and then it was into the familiar overtime routine.

Both teams played uninteresting, defensive hockey in a war of attrition to see who would tire first. "The clock wound on past midnight," Conn Smythe recalled. "We played period after period. King Clancy scored in the first overtime period, but the whistle had just gone. In the intermission the players lay on the benches, on the floor, anywhere flat, then went, and played the fifth overtime. By that time there had been one hundred and sixty minutes of hockey, one period short of three full games. It was 1:30 a.m. Many people had gone home, but others, listening to Foster at home on their radios, came down. I said, 'Let 'em in free.'"

During the fifth overtime intermission, Smythe convened with Ross and NHL president Calder in a little room down a corridor. This could not go on, all agreed, and the two managers, agreeing for once, suggested the game be declared a draw and continued at another time, or even decided right now by tossing a coin. The fretful NHL president said he did not know what to do, but that something must be done, because the winner was due in New York that evening (it now being morning) for the opening Stanley Cup game. Smythe dragged the little conference on for as long as possible to give his Leafs precious minutes of rest, then went back to the Toronto dressing room, where his men, dead tired, told him to forget the coin toss and to continue the fight. Ross agreed to this, but as the sixth over-time period began, both the Bruins and Leafs were practically asleep. Eddie Shore, perhaps worn a little by having played 165 minutes with his broken ribs strapped up, failed to get to the puck fast enough in the Boston end, and Toronto's Andy Blair, with fresher legs and his ribs intact, jumped on the disc and sent it to Ken Doraty, his teammate, who scored. It was one-fifty in the morning, and the Leafs were too tired to celebrate.

Later that day, the exhausted victors, having staggered into Toronto's Union Station at 3 a.m. for the train ride to New York, took to the ice at Madison Square Garden and, predict-ably, dropped the first game of the final against a well-rested Rangers team. In fact, the Leafs never fully recovered from their marathon with the Bruins, and lost the best-of-five cham-pionship series, three games to one.

The Shore family travelled to Alberta directly from Ontario after that epic overtime game in Toronto. Eddie, who had just been named winner of the Hart Trophy as the NHL's most valuable player, took two days off to recuperate and then, with the help of a small army of hired men, he made, as the saying goes, hay while the sun shone. That far north, there is daylight for up to fifteen hours a day in the spring, and Eddie used every one of those hours to plow the land and seed the soil with wheat, oats, and barley.

Eddie Shore had himself a model farm, complete with a modest house, a small barn in the Pennsylvania Dutch style, and a picturesque windmill, all set upon the fertile Canadian prairie. There was animal life all around: hogs, cattle, turkeys, ducks, chickens, workhorses (which were handsome Belgian and Percheron breeds), and a prized Guernsey bull named Taywater Warrior. The farm was no mere hobby, though, but a serious business proposition worth more than fifty thousand dollars. Eddie was not a penny in debt, and the grain he grew was of impressive quality and quantity. The Bruins' Vic Ripley and his father visited the Shore farm over that summer, and it was reported in Boston that the two "saw nothing in a two hundred mile journey through the grain lands the equal of what they found on the Shore property. They found, also, that Shore and his family were not over burdened with a lot of expensive machinery, eating up a lot of oil at fancy prices, and what machinery they have is nicely housed, preserving it from the weather and increasing its efficiency." In a good year, Eddie could clear $3,500 in profit from his crop; not an insubstantial sum in the middle of the Dirty Thirties, as the drought-plagued Depression years were known on the prairies.

Between the manic scramble of spring seeding and fall harvesting, Eddie could relax a little by playing horsy with Eddie Junior, presiding over the Alberta Belgian Breeders Association, shooting golf in the seventies, and playing outfield for a baseball team called, appropriately, the Professional Pucksters. In addition to Boston's great Eddie Shore, the Pucksters fielded such men as Leroy Goldsworthy, Murray Murdoch, Neil and Mac Colville, Roger Jenkins, Lou Trudel, Bill Carse, and Earl Robertson. On a hot Sunday afternoon, five thousand people

Shore at work on his farm in Daugh, Alberta. *(Courtesy of Edward W. Shore Jr.)*

would come out to Edmonton's Renfrew Park to see authentic NHL baseball, with all gate receipts going to charity.

As the summer of 1933 came to an end, Shore harvested his grain, butchered a three-hundred-pound hog, and, as he had yet to come to terms with Ross for the 1933–34 season, hunted deer. Meanwhile, two thousand miles away in Boston, those Bruins fans unable to attend the season opener could barely hear Foster Hewitt through the heavy static. "The Boston team without Eddie Shore doesn't look like a Boston team [static]," Hewitt was saying. "Eddie Shore makes a great difference to the Boston defense [static] Bailey up, gets right in and scores! The defense was wide open [static] Boston defense doesn't look too good at times." Without Shore, the Bruins were "shamboozled" during their season opener against the Leafs and lost by an undignified 6–1. This was Boston's worst defeat in over a year, and facing the prospect of having no Eddie to watch, Bruins fans were not bothering to buy tickets for the next game.

Shore continued shooting deer while negotiations dragged on. Ross informed Shore that his contract would be reduced in accordance with the league's new restrictions on player salaries, and Shore informed Ross that he would take no cut in pay. Ross was never a pleasant man to deal with, and just when Shore thought that everything was settled, a contract arrived in the mail for $2,500 less than the amount agreed upon. Shore, refusing to leave Alberta, could be found at the Civic Arena, practising with the Edmonton Eskimos, a minor-league version of his old WHL club. Shore enjoyed himself so much that he planned on buying and running the Eskimos should Boston not come to terms. No one knows how much money Shore eventually got, but it was certainly far more than the supposed "maximum" NHL allowance of $7,500. Soon the big boy was back in Boston and back with the Bruins.

SEVEN

=====

BOSTON GARDEN WAS THE PLACE, according to A. Linde Fowler, "for those who like their hockey mixed with fighting, wrestling, a black eye or two, perhaps a broken head, a riot thrown in, and perhaps a number of players and spectators thrown out." Art Ross was once accused of placing Beano Breen, a local hoodlum who later died under a hail of gunfire in the lobby of the Metropolitan Hotel, in a box seat just for intimidation.

"There is always something unusual going on in the Hub," Baz O'Meara complained. "It was there that Art Ross smacked King Clancy," O'Meara said. "Eddie Shore was in a row last year with Sylvio Mantha when Cooper Smeaton emerged from the fracas with damaged ribs. Tommy Gorman had a clinching-bee with Referee Bill Stewart. There is a belligerent attitude even in the press box. Frank Selke tells of how much self restraint he had to exercise to prevent himself from becoming embroiled with one of the writers of the Boston press. In most cities newspapermen refrain from loud comments in press boxes, cheering, or other signs of home town animation. Boston is a bit unfortunate in this regard. There is always an air of tension around the Garden. It has been a tremendous benefit to hockey in the Hub, whose fans are probably the most partisan on the circuit."

Referees at the Garden knew that Boston fans were the fiercest anywhere, as likely to throw lit cigars at them as they were eggs or oranges. The gallery gods had taken to hurling profanities, glass bottles, and the occasional monkey wrench down from their heavenly perch. The place could be a madhouse. "It's a tough town," Art Gagne admitted. "I'll say they are rabid. When I was playing with the Montreal Canadiens our toughest games were always in Boston. Your never knew what was going to happen there."

A dozen games into the 1933–34 season, Boston's record was a spotty six wins, six losses, and on the afternoon of the Bruins' thirteenth game, Tuesday, December 12, the Boston *Evening American*'s Bill Grimes said, "In some quarters it is felt that their frequent lapses are due to the less rugged type of hockey in vogue. For publicity purposes, a rumour was allowed to get around that the Bruins were going to revert to type and step into the Leafs tonight. We are waiting with interest to see just who is going to do the stepping and what happens to the 'steppees.'" Bruins fans were also waiting with interest, and so the Garden was sold out.

As expected, Maple Leafs coach Dick Irvin, as directed by his boss, Conn Smythe, planned to begin the contest with the Kid Line of Charlie Conacher, Joe Primeau, and Busher Jackson up front; team captain Hap Day and Alex Levinsky on defence; and George Hainsworth, now a Leaf after many years as a Canadien, in goal. Ace Bailey, Hec Kilrea, and Charlie Sands were the second offensive string, while King Clancy and Red Horner would relieve the top blueline pair.

The weather in Boston was cold and cloudy, and by nightfall, the thermometer was showing eight degrees Fahrenheit. The Maple Leafs, staying at the University Club, spent the day as "special sports assistants" at Santa's Headquarters on Washington Street, giving away autographs and collecting contributions for the Santa Fund.

Shortly before game time, the Garden customers, thankful for the warmth inside, were settling into their seats and eagerly anticipating an evening's worth of entertainment. Everyone was in an uproarious mood, and, upon seeing the portly referees Odie Cleghorn and Eusèbe Daigneault amble out onto the ice, the crowd let out a tremendous jeer.

The action started, and Bob Gracie saved Boston's hopes when he poked the puck away from Charlie Sands after a three-man Toronto break appeared ready to open up the scoring early. Shortly thereafter, Busher Jackson had a chance in front of the Bruins net with the puck right behind him, but Jackson was oblivious and the threat passed. Soon, the Leafs were storming the Boston end in a coordinated assault, and now it was up to Eddie Shore to rescue his club and burnish his reputation.

Since ending his holdout against Bruins management ten games earlier, Shore had spent a measly twelve minutes in the penalty box. His play was not up to the previous year's standard, and, it was reported before the game, "His attention has been called to the fact." With his reputation on the line, Shore stripped the rubber from the Toronto attackers and sped down the right side boards, where the clean-looking Red Horner, who could have passed for a college boy, waited to greet him in the Leafs zone. Horner, who was actually a brute, nailed Shore solidly, and Shore, thrown off balance, made a rink-wide pass that landed neatly on the wood of that rotund loafer, that deadly opportunist, Nels Stewart. Stewart appeared good for another one of his easy goals, but the diminutive Hainsworth, on a rare jaunt away from the net, was in an excellent position to make the save.

The hectic play continued, and at the midway mark in the period, Horner cursed himself for kicking the puck into his own net. Three minutes later, the Leafs equalized on a bizarre goal that put the Bruins, and Shore in particular, into a rage.

What happened was that Tiny Thompson was prostrate on the ice about twelve feet from his citadel, with the disc loose at the goal mouth. To prevent the Leafs from scoring, Shore leapt like a cat and landed flat on top of the puck. The sticks of Toronto's first line started to whack at his thighs, but, failing to dislodge the rubber from under him, the three over-grown adolescents of the Kid Line switched tactics and pushed him ever closer to the goal line. Outnumbered, Shore could do nothing more than wait for the whistle to blow, but referee Cleghorn did not oblige. Shore rode the puck in, and Cleghorn allowed the goal.

Thereafter, the game got rowdy and mean, although the slow-skating Cleghorn and Daigneault, officiating in a manner that would later be characterized as "eccentric," appeared to have not a worry in the world. "That's a mistake to send those officials," a clergyman was heard saying in the stands beforehand. "This game will end in a free-for-all." And a free-for-all it was. The Leafs checked and chopped the Bruins, Ace Bailey combed Shore's hair, and Shore glared at Bailey, storing the incident in mind for future reference. The skirmishes and misdemeanours continued unchecked for the remainder of the period, but then, at the start of the second period, as if in penitence for their laxity, and also perhaps because Cleghorn got cut on his cheek, the referees became incredibly strict. As part of this crackdown, Cleghorn sent Red Horner and Hap Day to the penalty box, and during the time that the Bruins had the two-man advantage, according to the Boston *Globe,* "Eddie Shore rushed with his old time vigor and just a touch of venom, and took many a hard bump during a succession of attacks which were fruitless. Tempers all around were wearing thin."

Boston's Red Beattie had a mix-up with King Clancy; Dit Clapper also had a row with Clancy; Boston's Joe Lamb had a fight with Toronto's Harold Cotton; and Ace Bailey and Bob Gracie had a go at one another. The referees paid no mind to any of this, but for some unknown reason, Cleghorn came down hard on Horner and Day once again, and once again the Bruins had the two-man advantage and embarked upon a series of attacks, with Shore leading most of the assaults and absorbing most of the punishment.

The cool George Hainsworth ably held the fort for Toronto while Horner and Day anxiously watched the clock from the penalty box. Free at last, the two jumped to the ice just as Shore was rushing deep into their zone on another one of his offensive sallies. Horner raced over and stick-tripped Shore, who slid into the boards. The referees' off-again, on-again whistle was off-again, and no penalty was called.

With Shore felled, King Clancy pounced on the unclaimed puck and tore away. "Shore picked himself up slowly and deliberately," according to an observer, "and he seemed peeved." There were six minutes left in the second period. Shore had taken plenty of unpunished abuse at the hands and sticks of the Leafs by this point, and Ace Bailey, who had dropped back from his position as centre to take Clancy's spot on the Toronto blue line, was the nearest opponent within reach. Bailey was watching the action unfold in the Bruins end and had his back to Shore, who, gathering speed and with his head down, charged at Bailey from behind like a bull. Shore's left shoulder slammed hard into Bailey's midsection, and the Leaf's skates shot out from under him. Bailey twisted around in the air as the crowd roared with delight, then he dropped backward, his head hitting the Garden ice with a dull thud that could be heard all over the building.

There was a collective gasp of horror, and then silence. Players froze in their tracks, and spectators rose to get a better look. All stared in disbelief at the sight of Ace Bailey, who moments ago was the very picture of perfect health, lying on the ice in a grotesque attitude and shuddering as if his neck had been broken.

Red Horner was the first to reach the stricken player. "I looked down on the writhing form of Ace Bailey," Horner recalled the next day, "and I went sick all over. The 'Ace' had an expression I will never forget. His mouth was hanging wide open, and his tongue was lolling. He was practically blue in the face, and my only thought was that Shore had pulled the

Bruins and Leafs gather around an unconscious Ace Bailey as one of the two referees, Odie Cleghorn or Eusèbe Daigneault, looks on. Red Horner, lower right, is going after Shore. *(Courtesy of The Sports Museum, Boston.)*

dirtiest trick I had witnessed in my five years with the Maple Leafs. I figured Bailey might die. I skated over to Shore, who had gone down to the middle zone, stood in front of him and told him in no unmistakable terms just what I thought of his dirty playing. He never spoke a word, just stood there with a vacant expression on his face. So I repeated my statement and with that let him have it smack on the button. Sticks never entered the argument. My fist shows how hard he was hit. With that I skated backwards and prepared to defend myself against the attack of the Bruins players and Manager Ross."

Horner's sucker punch to Shore was the second nause-ating event at the Garden in just thirty seconds, but more were promised as a wild-eyed Horner, with the large Charlie Conacher at his side, stood ready to take on all comers. The players cleared the benches, and the Boston Police Department rushed after the players. Ross ran up to Horner "and told me," Horner said, "I certainly had handed out a real knockout blow, but no better than what would be coming to me later." In the meantime, Smythe rushed over to Bailey, who had gone into convulsions, and Win Green went over to Shore, whose head was lying in an expanding pool of blood. Cleghorn, Daigneault, and the police prepared to separate the players, who were carrying their sticks high and ready to rumble, but Bruins and Leafs quickly realized the direness of the situation and no further peacekeeping was necessary. Boston and Toronto coaches, players, and trainers quickly attended each to their own. The unconscious and bleeding Eddie Shore was carried off by his kin, and the comatose Ace Bailey, covered in ten blankets in an effort to stop the shuddering, was borne away by his clan.

As he followed his injured player to the visitors' dressing room, Smythe was blocked by some Bruin fans who were milling around in the corridor for no other purpose than to make trouble. One of them menaced Smythe, who retorted that he would knock the fan's head off; the fan dared him to, and the stocky Toronto manager swung out and shattered the spectacles and injured the eye of one Leonard Kenworthy of 39 Maple Avenue, Everett, Massachusetts. With Kenworthy taken care of, an infuriated King Clancy, who had just been kicked in the leg, put the wood to rest of the mob and they scattered in a hurry.

There were two on-duty doctors in the building that night: the Bruins' Dr. Martin J. Crotty and the Boston Garden house physician, Dr. C. Lynde Gately. Dr. Crotty tended to Shore after doing what little he could for Bailey, but Dr. Gately knew nothing of either injury, having been busy in his office repairing a ticket agent who had been punched in the chin by a customer and a policeman whose finger someone had tried to chew off. Then Kenworthy was brought in, with his split eye, and the doctor flushed out the glass and was sewing the final stitch when the Garden electrician burst in and said, "This Bailey's a pretty sick man." Gately made his way to the visitors' dressing room where he found a berserk King Clancy shooting his fists out in all directions. "It looked as though an even worse row was coming," Gately recalled. "So I spoke with Clancy. I said, 'King if you want to help Bailey you have to be quiet, he's pretty bad.' King quieted down but there was still such a hubbub that we decided to move Bailey."

The dingy dressing room of the minor-league Boston Cubs was made available, and Bailey was moved there. "It was then that I diagnosed a lacerated brain," Gately said. "The boy would gain consciousness to some extent, and I asked him, 'What club do you play with?' He said, 'the Cubs.' I said, 'Who are you playing?' He said 'Pittsburgh.'"

Gately applied ice packs to the head, and Bailey dozed off. "I worked over him for a while longer and he again gained consciousness. I asked him again, 'Who do you play with?' He said, 'the Maple Leafs.' I asked him, 'Who is your captain?' He said, 'Day.' Those were his first sensible words and he picked up very well then. He wanted to get off the table and go back in the game but as soon as he made an effort he became nauseated and fell back. At that moment Eddie Shore and Art Ross came in. Shore just had seven stitches put in his head and he walked over, and Eddie said, 'I'm awfully sorry, I didn't mean it.' Ace looked at him and said, 'It's all in the game, Eddie.'"

A corps of extra policeman were called to the Garden to settle the crowd, a crowd that had become a good deal more uproarious at the conclusion of the contest (which resumed five minutes after Shore and Bailey were carried off ice) than it had been at the beginning. As the Leafs headed to their dressing room at the end of the game, they had to be protected by a phalanx of police and every usher in the building. Smythe's men had scored three unanswered goals after the Bailey–Shore knockouts, winning for the first time ever at the Garden after five long years of trying. The team was in no mood to celebrate, however, not with Bailey lapsing in and out of consciousness in the Cubs' dressing room next door.

Conn Smythe sat quietly and alone in a corner, and only a hushed voice or two broke the silence as his players towelled and slipped into their clothes. There was a pall of gloom when sports columnist George C. Carens came in to interview Smythe.

"What caused Shore to charge Bailey?" Carens asked.

"I have never seen Eddie Shore do a mean thing in a hockey game," Smythe replied. "I can't understand what possessed him. I've never seen a player take as much punishment as Shore took in our playoff series with the Bruins last April. My belief is that he is still punch-drunk from that series."

"Why does Frank Patrick assign such incompetent referees to a game between such fierce rivals?" Carens asked.

"I can't answer that one," said Smythe. "All I know is that up to the time of the rumpus we drew five penalties and the Bruins none."

"Tell me, Conn, are you and Art Ross as unfriendly as the reports have it?"

"Yes, we detest each other. The feeling is mutual. When I joined the National Hockey League, Ross told me a college coach would not last long in big league company. He said he'd run me out of the league in a year and a half. Well, he didn't do it, and now Toronto is a much better team than Boston and Ross can't take it."

A telegram for Smythe interrupted the interview. It read: "Have just heard Irvin was badly injured. Please wire details immediately."

"That's Ace's wife," said Smythe as he stood up to go. "I've got to get the doctor's report."

Eddie and Kate Shore drove home from the Garden that night, Eddie so dazed from Horner's hit and the subsequent crash to the ice that he couldn't drive straight. The next day brought news to the Shore apartment that Eddie had been suspended indefinitely by the NHL and that Ace Bailey, a five-inch fracture in his skull, had been taken to Audubon Hospital, where he was moaning incoherently and evidently in great pain.

That afternoon, two special officers, acting on Kenworthy's complaint, called upon Smythe at the University Club, and he was escorted to police headquarters, charged with assault and battery, and held overnight. That Art Ross lifted not one finger, nor one telephone receiver, to get Smythe out of jail did nothing to change how the Toronto man felt about his counterpart. Meanwhile, reporters were not allowed to see Bailey, although from behind closed doors they could hear the nurses and attendants talking to him constantly, even yelling, trying to keep the Ace from slipping into a coma.

For those who knew little about Irvin Wallace "Ace" Bailey, he was described as being a "slim, sharp-eyed, hard skating, hard shooting, aggressive Leaf forward," and, at 160 pounds, among the smallest men in the league. Immensely popular with Toronto fans and players alike, Bailey was said to be a gentleman who once returned a Canadien goalie's stick that had fallen to the ice. During the off-season, Bailey was a salesman for the City Dairy Company, and it was reported that Hap Day had been best man at his wedding. Ace and Mabel Bailey had one child, Joan, who was almost four, and now a distraught Mabel and Joan were on their way to Boston, to be met at the station by Conn Smythe. In the same train with mother and daughter was a huge floral piece for Ace Bailey, a gift from the Toronto City Council.

The Bruins' Dr. Crotty had wasted no time in finding the best possible care for Bailey, calling in the brain specialist Dr. John Hodgedon. After his examination, Hodgedon advised that Bailey be transferred to the neurosurgical department of Boston City Hospital, where he could be placed under the care of Dr. Donald Munro, the esteemed neurologist. Munro was a gruff, hard-shelled Scotsman who stood six feet tall, dry-smoked a pipe, and was a professional man of the highest calibre. The doctor immediately punctured Bailey's spinal cord to relieve the swelling, gave him hypotonic saline injections, took X-rays of his head, and waited for signs of recovery. Soon, Bailey was able to smile faintly and recognize his wife, and he asked how the game ended, remembering that it was 1–1 when everything went dark. In short order, however, Bailey lapsed back into a coma, his pulse dropped precipitously, and Munro decided to take drastic action.

Conn Smythe never once left Mabel Bailey's side during the gruelling three-hour operation. A husky, unnamed man sat outside Munro's office and was then taken down to the floor below and stationed outside the operating room, where he sat until the surgery ended. The stranger was sent home after being paid for his time. He was, it turned out, a professional blood donor, called to the hospital to be ready if a transfusion was necessary.

In a highly delicate procedure, Munro, assisted by Hodgedon and Crotty, removed a blood clot from under the left side of Bailey's skull where the fracture was, and three days later, Sunday, December 17, Bailey went under anaesthesia again as Munro prepared to relieve pressure on the right side of the brain, the side believed to be less damaged. Once he opened a hole, however, Munro almost gave up all hope. Bailey, the doctor saw, had also experienced extensive bleeding on the right side of his brain, meaning that he had suffered an intraventricular hemorrhage of the type that normally killed within four hours. The patient, as it turned out, had been dying all along. Over the next two and a half hours, Munro repaired what damage he could before placing a metal plate over the surgical opening and sewing Bailey up. "It is touch and go the rest of the way," Munro said afterward, but when asked directly whether Bailey would survive, the Scotsman pulled on his pipe and shook his head no.

In a hospital room filled wall to wall with flowers, Bailey, medicated with opiates, lay strapped to a cot in a semi-conscious struggle, with Mabel, his young wife, near collapse at his side. Canadian radio stations were reporting that Ace Bailey of the Toronto Maple Leafs had died of head injuries at the age of thirty-one, and in Boston, the newspapers were readying their readers for bad news, explaining that Bailey's chances of living were "very slim" and that a third operation was "impossible."

In Toronto and all across Ontario, according to the *Toronto Star*, there was "semi-hysteria" among the populace over what Shore had done to their native son, and a Boston paper said that Shore's most recent act was "deliberate and vicious." The Boston *Herald* received more than ten thousand calls from concerned citizens inquiring about Bailey's condition, and the Boston *Evening American* said, "The Bailey-Shore incident has aroused the ire of all fair-minded hockey fans. There is no place for such actions in any sport and, unless immediate steps are taken to eradicate the parties responsible, the game will not survive."

"Criticism of Shore is equaled or surpassed by the anger at the two referees who handled the match," the Boston *Globe* asserted. "The people who pay money to see pro hockey in Boston have been unable to stomach this latest affair. Shore's faithful public have turned against him with a high wave of critical epitaphs. . . . Shore's popularity . . . is passing."

Little Joan stayed with family friends in Boston's Back Bay, and Smythe shielded Mabel from the press and the public. On Monday, December 18, the still-unconscious Ace Bailey was running a high fever and was being given injections through the veins as well as inhalations of oxygen. Despite the odds, Bailey appeared to be holding his own, but at 3 a.m. his blood pressure soared suddenly, and he showed all the signs of having suffered a stroke. Dr. Joseph Hahn, Munro's assistant, performed an "emergency procedure," it was reported, but gave Bailey only minutes to live.

"Shore will probably never play hockey again," Weston Adams said in a prepared statement the following day. "He has expressed his desire to get away from this city."

The hated Bruin was a prisoner in his own apartment, blamed for killing Ace Bailey even though those who knew Shore personally found it incomprehensible that he could have done such a thing—or at least with deliberate intent. Shore's old teammate from the Eskimos, Duke Keats, telegraphed him from Edmonton, saying, "Everyone here realizes you are blameless. Knowing you, we are certain it was a mistake." In Montreal, columnist Baz O'Meara wrote, "Some years ago when Maroon-Bruin bitterness was at its height, Shore was the only player of the Boston squad to come into the Maroons dressing room when George Boucher broke his leg in the last game of the season. Shore shouldered his way into the dressing room to enquire after Boucher's health."

And in Boston, of course, there were many who knew Shore personally and knew that, unlike other professional athletes, particularly baseball players, he lived a quiet, law-abiding life, and reputedly never even drank alcohol or smoked tobacco (although, in actuality, he did both). Shore was a favourite with the spectators, and, skating over to the boards, he would thoughtfully return oranges that they had thrown at the referees. Once, when punched inadvertently by a Bruins fan who had been aiming instead at the Rangers' Babe Pratt, Shore accepted the fan's profuse apology and said graciously, "That sock was on the house." At the Bruins' downtown offices, located in the Jordan Marsh department store, the person who sold the tickets, a man named Fred Corcoran, told one reporter that Shore was inherently a decent person. "He's the kind who no matter what his rush will always stop to assist old people across a busy thoroughfare," Corcoran said. "He listens attentively to the story of every pan handler he meets, and invariably leaves a donation. On one occasion he left all that he had, a matter of nearly twenty dollars. They call him tough, but he is as soft as a kitten at the core."

Even a few writers from the Boston newspapers that were otherwise being so accusatory sided with Shore. "Everybody who knows Shore at all intimately, off the ice and away from the rink, knows that he wouldn't intentionally hurt a flea," A. Linde Fowler stated. "Off the ice he is a soft spoken, retiring sort of individual, and in the course of many conversations I have had with Eddie Shore one of the things that impressed me most has been his oft-repeated statement of the mortal fear he has of seriously hurting an opponent."

But none of this made any difference under the present circumstances, and Inspector John C. McCarthy of the homicide squad was sent to interview the man who had attacked Ace Bailey. According to McCarthy, who had never seen a hockey game in his life, Shore was careful to explain the "technical details" of the sport, telling him, "In the previous play I had been knocked down and my stick flew from my hand. As I got to my feet and picked up the stick I saw Bailey bringing the puck down the ice. If I was in the zone when he reached it an offside would have been declared. I dug in and sped as fast as I could with my head down to get out of the way . . . I figured I was going about twenty-two miles an hour. All hockey players skate with their heads down because to stand up straight would only reduce skating speed. I didn't see Bailey until it was too late to avoid hitting him. My left shoulder struck his right shoulder,

I didn't even remember if I was knocked down at the time. About twenty seconds later I was struck and knocked out."

The police tentatively absolved the bulky defenceman of "anything criminal," but front-page newspaper stories in Boston were drawing attention to discrepancies between what Shore had lucidly told Inspector McCarthy the day after the incident and the fuzzier version he later gave to the press. "First of all, let me say, that I am terribly, terribly sorry about this very unfortunate affair," Shore had told the Boston *Post*, "the whole thing was wholly and purely accidental . . . the thing began when I was tripped and fell headlong against the boards down near the Toronto goal line. I think I must have been dazed by that fall against the boards. I honestly think that I must have been 'out on my feet' after that because things were rather blurry to me . . . I didn't know who tripped me. I think probably it was Clancy, or it might have been Horner. . . . This reputation as the 'bad boy' of hockey who specializes in rough play is something that has been thrust upon me since this affair happened. I had not heard it before. I do not specialize in rough play. I am a hard, aggressive player and I am there one hundred per cent of the time. But the last thing in the world I want is to be known as 'rough' or 'tough.' I am not either."

In the days immediately following the accident, Shore was in a state of mental and emotional anguish. He asked if he could see Bailey. He asked that Kate be allowed to take care of Joan while Mabel was visiting the hospital. "Poor Eddie!" reporter Alexander Gibb wrote in the *Toronto Star*. "I saw him yesterday, looking only the ghost of himself. He can't sleep, he can't eat, he can't talk. He spends all his time trying to get the latest on Ace's condition."

The accused was being pressed from all sides. President Frank Calder and NHL managing director Frank Patrick, who were both in town to investigate, wanted to know the truth about the accident; Art Ross and Charles F. Adams, who was stepping in for his son Weston during this time of crisis, wanted to create a unified strategy to deal with the disaster; and Attorney Daniel Lynne, who was the governor's pick to sit on the Massachusetts Crime Commission, wanted to defend his client, Eddie Shore, against charges of manslaughter.

Austen Lake, in preparing for one of his overwritten sports columns, met with the condemned man and his manager at the Garden. "For the moment as we three, Eddie Shore, Art Ross and I sat in the Bruins' office," Lake recalled, "there was a thick and awkward silence, broken only by the steady ticking of the office clock, like drops of water leaking from a kitchen tap, and I noticed that a thin, blue vein at Eddie's temple pulsed to the same deliberate rhythm. As he sat now, hunched in the corner half-light, where a month ago he sat similarly while talking tersely and a little belligerently with Ross about his salary terms, he interlaced his fingers, locking them moistly and massaging the joints of his thumbs. When he spoke finally, the crisp rumble of his normal voice had melted to a throaty whisper and his words came gropingly a few at a time, bits of half-formed expression that trailed off and started at random, on some other track. And always he ended with a vague gesture, opening his palms emptily and muttering, 'Well, don't you see?' A cocoon of bandages, several inches in length, was plastered to the shaved back of his head, a trifle below the line where his hair thinned into baldness. There was a smoky glaze on the whites of his eyes and a charred look to the rims of his lids, mute evidence of sleeplessness, and I knew that in morbid curiosity, I had come to spy on a man close to nervous collapse."

That night, the Bruins played at home for the first time since the terrible events of exactly one week before. Boston's opponents were the Montreal Maroons, and knowing that the Montrealers were always a guaranteed draw at the Garden gate, Weston Adams pledged that every cent taken at the box office would go to Ace Bailey's family. The turnout, though, was disappointingly small, and only $6,642.22 was collected. From the gallery, the gods had chanted down at the rows of empty seats below, "We want Shore! We want Shore!"

After practically pronouncing Ace Bailey dead, Dr. Hahn remarked the next day that "I am amazed he is still alive." Bailey got no worse, and then, over the next forty-eight hours, began a miraculous turn for the better. On Thursday, December 21, which happened to be Joan's fourth birthday, Conn Smythe and Dr. Martin Crotty were seen leaving the hospital after visiting Bailey and, more significantly, seen smiling for the first time in over a week. Soon Bailey himself was smiling, and he was glad to see his father, who had come down from Toronto (and, according to a claim made decades later by the Leafs' Frank Selke, had a gun and planned to kill Shore). Bailey could also now laugh and joke around with daughter Joan, putting her little doll's hat on his head. "In a long fight," said Smythe, "give me the Ace."

Now that his player was out of imminent danger, the Toronto manager felt it time to return home. Earlier, Leonard Kenworthy had accepted Smythe's explanation that the punch in the corridor was in self-defence, and after seeing the two men make up, a Boston judge had dropped the charges. When it came to other matters, however, Smythe was not in a conciliatory mood. He retracted all of the nice things he had said about Shore the night of the accident, and, spewing venom at Art Ross and his "minor leaguers," vowed never again to play a Boston club that had Eddie Shore in its lineup.

The Ace Bailey incident had shaken the hockey world to its foundations, and reverberations were still being felt. Given the severity of his injury, Bailey would obviously be out of hockey forever. Red Horner, for his unprovoked attack on Shore, which could well have been fatal, was lucky enough to have been suspended for only six games. And for what he did to Bailey, Eddie Shore's fate hung in the balance as NHL lawyers continued to sift through the sworn testimony of fifty-one players, fans, and sportswriters who claimed to have had a clear view the event. All of this was very unsettling to hockey fans and it took no less a giant than Frank Patrick to put things in their proper perspective:

> The critics are ranting and deploring and declaring that this rowdyism will be the end of hockey. But it seems to me they just don't know what they are talking about. Rowdyism? Why they haven't seen anything in years. I think it was 1906 in Westmount that Hod Stuart was cut down by Alf Smith. That was rowdyism, assault, shambles, or what you will, beside which the entirely accidental and unpremeditated Bailey incident was nothing at all, except an unfortunate result which we all deplore. I wasn't playing in the game, for which I am very glad, as I have scars enough, but

was later called as a witness when three of the Ottawa players were arrested for assault. Cecil Blanchard of the Wanderers was the first to be cut down. I remember the blood just spouted out of his head when he was crashed deliberately by a stick. It was not a tap. The stick was brought down like a butcher swinging a cleaver. Then Alf Smith skated the width of the ice and cold-bloodedly carved down Hod Stuart. This wasn't an accident. It was done deliberately. Stuart was knocked senseless on the ice. He was bleeding unconscious. If such a thing happened in hockey today the offender would be at once ruled out for life—and still critics talk of murderous hockey and all such rot. They haven't seen anything. They didn't see the game in Ottawa where [my brother] Lester scored the winning goal for Wanderers. The rest of his teammates had been literally carved to pieces. They never saw the games in the old Soo League where it was just a matter of mow-them-down. They never saw Moose Johnson, butt-ended in the mouth, actually pull out his teeth and toss them on the ice.

Charles F. Adams sent Eddie Shore and his family to a secluded location in the countryside, and although Eddie would be taking his leave of Boston (after first fetching his skates at the Garden), his fans stood by him. "I think Eddie Shore is too fine a type of athlete to even insinuate that his collision with Ace Bailey was anything but accidental," said Grace Cody of Dorchester. "Of course it was an accident," Katherine Keenan of Brighton declared. "I don't think Eddie Shore would ever dream of injuring someone." Mary Healy, who worked at the RKO Keith Theatre, agreed. "It looked to me," she said, "that Shore was partially dazed and unconscious of any wrongdoing." These and other testimonials, such as "If Eddie Shore is ousted from hockey I will never go to another game," came cascading Shore's way, and any Boston sportswriter who had earlier criticized Shore found himself deluged with hate mail.

Frank Patrick announced on behalf of the league that Shore was innocent of having purposely hurt Bailey, and could return to hockey after completing a sixteen-game suspension, retroactive from the night of the accident. This decision, as everyone knew, was based entirely on the expectation that Bailey would live and not on anything the lawyers had found in their exhaustive investigation (in which witnesses for the Boston side saw an accident and witnesses for the Toronto side saw a crime).

The National Hockey League sought to put the whole awkward affair behind it, but Conn Smythe kept the episode alive by demanding monetary compensation from the Bruins for the injury to his player. This led to an acrimonious and public exchange of charges and counter-charges between Smythe and Charles F. Adams until the NHL Board of Governors imposed a gag order on the two. While Adams was battling Smythe over money, he insisted that Shore take an extended holiday to rebuild himself both mentally and physically. As Eddie and Kate were boarding the ship *Monarch of Bermuda* three days before Christmas, a telegram arrived:

We are all delighted with the wonderful news this morning about Bailey. We all appreciate the terrible strain that was inflicted on you and the trying ordeal that you have so courageously overcome. The New York Rangers wish you and your little family the happiest Christmas you have ever had.

Lester Patrick, N.Y. Rangers

The Shores returned from their vacation in mid-January, while the suspension was still in effect. "I'm still a little nervous," Eddie confessed in New York while waiting for the customs officer to inspect his baggage. "Right now I don't feel like playing hockey but I hope to regain my confidence when I strap on my skates." While her husband was off searching for two lost bags, Kate said, "Three weeks of rest and playing golf did wonders for Eddie. He's not nearly so nervous as when we left. Once he gets on the ice I'm sure he'll regain his confidence."

Some owners around the league, faced with a deepening economic depression and having difficulty filling their arenas, demanded that Shore be reinstated immediately. In Boston, interest in hockey without the superstar had all but disappeared, and Bruins fans could not wait for his return. Not wanting to disappoint when that day came, Shore wanted to get in shape, but when he went to strap on his skates, found there was no ice at the Garden. Instead, Shore practised on one of the naturally frozen surfaces in the area. His favourite was Boston's Jamaica Pond, and decades later, some local folk remembered having been little tykes back then, tottering around the pond on their runners, when who should glide up but the great Eddie Shore to teach them how to skate.

To wild applause, a tanned Eddie, accompanied by Kate, made his first public reappearance at the Garden on January

16, 1934. In the box next to the Shores' seats sat Mabel Bailey and Mrs. Jefferson, Dr. Munro's secretary, both happy, as everyone was, that the Ace was to be released from the hospital the following day. Just having Shore in the building was enough to snap the slumping Bruins out of a five-game winless streak, and they thumped the Canadiens 4–0. Two weeks later, his suspension ended, Shore took to the Garden ice and more than fourteen thousand fans gave their returning hero a howling welcome. While Shore had no part in the scoring and was looking a little rusty, even allowing himself to be knocked silly by an Earl Seibert check, the Bruins won for the first time in four games.

"Last night's game was more than a professional hockey contest," reporter Victor O. Jones explained the next day. "Long before game time it developed into something resembling a great hysteria, hero worship, or call it what you will. It was a great tribute to the personality of Eddie Shore. There is no other explanation to attach to the record crowd and the record enthusiasm. Shore may be anything you wish to call him, but, as far as Boston is concerned, he can do no wrong. Shore received the first of his thunderous ovations on his walk to the ice with the crowd pressing in on him and yelling 'Yeah Eddie,' 'Hello Eddie,' 'Whoopie' and making other incoherent sounds. Many a fan patted him affectionately on the back, while the eyes of the feminine contingent fairly popped with admiration and excitement."

In Chicago a few days later, the celebration of Shore's return continued. "More than 17,000 fans taxed the Coliseum capacity to its utmost," it was reported, "and there was such a distinctive reception for Shore that Manager Art Ross of the Bruins went on the 'air' between the second and third periods of Frank Ryan's customary re-broadcast of the game and thanked Chicago fans for their friendly treatment towards Shore."

Ace Bailey finally departed Boston for home with no memory of anything that happened between being hit by Shore and the visit from his father at the hospital ten days later. Bailey still showed the effects of his horrific injury. He tired easily, was quick to startle, and was unable to tolerate excitement. He also had an unpaid hospital bill of $1,200 and was out of work as a hockey player. The tightwad club owners of the NHL did not know what to do, when it was suggested that a benefit game be held for Bailey; this way, the fans would pick up the tab, while the owners would only have to donate the volunteer services of their players. Those wealthy men thought it an ingenious solution, and the idea was enthusiastically approved. There was just one sticking point, which was raised by the newspapers in Canada: Should Eddie Shore be allowed to participate? The answer was supplied by hockey fans all across the Dominion, who were unanimous in their insistence that he be invited to play.

At the all-star benefit game, held at Maple Leaf Gardens, the camera captured a healthful, youthful, and smiling Ace Bailey in hat and business suit, extending his hand to an Eddie Shore looking far older than his thirty-one years and a little sheepish under the newest addition to his wardrobe, the leather helmet he would wear for the rest of his career. As Bailey and Shore chatted with each other, everyone in the crowd roared their respective heads off for several minutes and then, moved by the spirit of the moment, Conn Smythe grabbed Charles

F. Adams, Ace Bailey, and Eddie Shore by the arms and took them out on the ice. For a magic moment, the four clasped hands to thunderous applause. On the sidelines, stewing, was Art Ross, whom Smythe had snubbed.

When all had quieted down, the Maple Leafs, dubbed the "Aces" for the game, took on Shore and his fellow "Stars," Howie Morenz, Aurèle Joliat, Lionel Conacher, Red Dutton, Bill Cook, and Hooley Smith among them. After sixty minutes of clean hockey, the Aces had crushed the Stars 7–2 and a sizable kitty of $20,909 was given to the real Ace. Shore grabbed the next train back to Boston and played a Bruins game at the Garden, and then, so as not to disappoint the people of Toronto, returned promptly with the Bruins for a regularly scheduled game in which he played only a symbolic two minutes, having previously suffered a thigh injury. "We want Shore!" the Toronto fans implored when they saw Eddie take to the bench.

As the regular season wound down, the Bruins were headed to a pathetic record of 18–25–5 with no hope of making the playoffs. The Ace Bailey episode had been a severe butt-end in the stomach from which the Rossmen, Shore no exception, took a long time to recover. And in another loss, the team's Rock of Gibraltar, the famous Number 3, Lionel Hitchman, announced his retirement.

On March 5, the Leafs made their final visit of the season to Boston Garden, and they brought Ace Bailey along with them. He visited Boston City Hospital for a checkup by Dr. Munro, and while there he gave thanks and souvenirs to the hospital staff. At the hockey game that night, he walked onto the playing surface to drop the puck, and was greeted by Shore at centre ice and by cheers from the stands so thunderous that they shook the rafters. After that, Bailey disappeared from the Boston scene, his hockey career seemingly over. Within a couple of years, however, the Ace, who was destined to live another six decades, became a regular winter visitor once again, coaching his Toronto Varsity Blues against the Harvard Crimson in thrilling games that packed the old Boston Arena with college bands and screaming fans.

EIGHT

=====

THE HOURGLASS HAD RUN OUT, perhaps never to be turned again, and for Eddie Shore, the last grains of sand had apparently fallen. It was January 1937, and the "Old Edmonton Express," as the sportswriters now dubbed him, was confined to bed. For how long, nobody knew. The previous summer, Shore had strained his back on the links in Edmonton while trying to extract his ball from a sand trap, and this injury was compounded when he took to the ice on the first day of Bruins practice and fell heavily on his neck. On opening night at the Garden, it was obvious the man was not fully functional, and then things deteriorated for Shore, especially after a wrench to the spine in a game against the Maple Leafs in Toronto. It all came to a head, so to speak, during a Bruins–Rangers battle in Boston when the puck was lying loose at the mouth of the Bruins cage. Shore dove for it, but Tiny Thompson lunged for it first, and Tiny came in under Eddie, hoisting him high in the air, where he turned half a somersault before crashing hard into the boards and landing on the base of his spine. He left the Garden in great pain. One vertebra, the doctors discovered, was cracked, and his spine displaced.

The artful Art Ross, always the showman and not always trustworthy, claimed that the Bruins superstar had not retired permanently and that, when Shore's body cast came off (sometime in the spring, it was hoped), he would have one last year of hockey left. But newspaper reporters were not convinced, and many were preparing to write the sports obituary for "old No. 2."

This was the year, it seemed, when all the aging ice warriors were dropping away. Roy Worters of the New York Americans, a superb goalie and Vézina Trophy winner, had seen his long career end arbitrarily with a hernia. Meanwhile, Conn Smythe, after seeing King Clancy struggle through the first six games of the season, had bluntly told him, "You're washed up, you're retired." King did not disagree, and he made a graceful exit from the sport he loved, saying, "I am leaving the game to the youngsters." Charlie Conacher's brother Lionel, who was Canada's most amazing all-around athlete and as good—or better—at football, wrestling, lacrosse, rugby, boxing, and baseball as he was at hockey (and he was a fantastic hockey player), let it be known that, after twelve seasons playing for the Pirates, Americans, Maroons, and Black Hawks, he would be departing the NHL to enter politics.

In another blow to the game, the man who once led the league, Howie Morenz, was felled by a freak accident in January, when the tip of his skate got caught in the boards, and bones in his leg and ankle were badly broken. Although only thirty-four years old, Morenz knew full well that his hockey days were behind him, and on March 8, 1937, Montreal was seized with grief when the awful news came that Howie Morenz had died, victim of a heart attack. "He was the greatest, most outstanding hockey player of all time," the convalescing Shore said when he heard of his rival's death, "but more than that he was one the few genuine sportsmen I have ever known."

The loss of Morenz hung like a dark cloud over hockey, a reminder that even the immortal are mortal. Baz O'Meara wrote in eulogy that "death loves a shining star," yet everyone knew that, by the time Morenz died, he was already a faded star, a slow and chubby shadow of his former self, a man who had been shipped to Chicago after eleven seasons with the Canadiens, before being shipped back to Montreal (by way of the Rangers) just before the season that he died. In Chicago, Morenz had had to endure the indignity of playing for Major Frederic McLaughlin's Black Hawks. McLaughlin was more huckster than hockey, a man whose 1936–37 "All American" club brought ridicule down upon himself and his organization when his Americans, rookies from Michigan and Minnesota, lasted only a few disastrous games before having to be replaced by Canadians. McLaughlin had earlier let his wife, Irene, design the Chicago uniform, and, according to reports, she "spent considerable time in museums and art galleries studying the war paint, feathers, and art of the original Black Hawk Indians. Then she incorporated her findings into her husband's team's uniform. As a final touch she had specially made hockey gloves with tessellated doodads similar to those worn by Buffalo Bill."

One night, Morenz had sheepishly shown Frank Patrick the gloves and said, sadly, "You never thought, Frank, did you, that I'd finish my career rigged out like this?"

Fans of Eddie Shore, the man they used to call the "Edmonton Eviscerator," had to be thinking that when his back healed it might be best if he hung up the skates, lest he play beyond his years, as Morenz had done. There were whispers even before Shore's injury that he had softened with age, and in fact Shore, who had averaged 112 penalty minutes a season between 1926–27 and 1932–33, had collected a mere 32 minutes in 1934–35. The Shore of yore, the thinking went, would not be seen again.

Without Number 2, the Bruins struggled through the remainder of the 1936–37 season before being eliminated in the first round of the playoffs. Shore, meanwhile, vowed that he would never return to hockey unless, he said, he reached his "old-time form." The doctors recommended back surgery, but Shore refused. He had healed himself many times before, and he was determined to do so again. Six weeks of bed rest passed before the body cast came off and Shore began exercising. As soon as he could, he made his way to East Lynn, Massachusetts, and the office of Dr. Phentonate Tonache, M.D. A virtual miracle worker, he put Shore on the road to full recovery, and he and his new patient formed a bond that lasted decades. Tonache become one of Shore's biggest boosters, and Shore became both a student of Tonache's osteopathic techniques and, as his many willing and unwilling "patients" could attest in later years, an avid practitioner himself.

For 1937–38, the Boston Bruins took on a fresh appearance when the teams' brown-and-yellow hues were replaced by a

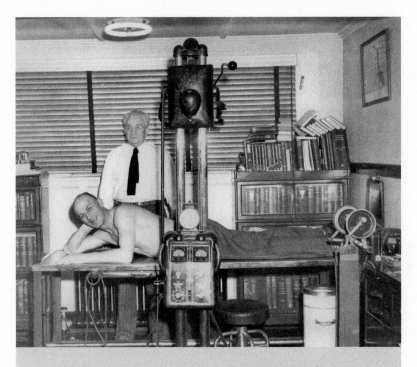

Dr. Phentonate Tonache and Eddie Shore. *(Courtesy of Edward W. Shore Jr.)*

sharper-looking black-and-gold colour scheme. The team itself had changed dramatically over the previous three years. Dit Clapper, Cooney Weiland, and Tiny Thompson remained, but the other greats of the past were gone. Lionel Hitchman was now coaching in the minor leagues, Percy Galbraith was playing in the minors, and George "Harvard" Owen had returned to the staid but respectable world of banking and investments on State Street. Owen, however, could not get the sport out of his system, and he became the coach of the MIT hockey team.

New to the Bruins this season were Mel Hill, Gordie Pettinger, Red Hamill, and Jack Crawford. The squad they joined had been assembled by Ross beginning in 1934, when he acquired the speedy right winger Charlie Sands and the large defenceman Jack Portland. A year later, Ross had signed Bill Cowley, Flash Hollett, and Ray Getliffe, all of whom would soon prove their worth, and in 1936, Ross had introduced three baby-faced youngsters, Bobby Bauer, Milt Schmidt, and Woody Dumart, to big-time hockey. The rookies comprised the youngest trio in the league, and because they hailed from Kitchener (formerly Berlin), Ontario, a city with a sizable German population, Bostonians affectionately baptized the threesome the Sauerkraut Line.

The "Krauts" worked ideally together, despite being outwardly different. The eldest, Bobby Bauer (no relation, unfortunately for him, to the hockey equipment company), was twenty-two years old, personable, poised, and the least self-conscious of the three when off the ice. Bobby was also the smallest Kraut, at five foot eleven and 150 pounds, but this did not stop him from becoming the line's goal-getter, and in his first season with the Bruins he netted twenty of them. Woody "Porky" Dumart, age twenty-one, was the largest of the kids, and he used his sizable frame to carve a passageway down the left side of the rink, and woe to anybody who got in his way. He was a quiet young man not much given to humour, yet he had an even temper that he rarely lost, even when fouled upon. Dumart also may have been the least imaginative player of the three, but he played steadily in his own groove, and in his second year with the Bruins, he scored thirteen times. Milt Schmidt, who would one day coach the Bruins, centred the Sauerkraut Line to perfection. The boyish, shy Milt was long and lean, and when on the ice he forgot his bashfulness entirely, becoming the meanest of the Krauts, flaring the fastest and fighting back the hardest. In his first full year with the Bruins after missing most of the 1936–37 season with a broken jaw that had to be wired shut, Milt scored thirteen times.

A recuperated and rejuvenated Eddie Shore, now the longest-serving member of the Bruins, rejoined this crew of a few veterans and lots of fuzzy-faced youngsters at the beginning of the 1937–38 season, and Boston promptly won its first six games for its best start ever. Eddie drove his mates hard. "You just shook in your boots when the great Shore came over to say something to you," Schmidt remembered. "'Mister Schmidt'—it wasn't 'Milt' or 'Conrad,' my second name, it was always 'Mister' all the time; or, if he didn't have time to say 'Mister' it was 'Joe'—so I skated over and said, 'Yes, Eddie?' and he says, 'Let me tell you something, son,' he says. 'Your days in the National Hockey League will be numbered if you do not change your style of skating.' I says, 'Eddie, I'm nineteen years of age, how am I gonna change now?' He says, 'You will change, or you will not last.'"

Shore had many peculiarities, and he could be a hard guy to figure out. He cut his perfectly good two-dollar hockey stick almost down to a stub, and off the ice he kept his distance from the other Bruins. "It was strange," Dumart recalled, "but you'd never see him in any of the cities we visited until game time. Nobody knew where the hell he went. He was a real loner. I used to bunk across from him on the long train trips and I don't remember having a single real conversation with him." But Shore's understanding of hockey was without equal. He was even planning to write the definitive book on the subject, and had invested five hundred dollars on illustrations (alas, none seem to have survived). "It's to be a treatise on skating and hockey balanced with advice to the young," Shore explained of the book that he would never finish, adding, "Hockey is on a higher plane today, it attracts better types. I can look at a hockey player and tell you within a few months when his career will end. That comes from study and observation. Men are not unlike stock. You learn to separate the good cattle from the dolts from observing them closely."

At age thirty-five, Shore was nearing middle age, but "Mr. Hockey"—as he was called in the days before Gordie Howe—continued to play as if there were four Shores on the ice. There was the Shore taking Tiny Thompson's place in the crease to stop the puck; there was the Shore at centre ice, grabbing the puck; there was the Shore always parked beside the opponent's cage, ready to pass or shoot the puck; and there was the Shore back again in the Bruins zone, ready to dynamite the onrushing enemy. That season, Shore was playing some of the best hockey of his career, and still making two or three times as many extraordinary plays as the average NHL defenceman. He was still the storm centre of every game, his baritone voice could still be heard arguing heatedly with the referees, and he could still galvanize his teammates. "It is hardly possible to exaggerate the value of Shore to the Bruins," a reporter explained. "More than anything, Shore is the morale of the Bruins."

If Shore thought any of the Bruins were acting doltish, he would use his "whip," meaning an unexpected pass of the puck with an order to "Really hit them this time." If he thought anyone could use some coaching, he was happy to oblige—that is, before Art Ross caught wind of this and threatened to fine him unless he stopped. Shore later told his son, Eddie

Junior, that he'd stopped and the Bruins had promptly gone into a slump. "Look, Eddie," the men said, "we're losing, you've got to coach us," but Shore, who knew from experience that threats from Ross should never be taken idly, replied, "No way, I'm not going to be fined." His teammates, though, insisted, and with Shore again coaching on the sly, the Bruins began to win again, Boston went crazy for hockey again, and the gallery gods were delirious. One of their frequent moves was to rip seats from the concrete floor and throw sharp splinters of wood—with nails sticking out—onto the ice: miraculously, no one was ever hurt.

The best NHL team to have come out of Boston in half a decade finished the season in first place—and then folded like an accordion to Toronto in three straight games in the first round of the playoffs. For Ross, it was the lowest point of his career.

Although greatly disappointed, the Garden fans still adored their men in black and gold, and, with Shore back to his old-time form and the Sauerkrauters getting better all the time, they could hardly wait for next year. "Boston was a great hockey town," said Ray Getliffe, who later became a Canadien but was a Bruin starting in 1936–37. "I had four very enjoyable years in Boston. The fans took you home for dinner, and there are not many other cities where they did that."

While war clouds were gathering over Europe during the summer of 1938, the citizens of Edmonton could look up to peaceful Canadian skies and see their hometown hero, Eddie Shore, tooling around in an airplane. Now age thirty-six, he had tried to join the Royal Canadian Air Force, but his services were respectfully declined. When the hockey-pilot landed on his wheat farm in Daugh, he stepped onto a thriving operation complete with the latest machinery. Shore worked the land from dawn to dusk, played exhibition baseball and endless games of golf, rode horseback for miles, and for his exercise swam laps in the Sturgeon River. After one swim, he heard the cries of sixteen-year-old Beatrice Pengally coming from across the water. The young woman was drowning, as were her friend Howard Davis and another swimmer who had gone to her aid. Fully clothed, the NHL superstar plunged into the water, and, as astonished newspaper readers would learn the next day, rescued all three.

Bruins training camp customarily got under way in October, and that was when Eddie Junior had to leave both his school and his ideal boy's life on a western farm to take up winter quarters with his parents in Brookline, Massachusetts. Back in Daugh, the young Eddie could ride his horse to a one-room schoolhouse, and the education he got was superior: coming to Brookline in October, he would find himself ahead of his American classmates; returning to Daugh in April, he would find himself behind his Canadian classmates.

This year, 1938, the Shore family was in Brookline in time for training camp, but Eddie Senior had not returned to work because he was out on strike. The previous spring, Shore had capped his comeback year by winning the fourth Hart Trophy of his career, and he expected his just rewards from Weston Adams and Ross when it came time to sign a new contract. Negotiations, though, had gone nowhere, and with the NHL season now about to get under way, Shore had been locked out of Bruins practices and was instead scrimmaging with the minor-league Cubs. No one knew what was happening regarding his contract, and cynics suspected the whole thing was a publicity stunt to drum up early-season interest in the Bruins. The drama increased when Adams and Ross announced that they had given up trying to reason with Shore and had turned negotiations over to NHL president Frank Calder. Adams, however, was not interested in negotiating; he had heard the diminished crowds at the Garden booing the home team and chanting, "We want Shore," and he had watched the dispirited Bruins falter out of the gate with two wins, a loss, and a tie. Having heard and seen enough, Adams secretly ordered "rubber-stamp Calder," as the Boston press called the NHL president, to accept Eddie's terms at whatever cost. Exactly how much Adams agreed to pay Shore is not known, because in those days NHL club finances were as secret as Mafioso dealings, but the contract likely made Shore, as he was always rumoured to be, the highest-paid player in the league once again.

The one-man labour action was a win for Shore, but it soured some Bostonians on hockey, and there were also disquieting signs that the great goalie Tiny Thompson was going to be pushed out by an obscure minor-leaguer named Frankie Brimsek. Ross responded to this talk by insisting, "No sir; absolutely not. There's not a chance in the world of our getting rid of Tiny," before sending Tiny packing as part of a fifteen-thousand-dollar deal with Detroit.

Bitter at the loss of Thompson, who had just won his fourth Vézina Trophy and had, over the years, saved an estimated 16,500 shots fired at the Bruins net, Boston fans were not ready to accept his replacement. Compared to the tall, acrobatic Tiny, who flew boldly here and there and stood

Shore in a publicity shot, mid-1930s. Note the helmet Shore had taken to wearing. *(Courtesy of Edward W. Shore Jr.)*

like a sentry in front of the net, little Frankie Brimsek stood a mere five foot nine, wore an old pair of red pants for luck, and crouched between the pipes. Many in Boston thought the whole thing a disgrace, and some considered the loss of Thompson to be the worst thing to have happened to the city since the Red Sox foolishly sold Babe Ruth to New York in 1920 (an event Bostonians can still get weepy about today).

Hockey observers who had warned in the midst of the contract holdout that the Bruins needed Shore more than he needed them, now had the perfect right to say "I told you so" when he came storming back into action. After taking a bow as he stepped out onto the Garden ice for the first time that season, Eddie was soon leading power plays, knocking down rivals, and checking like a wildcat on skates. He was forever floating in on the play, intercepting passes, smothering shots, icing the disc, and hitting hard. "In physical strength," one reporter noted, "concentration, and quickness of temper, Shore has an edge over all other hockey players, although he is approaching his fortieth birthday." Finally, and with the score tied, "Shore made a headlong rush with the puck, hurtled untouched between two Detroit defensemen, and laid a back-handed pass onto Bobby Bauer's stick which was quickly converted into the winning goal."

The Bruins won the next two contests, subsequently lost a game to the Canadiens, and then something amazing happened: Frankie Brimsek absolutely refused to let the puck into his net. In the twelve games that the Bruins played in the month of December 1938, the young man from Eveleth, Minnesota, stayed stubbornly in his crease, his hands working in a blur, and held the opposition scoreless on six occasions. Brimsek eventually went 231 minutes and 54 seconds without allowing the rubber to slip in behind him.

Bruins fans baptized Brimsek "Kid Zero," and before the season was over Mister Zero humiliated every team in the NHL by shutting out all of them at least once. He was the anchor between the pipes for, according the Boston *Evening Transcript*'s Harold Kaese (A. Linde Fowler having retired), "the best hockey team Boston has ever rallied to cheer." And cheer Boston did, in particular the gallery gods, who also bombed the ice with sugar, flour, pennies, eggs, umbrellas, vegetables, oranges, tin cans, and sandwiches. By early January, the Bruins, who were even better by some accounts than the great Boston teams of 1928–31, looked unstoppable.

Perhaps invigorated by his boys' brilliant play, Art Ross was coming up with new ideas every day. The catalogue of his innovations already included an improved hockey net, an improved hockey puck, an improved hockey helmet, the season-ticket plan, the rule against icing, the referee/linesman system, and the tactic of pulling the goalie for an extra attacker. To this list, Ross was currently planning to add special pads for hockey players to go over their hips and kidneys, a hockey suit made of flexible aluminum, a skate covered with steel mesh to protect feet and ankles, a spring-loaded device to be attached to the goal posts to save players who collided with them, and—his two most outlandish ideas of all—a hockey stick with a wooden blade and metal shaft built for lightness and strength, and the elimination of the red line for faster play.

In early February, with the Bruins a blistering-hot 25–7–2, Ross had to take a break from inventing to respond to rumours that the team was on the brink of trading Shore for a large amount of cash. Boston braced itself for the third hockey scandal of the season, while its star, not waiting around for any trade to happen, sped (Shore drove like he skated—fast) through the scenic New England countryside to Springfield, Massachusetts.

Springfield was ninety miles due west of Boston, and while much smaller, it too had a long history (for an American city, that is) of professional hockey. The Springfield Indians had come into being in 1925, a year after the Bruins, and the team was presently owned by insurance man J. Lucien Garneau, whose playboy lifestyle and spending habits had driven it into bankruptcy. The International-American Hockey League (successor league to the Can-Am), wanted to keep the pro game in Springfield and announced that the Indians were up for sale. This news coincided exactly with reports that Shore might not be a Bruin much longer, and got the mild-mannered and soft-spoken Walter Graham, sportswriter for the influential Springfield *Daily News,* thinking. Graham contacted Shore and suggested that he take a drive out to see the team firsthand.

Shore parked his car at the Indians' arena, made a mental note of all the free parking available, and anonymously bought a fifty-five-cent ticket for the game—the cheapest ticket there was—so that he could observe the operation from the highest point in the stands. The most renowned hockey player in the world, watching the game in silence, managed to hide his identity with only one close call.

"You're Eddie Shore, I presume?" an astute young reporter asked.

"I guess I do look a bit like him," Shore said modestly. "But I'm glad I'm not. The things I read about Eddie Shore, he must be a bastard."

Shore had only a passing interest in the hockey being played that night, and in later years he couldn't recall who the opponents were. What interested him—a lot—were the crowd's size, which he reckoned to be around five thousand, and its enthusiasm. "They hollered, they screamed like maniacs at everything the Indians did," Shore said, "even little things like poke-checking the puck, putting an elbow in somebody's face. Those are the kind of fans an owner, naturally, likes, because they support their club win or lose." Another interesting thing, Shore said, was that "there were ticket-takers on just about every gate, front, side and back of the building, and the gatemen were looking the other way much of the time as the fans kept pouring in."

Boston's third hockey scandal of the year never came to pass because Shore was not traded, and attention turned to the Stanley Cup playoffs. That Art Ross's first-place Boston Bruins and Lester Patrick's second-place New York Rangers were destined to face each other in Series A, a best-of-seven semifinal, had seemed inevitable since early in the season. The Bruins and Rangers were easily the class of the league, and each had all the markings of a Stanley Cup champion, although sportswriters pegged the Bruins as favourites to win.

In their favour, the Bruins had the remarkable Brimsek, who would end the regular season with a record of 33–9–1, including ten shutouts. He would also win the Vézina Trophy, the Calder Memorial Trophy as rookie of the year, and the honour of being the first rookie ever named to the NHL's First All-Star Team. Also in its favour, Boston had three exceptionally strong forward lines. There was the powerful first unit of Bauer, Schmidt, and Dumart; the second of Cowley, Sands, and Getliffe (which was actually supposed to have been the first line, but the Sauerkrauters had been promoted); and the third line of Gord Pettinger, Roy Conacher, and Mel Hill. So good was the third line that it could have been the first on many other teams. Hill was considered by the sporting press to be a small and "delicate" player, even though, at five foot ten and

Art Ross with his Rossmen, 1938–39. *(Courtesy of Edward W. Shore Jr.)*

175 pounds, his size was hardly unusual for the NHL of his day. Earlier rejected by the Rangers, with the Bruins, Hill turned in an impressive performance during key moments, and equally impressive was his linemate, Roy Conacher. A twenty-two-year-old rookie, Conacher led the NHL with twenty-six goals, a record for a first-year player, and he came in second only to Brimsek in the Calder Trophy balloting. Also in Boston's favour was the team's dynamic defence quartet of Portland, Crawford, Shore, and Clapper. Clapper, having lost some of his step with age, had dropped back to the blue line, and on some nights, he and his three colleagues defended their zone so well that Brimsek might as well have taken a seat in the stands, for all he was needed.

"Our defense was so strong," Ross recalled in 1963, "that we used to do something that would be suicidal today. I used to order my forwards to play outside when back-checking against the opposing wings. In other words, instead of driving the play to the outside, which is normal, I had them driving it inside, toward the goal and not away from it. That way, my forwards could be looking at their defensemen at all times and be ready for a pass or a loose puck. You had to have a great defense to play like that, and we had it."

The Rangers, however, did not go without chances to upset the Bruins, and, like the Bruins, had undergone an almost complete transformation in recent years. Gone from the current New York lineup were Bill and Bun Cook, Frank Boucher, Ching Johnson, Murray Murdoch, Taffy Abel, and the other colourful personalities of the Rangers' past. In their place was the core of the new Rangers: centres Phil Watson and Neil Colville and wingers Bryan Hextall, Mac Colville (Neil's brother), Alex Shibicky, and Dutch "the midget" Hiller, who smiled even as he was being run down by much larger opponents. On defence, the Rangers had Babe Pratt, with his freight-handler's body and Girl Scout's face, Art Coulter, Ott Heller, who could weave through an entire opposing team, and Lester Patrick's twenty-four-year-old son Murray, known as "Muzz," a former Canadian amateur heavyweight boxing champion. Among the spare players carried by the Rangers was Lester Patrick's other son, Lynn, age twenty-seven, who played on the forward line and with a good deal more finesse than Muzz, and who was the better hockey player. In the New York net stood the solidly built Davey Kerr, an agile fellow who could do the splits.

Because they had finished first in the league, the Bruins chose where to open the series, and Ross opted to start slowly in sedate Madison Square Garden rather than Boston Garden, with all of its craziness. The team arrived in Gotham on March 20, 1939, to spend a quiet night at the Lincoln Hotel, where Ross patrolled the corridors on the lookout for "bar flies" who maybe wanted to go out for a drink. Attendance at Rangers home games had been unusually small of late, but New Yorkers had apparently been saving their money for the play-offs, because the next day there was a sizable number of fans waiting the start of the game, puffing on cigarettes and filling the cavernous building with smoke.

The game got off to a boring start. Both teams watched each other so closely that neither had even half a chance to score. Rangers captain Art Coulter was benched for elbowing Conacher, Dumart was sent off for cross-checking, and Coulter and Dumart both ran afoul of the referee and were sent off together. By way of excitement, that was about it.

The Rossmen did little to enliven things in the second period, sticking, as they would all evening, to a coldly calculated defensive style from which they rarely diverged. The one occasion when they did show some life was when Phil Watson dashed down on them from the right and tried to get the puck to Bryan Hextall. Crawford intercepted, reversed the play, and passed Cowley the disc. Skating like the wind, Cowley swooped in close enough to Rangers goalie Davey Kerr for a straight shot, but Kerr caught it in his gloves. More heavy action followed when Shore slammed Ott Heller into the boards and was immediately sent to the cooler. With Shore safely locked up, Bryan Hextall, Phil Watson, and Dutch Hiller attacked the

Boston end until Shore was let loose, whereupon the three Rangers quickly went back to minding their manners.

The period was headed towards an inconclusive final when Gordie Pettinger tripped Lynn Patrick with less than two minutes remaining and was whistled to the penalty box. Up one man, the Rangers thought it a good time to score a goal. Mac Colville sent the puck to brother Neil, who sent it to Pratt, who passed to Alex Shibicky, who drilled it fifteen feet and between the legs of Frankie Brimsek.

The third period had its moments as well, such as when Muzz Patrick hit Milt Schmidt so hard that "Schmiddy" went flying over the fence, taking referee Micky Ion with him, just as Bobby Bauer poked the puck into the Rangers cage.

Linesman Donnie McFadyen saw the goal, the seventy-eight members of the press saw the goal, all of the Rangers and Bruins saw the goal, the 14,886 spectators in attendance saw the goal, but Mickey Ion did not see the goal because he was prone in the aisle between the rail seats. "No goal!" Ion ruled firmly as he got up. Mindful of the league rule that managers were liable to a thousand-dollar fine for "commenting adversely for publication on any NHL referee," Ross, his face red with anger, withheld comment. The Bruins made up for Bauer's disallowed goal moments later, when the brilliant Bill Cowley deflected a lightning-fast pass from Dit Clapper that went past Kerr. This time, Ion saw the puck cross the goal line. The period ended with no further scoring, and, as the ice was being scraped and watered in preparation for the first overtime session, the spectators were resigned to staying up until the wee hours.

In the first overtime, Schmidt caged the disc, but Ion had

just blown the whistle and the goal was disallowed. Neither team dared to take any chances for the remainder of the period, nor did they attempt any heroics during the next overtime period, nor the one after that. Exhausted Madison Square Garden workers were just about ready to clear the ice for the seventh time in five hours when, suddenly, at 1:05 a.m., Bill Cowley shot down the right side boards and made a pass to Mel Hill, who was coming in fast. Hill met the puck perfectly. Kerr never had a chance. New Yorkers love a winner, and, rising from their seats to make their weary way to the subway, the spectators applauded the Bruins.

Hill was the overtime hero again two nights later in Boston. After sixty minutes, the score was tied at two. Eight minutes into the first extra session, Bill Cowley, who was eel-like in his ability to slither away from opponents, escaped from a gang of Rangers to feed the puck back to Hill, who was skating up ice behind him. Hill lifted the disc into the upper left-hand corner of the Rangers net from twenty-five feet out. Exiting the Boston Garden, which had hosted a wild crowd of 16,702 that evening, Hill's arm ached from all of the programs, papers, and even shirt cuffs that he had had to sign.

Going into game number three, the Bruins were a healthy lot, but the Rangers were not. Lester Patrick was without his goaltender, Davey Kerr, who had been bumped hard by the child prodigy Roy Conacher in the first game. X-rays revealed that the muscle attached to Kerr's right shoulder bone was severed. "We are definitely without the services of Davey Kerr in goal," Patrick acknowledged. In Kerr's place would be minor leaguer Bert Gardiner, whose first and only previous appearance in the Rangers net had come three years earlier.

Gardiner was an instant hit with the Boston fans, and the over-capacity crowd of 16,981 cheered wildly every time he let the puck into the net behind him. The Rangers' George Allen opened the scoring against the home team in a laughable (for the Bruins) manner when the disc bounced off his chest and past the team's substitute goalie. Following this debacle, Gardiner gave Milt Schmidt the time of his young life when he allowed the kid to tally in both the second and third periods, giving the Sauerkraut Line its first goals of the series.

Gardiner, however, was no amateur. He put on a flashy display of goaltending, complete with expert slides, and in sixty minutes of play he faced twenty-nine shots and was scored upon four times—a weak, but hardly disastrous performance, considering that there was little in the way of a Rangers defence or offence in front of him. The Blueshirts may have snapped around in the razzle-dazzle "streamlined" style that they had made vogue, but when it came time to attack the Bruins zone, they were repeatedly swept away by the backchecking fiends of the Boston defence. The game belonged to Boston, and, after a Conacher goal in the third period (a pretty one after he swooped in from behind the Rangers net and then swooped out to score), it was clear that the Bruins would win, and they did, 4–1.

The Rangers were down three games to none, and the Bruins, with their eleventh win in a row, were on top of the world. They belted out their favourite song, "Paree," in the showers afterwards, and they argued about what each would do with their championship bonus money. Bill Grimes of the Boston *Evening Advertiser* wrote the next day that the Bruins were now definitely in the Stanley Cup final, "unless they get mixed up in a train wreck."

Rangers fans gathered in Madison Square Garden on March 28 to see the last game of the season and to bid farewell to their beloved men in blue. They were also looking forward to giving Shore the "raspberry." "He draws the biggest boos of any player in the circuit," the New York *Herald Tribune*'s Al Laney explained, "because he is generally recognized as about the best. The New York fans love him, a fact that was easily discernable in their booing. And the reason for it was plain for all to see. Shore is a throwback to the day when hockey was a lusty if less streamlined game. He plays a crushing defence. And there is no denying that when he is on the ice things are more exciting. There is hardly anyone left in hockey any more against whom the fans can let loose such a volley of raspberries."

The raspberries turned to groans just forty-nine seconds into the contest, when Milt Schmidt, assisted by Bauer and Dumart, made a neat spank from eight feet out for an all-Kitchener goal. The Rangers, however, refused to go quietly, and minutes later, the spectators may well have thought that they had mistakenly bought tickets not for a hockey game, but for Fight Night at Madison Square Garden.

It all began when Phil Watson veered into Boston territory and fired a shot that cut through a dozen legs and staggered Brimsek. Brimsek had shifted his body into the path of the puck and made the save, kicking the disc out to the corner, where Watson and big Jack Portland rushed for it and, not liking the looks of each other, started swinging away. Hextall came up to make it two against one before Shore jumped into the fray and separated everyone. Hostilities momentarily suspended, an angry mob of hockey players was milling around, eyeing each other distrustfully, when the butt end of Phil Watson's stick emerged from a group of Blueshirts and hit Shore in the nose. In a second, gloves were off, sticks thrown aside, and every available player was spraying punches, grabbing jerseys, and pulling one another down. The crowd was in an uproar; the players slugged and tugged, flailing away at one partner before switching for another. Shore was backing away from the battle to see where he was needed most, when Muzz Patrick's fist connected with his chin.

The Shore–Patrick bout was the main attraction of the night, but for all its entertainment potential, it turned out to be a disappointment. Shore was no match for the youthful pugilist, and Muzz had the upper hand throughout. According to John Kieran of the *New York Times,* Muzz "was having a fine time and would have lingered longer over Shore except that the referee and gendarmes interfered. By that time the Very Good Eddie looked as though he had gone through a threshing machine on his hands and knees, and it took a good half hour to paste and patch him together again so that he could go back and play with the boys."

In the dressing room, as his nose (broken in two places), a cut under the right eye, and badly lacerated mouth were being tended to, Shore complained from beneath the cold packs on his face that not all was fair. Art Coulter, Shore said, had snuck in some licks, and Watson had smashed him over the head with his stick. Fearing that Shore might reappear at any moment, the Rangers made the most of his absence by pushing into the Bruins end, where Mac Colville managed to get the puck through Brimsek. Then Lynn Patrick—only seconds before a stitched-up, plastered-up, and bandaged-up Shore stepped back onto the ice—kicked the puck into the

Boston net and was lucky enough to have Ion allow it. With Shore back, there would be no more Rangers goals, but the damage had been done, and by the end of the third period, the Rangers had won, 2–1.

Ross was irate, accusing the Rangers of abandoning hockey for the rough stuff and baiting Shore just to get him off the ice. "It's a well known fact," Ross fumed, "that whenever the Bruins get into a fight, Shore is one of the first players to race into the melee. Time and again, you've seen him dash down the ice and horn into private fights which didn't concern him. He just can't resist the temptation and every club in the N.H.L. is wise to this, you might say, weakness." Not everyone, though, shared Ross's outrage. Boston sportswriter Austen Lake visited the Bruins' dressing room after the game. "Shore for his part was philosophic," Lake wrote, adding, "Later as he sat while Dr. Crotty probed his nasal passages and added new layers of adhesive, he mustered a grin which was painful to watch and remarked that it was part of the game."

Bruins fans were more than ready for the fifth match, and 16,409 of them arrived at the Boston Garden the night of March 30, armed with glass bottles, lunch pails, hunks of metal, chunks of concrete, rotten fruit, lead ballast, eggs, drinking flasks, beer cans, and, the newest thing, a ten-inch firecracker called a cannon. The crowd had been incited by Boston press reports that described the Rangers as "hairy apes . . . just swung down from the limb of a tree" who had "gouged, garroted, and ganged Eddie Shore." The newspapers had described Shore's injuries in such lurid detail that for Bruins fans to read this was, Austen Lake said, "like poking grizzly bears at the zoo with rake handles."

Missiles of every conceivable type greeted the Blueshirts as they made their way onto the ice for the warmup. Someone with a strong arm, and perfect aim, threw a piece of steam-fitter's pipe at Muzz Patrick's head. Thomas P. Foley, a twenty-six-year-old spectator, collapsed from the excitement and was later pronounced dead. Frank Calder had, wisely, prepared for the worst. Sitting in a box seat and hoping he would not be recognized, he was wearing a hard hat. With Calder refusing to show his face and lay down some law and order, Lester Patrick was fearful for his sons' safety, not to mention that of their teammates. He had begun pulling the Rangers in the direction of the entranceway to the rink when referee Norm Lamport barked, "Take your team off this ice and I'll forfeit the game." To which Patrick replied, "Forfeit and be damned." Finally, the Boston Police made an example of one or two offenders, and the rain of fruit and hardware tapered off. Now that the weather was clear, Patrick decided to stay and fight.

The puck was dropped, and the ensuing game was a low-scoring, hard-charging contest—playoff hockey at its best. The two teams engaged in disciplined play with just the right amount of desperation to make it a memorable night. Each side was hungry for victory, and both clubs deserved to win. In the end, New York again prevailed 2–1 on an overtime goal by the Rangers' spare centre, Clint Smith.

Having now lost twice, the jittery Boston Bruins were not in a joking mood when they took to the ice at Madison Square Garden on April 1 for the sixth game. The first period was scoreless, as was the second, but then a misunderstanding by the Rangers on their own blue line allowed a Bill Cowley-to-Mel

Hill combination to hang the rubber in the twine behind Bert Gardiner. The lead lasted only minutes, though, before Phil Watson rushed around a winded Shore and tossed a backhand shot over Brimsek's shoulder as the goalie was readying for a low-corner shot. Penalties in the third period doomed the Bruins, as New York made the most of Mel Hill's illegal interference with Mac Colville and of Eddie Shore's hold on Dutch Hiller. The Rangers' 3–1 win would have been by an even larger margin if they had scored on any of the many breakaways the Bruins gave them.

The series was deadlocked at three wins apiece and, with less than twenty-four hours before the deciding seventh game was set to begin, neither team had time to rest. At Boston Garden, a crowd of 16,981 awaited the start. Tickets had been so hard to come by that not even Charles F. Adams could get four seats together and had to settle for two singles in the first balcony and two behind a post. There was a great deal of nervousness in the Bruins dressing room before the game. "Eddie Shore," Ray Getliffe remembered, "called the team together and told us we needed to give it our all if we were going to be successful."

The contest was bitterly fought, intensely exciting, and played at breakneck speed. Ott Heller tried an early rush, but tumbled over Shore; then the Bruins came down on a rush of their own, but Heller tripped Dumart and sent him sailing into the Rangers cage. Dumart had the last laugh when Heller, now sitting in the penalty box, watched helplessly as his scoring blast shook the Ranger goal posts. The struggle raged on, end to end, but with little to show for it: what looked like a promising Cowley–Hill combination went nowhere; a Heller kick of the puck almost sent it into his own net; and an assault on the Boston cage by the Colville brothers was nipped in the bud by the Bruins defence.

The first "barrage" of the evening occurred eighteen minutes into the first period, after Mickey Ion failed to penalize Lynn Patrick for Lynn's generous application of his elbow to Flash Hollett. Instantly, cannon firecrackers dropped down from the balconies and burst all over the rink. One of the bomblets detonated near big Art Coulter. As if on cue, the enthusiastic crowd started to pelt the ice with garbage, and a spectator in a box seat, after a struggle with four policemen, was ejected. When the Garden scrapers had done their job, play resumed until linesman Donnie McFadyen drew the ire of the fans by calling a faceoff in the Bruins zone. Bowing to the wishes of the public, the agreeable McFadyen moved the faceoff to centre ice, yet this was not enough for some, and from the galleries came the second barrage of the night. A cannon exploded right next to Miss O'Bey of Worcester, Massachusetts. Her hair was singed almost to the top of her head, she was bleeding under the left eye, and she had powder burns on her forehead and neck. Her companion in the next seat had her eardrum ruptured. Miss O'Bey was taken away by an usher, and it was a while before she returned to her seat, where she was seen yelling and hollering with the best of them.

After the second barrage had subsided, the Rangers' seldom-used Bill Carse had a chance to put his team out in front, but Brimsek blocked the long drive. Then, with Dit Clapper sitting in the cooler, the Rangers tried again and skated deep into the Bruins end, but got nowhere. In return,

Shore organized a powerful counterattack, but could not complete it before the period ended.

Schmidt golfed the puck down the ice at the start of the second frame, and this was the sign for the Bruins' attack to begin again. With Boston hammering away, the puck flew high and all but landed in the Ranger net. The pace was terrific for about eight minutes, before both teams eased off. The Rangers were the first to resume at full speed, and the battle once again flowed both ways. Lynn Patrick lashed a shot that Brimsek staggered into, and Boston came back with a charge that clicked when Ray Getliffe sent the puck into the cage at 15:52. The Rangers did not have to wait long to exact their revenge. They crushed the Bruins defenders, and after numerous shots and passes, Muzz Patrick rifled a shot that beat Brimsek completely and evened the score, 1–1.

At the start of the third period, Shore made one of his classic rushes and poked the puck towards Bauer, who shot it at Gardiner, who caught the puck with his skate. Then Shore took a shot that went wide. Shibicky had to leave the ice with an injured shoulder. He did not return. There were five minutes remaining in the game, and the Rangers forgot about their voguish "streamlined" hockey and scrambled any way they could to get into the Bruins zone. The Bruins responded in kind. Dumart rushed past Pratt and shot the puck cleanly across the crease, where Gardiner stopped it before it could go in. The play reversed, and a blast from Mac Colville grazed the Boston post. With a few seconds remaining, the players got into a jam on the boards. Coulter and Clapper crossed sticks and looked ready to murder one another. Then the whistle blew, sixty minutes of hockey had been played, and it was time to scrape and water the ice.

Two minutes into overtime, Bauer shaved Gardiner's post with a backhand shot. Carse gathered the puck, and he and Neil Colville went down on a charge until Portland rudely blocked their path. The Bruins then rushed through the Rangers blue line, leaving Pratt alone in front of Brimsek. Only Pratt's miss saved the Bruins from losing the game. Smith then led the Rangers on the warpath, but Boston vigorously counterattacked. Gardiner ably protected his net and saved a Crawford shot, and shortly afterward, at the other end of the ice, Neil Colville missed the corner on a pass from Carse, losing his stick in the ensuing scuffle.

As overtime ground on, Bryan Hextall came within a fraction of an inch of cinching victory for the Rangers, but Brimsek, just barely, managed to reach the disc with the tip of his outstretched skate. The Rangers then withstood a terrific bombardment, during which a shot by Conacher hit the post and Hollett nearly scored. The first overtime period was over.

High above the rink, the Garden press box must have emptied out, as there are no detailed accounts of the rest of the game. The winning goal, however, came at 12:40 a.m., after 108 minutes of play. In the eighth minute of the third overtime period, Bill Cowley recovered a wild shot taken by Roy Conacher, and he fed the puck to Mel Hill. Hill, twenty feet out and taking his time, rifled the disc with a fine forehand, and it flew past Bert Gardiner. Almost before the red light blazed, perfect strangers were leaping up from the stands to kiss each other and dance in the aisles, while down on the ice, the ecstatic Boston Bruins tore towards Hill to practically rip him from limb to limb.

Mel Hill left the building with his housemates, Conacher, Dumart, Bauer, and Schmidt, but was much too excited to sleep. The twenty-three-year-old from Saskatoon—who would forever after be called "Mr. Sudden Death"—walked the streets until six o'clock that morning, trying to calm his nerves, in the company of Patrolman James Travers, Brookline Police Department, who was out on his normal beat.

Boston now faced Toronto in the Stanley Cup final, and Shore informed the Bruins that he had bought the Springfield Indians. This came as a bombshell to Adams, Ross, and the NHL. The league's hockey players were supposed to be sub-servient to their masters, and the idea of one of them owning a team on the side was not only a shocker, it was completely unacceptable. The Bruins categorically said no to Shore's plans, even though he had already paid the International-American Hockey League's fifty-six-thousand-dollar asking price.

Predictably, the Bruins–Maple Leafs series, which the Bruins won four games to one, was a letdown after the epic battle with the Rangers. That Boston–New York series, con-sidered at the time—and long afterward—to be one of the best ever held, was remarkable for having lasted, including the overtime periods, the equivalent of nine full games.

At the conclusion of the fifth and final game of the Bruins' series with the Leafs, a 3–1 win on April 16, NHL president Frank Calder stood nervously on the Boston Garden ice with the Stanley Cup in hand, cannons exploding all around him. "We want Shore! We want Shore!" the crowd chanted, because their hero had disappeared into the dressing room. Having fulfilled his Bruins contract for the season, and disgusted with Bruins management and their refusal to let him own the Indians, Shore saw no reason to dally at the Garden a moment longer. The rest of the Bruins had all assembled at centre ice and were ready to receive the Cup, but "the crowd," Milt Schmidt recalled, "simply would not let Mr. Calder present the trophy until Shore came back on the ice." A riot threatened, someone went into the dressing room to plead with him, and, Schmidt said, "The uproar was stunning when Shore finally came out. The crowd gave him such an ovation it made goose bumps run up and down your back."

NINE

===

PRESIDENT EDDIE SHORE PARKED his car, a powerful Lincoln Zephyr, in the middle of the Eastern States Coliseum, the home of the Springfield Indians in West Springfield. If the rink had been frozen, this would have been centre ice, but it was summertime and there was neither ice nor skating, just a lot of hard work to do. For this purpose, Shore had transformed the Lincoln into his presidential tool shed and office. He had his rugged clothes strewn out on the car floor for the manual labour, and for the financial side of things, he had his finer togs—his fedora, shirts, suits, and ties—neatly dangling from hangers in the back seat. The dirty chores included getting down on his hands and knees and crawling into the Coliseum's grimy tunnels. Shore had to repair eight miles of refrigeration pipes and headers, which, like everything else about the arena, former owner J. Lucien Garneau had let deteriorate. Garneau had also let the Indians run up various debts, including hundreds of dollars in liquor bills, and whenever the creditors and bankers came calling, Shore would emerge from the tunnel, change quickly into a suit, and become all business.

Shore's prairie frugality had always served him well, but now more than ever. He kept a lean front office and, printed in the Indians' official game program, listed son Eddie Junior, age nine, his vice-president. Shore maintained tight control over spending by keeping the payroll down and doing almost everything himself. For example, with no experience or instruction of how to do it, when the time came to set up the rink, he did it alone. "I always," Shore explained, "observed whenever I saw men putting one together. I learned from watching, and then added a few of my own ideas." An employee of Shore's, Charles Leopold, recalled, "Whether it was ice-making, shovelling snow, carpentry, pipe-fitting, welding, mixing cement, no matter what, Shore usually had his own way of doing things. He was seldom wrong." Occasionally, Shore would have to bring in experts to help, but even when surrounded by men who knew more than he did, another employee recalled, "Everybody focused on him. If he pointed a finger in one direction, all eyes would turn that way. He was an extraordinary leader in so many ways."

For Shore to make a return on his investment, which was the sum of all his life savings plus a mortgage on the Alberta farm, he had to bring cash customers through the Coliseum doors starting in November. This meant getting everything ready, not least of which was a hockey team that the fans could watch when not lined up to buy popcorn, hot dogs, and beer at the concession stands. Over the years, Shore had witnessed Art

Eddie Sr. sends Eddie "Ted" Jr., age ten, out onto the ice, 1941.
(Courtesy of Edward W. Shore Jr.)

Ross in operation, and, following the Ross example, he let some of the veterans go and tried out an army of prospects before accepting a promising few. Then, also in imitation of Ross, he offered his players minimal salaries, because Shore knew what all his Indians knew: trains for Canada left Springfield every day.

On opening night, the Coliseum under president Eddie Shore resembled a police state. No one was getting in for free, as they had under Garneau, because Shore had seen to it that the arena was as secure as Fort Knox. The fire exits were sealed with tape and guarded, and the ticket-takers were watched by the president himself. Shore also wanted everybody, employee and spectator alike, to be on their best behaviour, and had hired an extra-large police detail to enforce peace. Then, with everything running the way it should and the unheated Coliseum a bracing forty degrees Fahrenheit (which led to brisk sales of hot coffee), Shore went to the dressing room, stripped off his business suit, pulled on Indians jersey Number 2, and skated out to his position on the blue line just as the band struck up the Indians' song, "Lucky Day." The sight of Shore gave the spectators a case of the screaming meemies. Their reaction proved that he was the main attraction and worth, by his own estimate, twenty-five thousand dollars a year in gate receipts. Then, looking up into the stands, Shore checked to see that his ushers were doing their jobs, while also making a quick calculation of the crowd size. (The Boston press joked that Shore's calculation had better match the number of tickets sold, or else someone was going to get fired).

This was an exhibition game, played before the start of the 1939–40 season, and in another pre-season tune-up, the Indians played in Boston Garden. It was bizarre: Eddie Shore playing for his own team, the Indians, against his own team, the Bruins. Equally unusual was the "gentlemen's agreement" between Shore and Weston Adams. Shore, according to the arrangement, would sit out the first half of the Bruins' season and then, starting December 15, play Bruins home games at a flat rate of two hundred dollars per game (three hundred during the playoffs). In return for this light duty, which was designed to give Shore time to man the Coliseum front office, he promised not to skate for any other hockey club—most significantly, his Indians. The agreement, however, was broken by the defending Stanley Cup champions as soon as they dropped their first game, 5–0, and their second, 2–1. Ross declared an emergency and drafted Shore in time for the Bruins' third game, a bout with Chicago in the Garden. The move was hailed by the Boston press. "Eddie on skates," it was explained, "will give the Bruins the great physical and moral support of which he is capable."

The timing of the call-up could hardly have been less convenient for Shore. His Indians had just begun their regular season, too, and, coincidentally, the Ice Follies were at the Coliseum right then, meaning that he personally had to keep an eagle eye on the gate, guard the till, write a blizzard of cheques to cover expenses, and boss his employees around. Shore was down to three hours of sleep a night and had not skated in two weeks. Exhausted, he made the ninety-mile trip over winding country roads from Springfield to Boston in less than two hours and, it was reported, "played a smashing game." Shore helped notch the victory for Ross by being on the ice for all three Bruin goals and then, job done, he roared back to Springfield. Days later, he received another urgent telephone call from Ross: Jack Crawford was out with a chipped elbow bone and Shore was to report to the Garden immediately.

This time around, Shore's play was mediocre, and the Bruins lost, which told Ross that he needed his defenceman's undivided attention on a full-time basis. Henceforth, Ross informed Shore, he was to play all Bruins games, home and away, before December 15 and after December 15, no exceptions. Shore refused, yet as a final favour to Ross, he did suit up for a bout against the Rangers that ended in a 2–2 tie. Shore, who scored one of the Boston goals and assisted Herb Cain on the other, got a cracked lip (courtesy of Alex Shibicky's stick) and a bruised chin (from a flying puck), and apologized that his play was not up to his usual standard. "I haven't skated since Tuesday," he told the press. "A man can't do himself justice or his team unless he is in condition. I'm too busy at Springfield. A man can't burn the candle at a half-dozen ends like I've been doing and get away with it. I want to quit." Before leaving the Garden that night with a suitcase full of hockey equipment, Shore had a ten-minute meeting with Ross and Adams, and the two told Shore that he was not to do as he pleased.

Bruins fans had been baffled by Shore's decision to buy the Indians, but they respected his wish to own his own team and play for it if he wanted to, and when they learned that Ross would not grant Shore the outright release from the Bruins that he wanted, a banner appeared at the Garden reading, WHY NOT TRADE ROSS? Ross and Adams were earning heaps of bad publicity, and the NHL, facing intense fan sentiment in favour of Shore, refused to intervene on their behalf. Shore, for his part, kept his word that he was through as a Bruin—for two weeks. Flash Hollett, the popular Bruins defenceman, learned that his small son had died, and Shore, to give the grieving father time to fly home to Toronto, volunteered to take his place on the blue line. It was December 5, 1939, and, in what would indeed be Eddie Shore's last game wearing the black and gold, he broke a 1–1 tie, scoring the game-winning goal.

Shore with defenceman Flash Hollett. *(Courtesy of Edward W. Shore Jr.)*

Ross and Adams, who could have sold Shore for at least fifty thousand dollars the previous year (and undoubtedly wished they had), decided that the best way to keep their rights to Eddie was to "loan" him to the Indians on the condition that he play in Springfield's home games only, and be ready to play for the Bruins on a moment's notice. The compromise was acceptable to Shore, but not to the International-American Hockey League. The IAHL wanted to spread the Shore cash generator around and demanded that he play not just at the Coliseum but in its seven other arenas, from Providence, Rhode Island, to Cleveland, Ohio. Shore chose not to jump his Boston contract entirely, and risk enraging both Ross and the NHL; instead, he defied the minor league. The three-way custody battle finally ended on January 25, 1940. Accepting the fact that Shore's years in Boston were finally over, the Bruins traded him to the New York Americans, where it was thought he could do no harm. "I'm tickled to death," the Americans' manager and Shore's old friend, Red Dutton, declared. "He'll help the Americans—help them plenty. He can play with his Springfield team any time and any place he wants to."

Boston sports columnist Dave Egan telephoned Springfield the night of the announcement and found Shore unusually emotional. "His voice," Egan reported, "was tired and beaten and his words clutched in his throat." Shore had one request for the journalist: "Tell the hockey fans of Boston that I appreciate what they've done for me over the years. Tell them strong."

In his column the next day, Egan wrote, "Shore knew he would be traded this year, so Shore purchased the Springfield Indians. But then Eddie Shore was shipped down the river to the last-place New York Americans because there can be only one great man of Boston hockey and his name is Art Ross. It was never complicated. Shore could not play for Springfield because Art Ross said so. After purchasing the Indians he could not play out of town games because Art Ross said so. That is all there is to this dreary story. The winner of course, is Art Ross."

Shore got to work for Red Dutton while not having to neglect his own team. "Shore is slated to play for the New York Americans in their Madison Square Garden game against Canadiens on Sunday," Walter Graham of the Springfield *Daily News* reported. "On Tuesday, Eddie will play against Hershey here and on Wednesday he will be with the Indians at Philadelphia. He is likely to play for the Americans against Bruins at New York on Thursday before going on to Boston for the Saturday return game. Outside of that, Eddie won't have anything to do."

The schedule was hectic for Shore that season. He was playing for two clubs in two leagues (during one stretch, he played five games in six nights), besides which he had other obligations that called for his attention. These were the visits to the boys and girls at the Shriners Hospital (Shore would join the Shrine in 1942), the radio interviews, the awards he gave out to local sportsmen, the scouting trips to Canada, the creation with several other investors of the Ice Capades, and the resurrection of the Greater Springfield Junior Amateur Hockey League. The junior league—the largest in the United States, with more than two hundred boys participating—had declined in recent years, but Shore revived it with his energy, advice, and enthusiasm. Every Saturday morning, bright and early, Eddie Shore, squeezing in time between his NHL and IAHL appointments, could be found out on the Coliseum ice, teaching a mob of youngsters the fundamentals of skating and hockey, and all for free.

Red Dutton's New York Americans could have used some training in Shore's schoolboy hockey league, because while the "Amerks" were an NHL club (and one as old as the Bruins), they certainly did not play like one. As early as November, the Americans had found themselves nearly out of the play-offs, which, had it happened, would have set an NHL record for futility. "What are we going to do?" Dutton had publicly lamented, but with Shore on board, all of that now changed. Shore played the hero's role that Dutton knew that he would and could, and although there was not much remaining of the season, the Americans edged into playoff contention, as did Shore's other team, the Indians. As luck would have it, both the Americans and the Indians' opening playoff games were scheduled for the same Tuesday night. Springfield fans wanted Shore to spend the evening with them at the Coliseum for the bout against the Pittsburgh Hornets, but the NHL ruled that he had to be with the Americans in Detroit for their first match against the Red Wings.

So, Shore took an airplane and played on Tuesday for the Americans in their first game against the Wings in Detroit. On Thursday he took another plane and played for the Indians in their second game against the Hornets in Pittsburg (having not been able to play the first game in Springfield). Friday, after more flying, he played for the Americans in their second game against the Wings in New York. Saturday he left the airport to play for the Indians in their third game against the Hornets in Pittsburgh. Finally, he was back in Detroit on Sunday, to play for the Americans in their third and final game against the Wings.

Red Dutton had his defenceman Pat Egan team up with Shore on this two-league, three-city, five-game, six-day odyssey, and Egan, who was half Shore's age, recalled, "When we [arrived] for that last game, I tell you I was gassed. We both got off the plane to go into town. Eddie says, 'Where you going?'

I said, 'I'm going to bed, I've had it.' He says, 'I've got some business to do, see you at supper.' Talk about stamina."

Despite Shore's and Egan's best efforts, both the Americans and the Indians failed to advance beyond the first rounds of their respective playoffs. In the spring of 1940, the Shores returned to the farm in Alberta, and Eddie told a disappointed Red Dutton that he would not be returning to the Americans, the better to devote more time to his own club, the Indians. That fall, the Shores returned from Alberta to their large apartment in Springfield, and Eddie Shore Jr.—whom everybody called Ted—made a new friend in Rodney Macaulay, a boy who became a frequent guest at the Shore's place. "When I would see Eddie Senior, it was usually dinnertime," Macaulay remembered, "and often times the Shores would invite me to the hockey games in West Springfield. Eddie Senior used to drive a hundred miles an hour. I will never forget that. The four of us would get to the game early, because Eddie Senior had to dress. We watched the game from the Shores' box, and then, after the game Kate and Ted and I had to wait because he always had a news conference in his office. And so it was a long night for us kids."

The Coliseum was really nothing but a humble old barn, built in 1916 to house horse shows, but the building was beloved by hockey fans for being both beautiful and cozy in its own way; and, thanks to Shore, it now had the slickest, best ice in hockey. Between October and May, which was the duration of his yearly lease, the Coliseum became Eddie Shore's second home, and there was nothing he would not do there, from cleaning the toilets to climbing the girders eighty-five feet above the ice to change a light bulb, both to save money

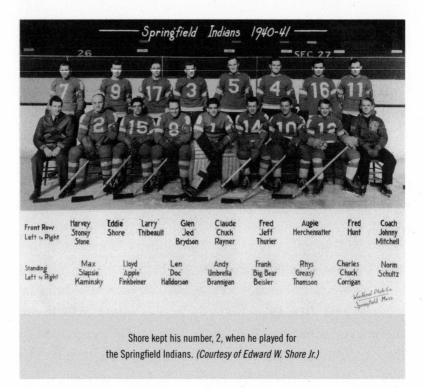

Front Row Left to Right	Harvey Stoney Stone	Eddie Shore	Larry Thibeault	Glen Jed Brydson	Claude Chuck Rayner	Fred Jeff Thurier	Augie Herchenratter	Fred Hunt	Coach Johnny Mitchell
Standing Left to Right	Max Slapsie Kaminsky	Lloyd Apple Finkbeiner	Len Doc Halldorson	Andy Umbrella Brannigan	Frank Big Bear Beisler	Rhys Greasy Thomson	Charles Chuck Corrigan	Norm Schultz	

Shore kept his number, 2, when he played for
the Springfield Indians. *(Courtesy of Edward W. Shore Jr.)*

and to guarantee that it was done right. It was not uncommon to see the Indians star expertly driving a snowplow in the wee hours of the morning, clearing the Coliseum parking lot.

The Shores headed back to Daugh after the 1940–41 season, as they had done for more than a decade, not knowing that this would be their last year of farming. During the season that had just ended, Shore's second in Springfield, he had led his team to a 26–21–9 record, scoring four goals in fifty-six games and spending a hefty sixty-six minutes in the penalty box, the most since 1932–33. In the summer of 1941, Shore was diagnosed with cancer of some type and given six months to live. He bought a house-trailer, and, along with Kate and Ted, left for treatment in California. Cured after he passed the cancer rectally—or so he claimed—he returned to Springfield that fall and dove into Indians hockey again. Eddie played thirty-five games in 1941–42, scoring five goals and almost matching his previous year's record by sitting in the box for sixty-one minutes. The Indians won their division title that season, but not the American Hockey League (the IAHL had changed its name) championship.

All this time, Shore had mellowed not at all, and columnist John Lardner gave his readers an update on the "Edmonton Terror" in January 1942:

> Word reaches us from New Haven, Connecticut that on the night of the 18th in pursuance of what he no doubt considered to be his business duties as owner of the Springfield club of the American Hockey League, Mr. Edward Shore did feloniously assault one Eddie Kuntz, a referee, and attempt to detach his ears and cram them down his throat two abreast. Further word says that Mr. Shore, failing to achieve this goal the first time, pursued Mr. Kuntz into the dressing room after the game and resumed his efforts. Ultimate word says that Mr. Shore has been hurled out of the American Hockey League on one bounce, "pending further notice."

Weeks earlier, a high-school hockey game at the Coliseum had been disrupted by news that the Japanese had attacked Pearl Harbor, and the first question on everybody's lips was, "Where's Pearl Harbor?" The game continued, but shortly thereafter the U.S. Army Quartermaster Corps announced plans to occupy the Coliseum and fill it to the girders with textiles. Shore put up a brave fight against the Army and held the Coliseum just long enough to install new piping, pour a cement floor, and replace a compressor, but then he had to go. Evicted from his arena, Shore suspended his Springfield franchise and decided to retire as a professional player after a spectacular eighteen-year run. For the next three seasons, from 1942–43 until 1944–45, Shore managed the Buffalo Bisons hockey team for his friend Lou Jacobs, the concession magnate who owned Sportservice and whose son Jeremy would buy the Boston Bruins in 1975. Shore did well by Jacobs, even coming out of retirement to play one game for the Bisons in 1943–44, and won the AHL championship, twice.

When Allied victory was declared, Shore was eager to resume operations in Springfield, but the Army had come to like the Coliseum as much as he did and refused to move out, forcing Shore to reactivate his AHL franchise in New Haven for 1945–46.

It was a terrible year for Shore. He lost a lot of games and a lot of money in New Haven, but that was nothing compared to the loss of Kate, his wife, golfing companion, and dance partner, to breast cancer. When the Indians owner was finally allowed to move his team back into the Coliseum the following fall, he was a single parent. Eddie sent his VP and teenage son Ted to Wilbraham Academy, not far from Springfield. Because of wartime travel restrictions, the Shores had been unable to get back to Alberta after 1941, and Eddie had given up farming (and sold the farm in Daugh sometime in the late 1940s). Springfield was now home for father and son, and in the years to come, during Ted's school breaks, the two would spend

As manager of the Buffalo Bisons, *circa* 1943.
(Courtesy of Edward W. Shore Jr.)

as much time at the Coliseum as they did in their Springfield apartment, Ted learning everything there was to know about running an arena and a hockey team.

In the late 1940s, Eddie Shore made up for the lost war years by adding, on the strength of the revenues that the Indians were bringing him, a few teams in the lower minors, creating a little hockey empire. Shore drafted his nephew Jack Butterfield, the son of his older sister Lizzy, to help run the operation. Butterfield was from Regina and fresh from the Royal Canadian Air Force, where he had served as a torpedo bomber pilot (and broken his back in a crash). The moment Butterfield arrived in the States, Shore sent him to Texas to manage the Fort Worth Rangers of the United States Hockey League. In addition to the Rangers, Shore also had a Pacific Coast Hockey League franchise in California, the Oakland Oaks, and was part owner of another club in San Diego. In a search for able bodies to staff his teams, Shore had friends up in Canada who would alert him to potential talent, but Shore also travelled north to scout practically every single arena, small and large, in the country, and at one time he had as many as eighty players under contract. Some of these boys and men he recruited himself, some had been cut from other teams and wanted a second chance, and some had been sent to him by NHL clubs for some much-needed improvement.

Every year for decades, sixty or seventy recruits travelled to Shore's annual training camp, which was usually held in Barrie, Ontario. Players streamed in from all across Canada, and all had to sign the infamous "C Form" binding them to Shore for one year and, at Shore's discretion, every year after that forever. A budding professional, Brian Smith, who later played for the Los Angeles Kings, tried to escape assignment to Shore's camp by playing pro hockey in Europe, but Shore smoked him out and Smith had to report. The reluctant recruit recalled arriving in Ontario and signing his life away. "Shore invited me to his room for contract negotiations," Smith said. "Forget the negotiation part. It was 'take it or leave it' when it came to money. I realized that in a hurry and decided to sign just to get it over with. As I was writing my name he said 'Hold it Mr. Smith, why would you hold the pen so low on the shaft? You should hold it higher, that way you can write much more clearly.'"

At the camp, Shore examined how each player walked and made corrections if his legs were not properly bent, his knees were not the right distance apart, or his stride was too long. The meal allowance was four dollars a day, lodging was provided—three players to a room—at cheap hotels, and some of the equipment was old Bruins stuff from the 1930s. Twice a day, once in the morning and once in the afternoon, Shore held gruelling, two-hour-long ice drills, preceded by one-hour warm-up sessions.

First and foremost, Shore taught everyone, from those in Junior A to NHL veterans, how to skate. Skating the Shore way meant having your weight directly over the blades, knees bent almost to a sitting position, legs six inches apart, feet eleven inches apart, and pushing straight to the side in short, strong strokes. Shore demanded that everyone do this properly. "To teach the technique," Brian Smith said, "he used a variety of methods, but the most effective, and least enjoyable, was to tie us up. He used hockey laces to tie our elbows behind our backs to the get the right arm position. He would tie our knees together so we'd have to take the desired, short, choppy strides he believed were necessary for good balance."

Shore also taught tricks like the neat sideways slide he had developed to elude onrushing attackers, but he mainly taught the basics, like how to hold the hockey stick. The stick, he insisted, must be held with both hands positioned exactly twenty-four inches apart. The stick itself was to be kept below the hips, with the blade touching, or almost touching, the ice at all times. To avoid getting the butt-end in the stomach, the stick was also held parallel to the feet and never towards the body. And the blade of the stick must always be taped toe to heel. "I got a phone call at home about 7:30 in the evening," Smith recalled. "It was Eddie Shore. He said, 'Mr. Smith, come down to the rink and see me immediately'—click." Smith did as ordered and arrived at the Coliseum to find Shore with "his sleeves rolled up to the elbows, revealing those massive forearms, his tie loosened, the bald head wet with sweat, and a wild look in his eye. When he spotted me, Shore roared, 'Mr. Smith, Why, why, why . . . would you tape your stick from the heel to the toe instead of the toe to the heel?' Before I had a chance to answer, he fired the stick the length of the room where it became part of a pile started before I had arrived. Then he grabbed other sticks, screaming, 'Look at this one, the knob is too big . . . look at this one, not enough tape,' and so on."

Dissatisfied with what was available on the market, Shore had the Wally Company in Canada manufacture a special hockey stick just for him. The Wally sticks were kept in a big bin for everyone to share, and with their heavy weight and short, seven-inch reinforced blade, the Wallys were indestructible. The players hated them. All the Wallys were the same: of equal length, with straight blades, and with a lie value of six. "Shore's idea," explained one of his Indians, Kent Douglas, of the high lie, "was if you handle the puck here, at your feet, whoever was checking you had to get in close, they shouldn't get the puck away from you. There was a method to his madness."

Douglas did not agree with Shore most of the time, and once, in Shore's office, got into fisticuffs with him. The argument was over how best to hold a hockey stick, which to most people might have been a minor matter, but not to those two. Although Douglas had his run-ins with Shore, he also learned a lot in Springfield, and later won four Stanley Cups with the Maple Leafs in Toronto. Giving credit where credit was due, Douglas said of Shore, "My feeling has always been that the old man knew more about hockey than anyone else before or since."

With the bark of a German shepherd, Shore hammered home his hockey system. His number one rule was that all players must face the puck at all times. Other dictates included no slap shots, because not only did they mark up the white boards but, more importantly, they were inaccurate. Always, Shore said, use the wrist shot. He also directed that no more than one man go for the puck at the same time, that nobody chase the puck behind the enemy net, and that everyone constantly keep passing the disc. "With that puck movement," Brian Kilrea, a former Indian, noted of the last point, "we appeared to be a faster team than we were." Shore pummelled his hockey system into his players' heads until everyone got it, and a dozen and more of his Indians—including Kilrea, who later coached the Ottawa 67's for twenty-eight years—got it so well that they took his system and made successful coaching careers out of it.

"He was always interested in the little things," Ted Shore recalled, "and the little things make the big things easier. In other words, if you can't pass the puck, if you can't give and receive a pass, if you can't turn, if you can't flip the puck, you are going to have a problem playing this game. How to take a guy out on the boards, how to balance—balance, he was big, big on balance. Whether you are playing hockey or playing golf, or just standing there, you better have your knees bent and be balanced, otherwise he is liable to walk up and knock you over."

Having spent much of his adult life in the penalty box, Eddie Shore did not wish this fate on anyone else. "He didn't want you to be pushed around," Shore's top scorer, Jimmy Anderson, explained. "He wanted you to retaliate, but he didn't want you to do it so you went in the penalty box. Like, he'd show you how to hit a guy with your hip and not have to use your hands and stick. You just hit just a part of him so he will hit the boards, and the boards will roll him right around. He taught little things like that, you can't believe it, little things, and they all worked. And we had to do these things, you know, we had to do these things. He'd either bench you or penalize you if you didn't do them, and then the next day, he'd get you alone and talk to you about it."

Shore's expertise was in taking those with marginal hockey skills and sending them on their way to professional careers. "One especially was Teddy Harris who later played with Montreal," remembered Harry Pidhirny, one of Shore's Indians. "When Harris first came to Springfield, God, he could hardly skate. By the time he left he was good." Not everybody, however, flourished under Shore's harsh tutelage, and some quit hockey outright after a short time with him, or even threw in the towel when told to report to his training camp. Other players outwardly went along with Shore but got little out of it, and ridiculed his theories. And Shore had plenty of theories, such as his belief in the similarity of tap dancing and skating (which, upon reflection, hardly sounds far-fetched). What Shore was teaching may have seemed peculiar at the time, but it bore a striking resemblance to such later innovations as power skating, visualization, the neutral-zone trap, and year-round physical conditioning. "Shore was years ahead of his time," said Brian Smith.

"Whatever they teach now in hockey schools," added an Indian from the 1950s, Gordie Howarth, "it'll be what Shore taught."

For Shore's recruits, training camp lasted a month, and candidates who made the cut boarded the bus for the first Indians game. Those who did not were either sent home or to any number of teams, from Halifax to San Diego, to which Shore had a connection (and Shore had a connection with everybody in hockey). All, though, left camp having learned something. One year, a young man wearing a Maple Leafs jersey appeared uninvited. It was obvious that he was not quite right in the head. Shore took him aside and told him he was going to teach him some things, and worked with him on the fundamentals of skating. After a couple of days, he released the young man from camp, saying, "You'll do all right, I know you will, keep in touch."

In 1947, Shore was inducted into the Hockey Hall of Fame, and, like everything else when it came to Shore and the Bruins, the process had been contentious. Art Ross was a member of the NHL Board of Governors, and he recommended that Dit Clapper be added to the Hall, and in short order Clapper was voted in as its first living member. Bruins fans were, naturally, thrilled, but one pedestrian on Boston's Washington Street wanted to know, "Why are they keeping Shore out of it?" Shore was asked about this by a reporter. "I guess I don't belong in it," Shore deadpanned. "Possibly the ability wasn't there." In Boston, there was a storm of protest and renewed anger at Ross, and within weeks, Shore received a message from Weston Adams congratulating him on his induction and inviting him to a special ceremony at the Garden, where Bruins jersey Number 2 would be sent to the rafters and would never come down.

Eddie Shore made good money in West Springfield, whose out-of-date arena, home to his Indians and other events that he booked, had made him the most successful rink operator in the United States. Shore was happy where he was; by 1950, he had pulled out of the Texas hockey market (there being, it turned out, *no* Texas hockey market), closed down his Oakland team in midseason due to poor attendance, and, because of conflicts with his fellow owners, got out of San Diego. Then the AHL told him that a new arena, the Onondaga War Memorial, had just gone up in Syracuse, New York. It was a four-million-dollar beauty in need of a hockey team.

In those days, as now, the AHL was the premier minor hockey league in the United States, often just a shade below the NHL in terms of quality of play (and sometimes even better). Also in those days, as now, AHL franchises were constantly engaged in an annual game of musical chairs. The league's clubs moved, closed, and opened at a dizzy pace, sometimes arriving in new AHL cities and sometimes returning to old ones. Concerned that the league would take his franchise away from him if he did not play along, Shore reluctantly got up from his chair in 1951, and, when the music stopped, plunked down in another, renaming his Indians the Syracuse Warriors.

At the Onondaga War Memorial, everything went wrong. The Warriors were awful, attendance was poor, and in three years Shore burned through seven hundred thousand dollars of his own money before the AHL let him return to the Coliseum in West Springfield. (The AHL returned to Syracuse in 1974, left in 1975, returned in 1979, left in 1980, returned in 1994—and is still there.)

In 1954, the Korean conflict was over, Dwight D. Eisenhower was in the White House, and the golden era of hockey had arrived in Springfield. Their first season back, 1954–55, the Indians enjoyed their first winning year since 1942, and rookie Jimmy Anderson got the first 39 of his eventual 425 goals. Springfield was high on hockey, and the Indians were the talk of the town. Ross Lowe at centre ice and Gordon Tottle on defence were named AHL all-stars that year, and the Coliseum rocked with rabid fans—5,934 of them most nights—stomping like mad on the wooden floors of the stands.

Indians games were on Saturday nights, and on Saturday night the Coliseum was the place to be. Television had just come to Springfield on channels 22 and 40, but it was black-and-white fare and no competition for the live color of the Coliseum. The arena was where you went to see, be seen, and see hockey. "If you weren't at an Indians game Saturday night," a Springfield fan remembered, "then it was thought there was something wrong with you." Politicians, judges, and gangsters were all there, and nearly every game was a sellout. The team song was Bill Haley's "Shake, Rattle and Roll," which blared from the loudspeakers as the Indians took to the ice and the spectators went crazy. Intermissions were vast social affairs, thanks to a unique ten-foot-wide corridor between the box seats and rinkside seats that served as a walkway along which fans could meet and greet. It was said that marriages were made at the Coliseum, but not in every instance. "You'd take your first date there," one spectator, Pat Pompei, recalled, "and if she didn't like hockey, it would be the last date."

The next several seasons disappointed in comparison to 1954–55, yet Indians fans never blamed a loss on their team. Instead, they took out their ire on opposing players by yelling at them, dousing them with beer, chasing them into the parking lot, and stoning their bus. The Indians regained their glory at the end of the 1950s, when Shore collaborated with the New York Rangers and, in return for developing Rangers talent, got a bucket full of first-rate players. For three years running, the AHL championship Calder Cup (named after Frank) stayed in Springfield. From his seat in Section 25, Box 1, Eddie Shore had a direct telephone link to Pat Egan, his old New York Americans/Springfield Indians defence partner of 1940, who was now his coach. Standing behind the Indians bench, Egan had to take Shore's telephone calls, and, following his orders, he led Springfield to dominance in 1959–60, 1960–61, and 1961–62 for a natural AHL hat trick never repeated by any other team in the league before or since.

The Indians had outstanding players in men like the tragic Bill Sweeney, winner of the AHL scoring title every year from 1960 to 1963, who played while drunk and, at age fifty-four, died an alcoholic. The Indians also had greats in Jimmy Anderson and Harry Pidhirny, Teddy Harris, Dennis Olson, Kent Douglas, Bruce Cline, Bob McCord, Brian Kilrea, Billy McCreary, and George Wood. Anderson, Harris, Douglas, and McCord advanced to the NHL, but it is a crime that the others did not, because each would easily have done so today. However, so entrenched was the six-team NHL in the pre-expansion era that, the joke went, you had to wait for an NHL player to die before you could move up.

One of those minor-leaguers-in-waiting was Don Cherry, the future Bruins coach and television commentator. When Cherry came to Springfield via a trade with Hershey in 1957, he was already fearful of his new boss. "Having heard so much about Eddie Shore before actually meeting him," Cherry remembered, he had thought Shore would be large and ominous. "That, however, was not the Eddie Shore who shook my hand and welcomed me to the Springfield Indians." Shore, according to Cherry, was small, bald, and obviously tough. Although Shore's face was scarred, for someone in his fifties he appeared to Cherry "to be in mint condition. In no time at all I learned what Shore thought of me. He gave me a nickname—the Madagascar Kid. I think that's where he would have sent me, given the opportunity."

Cherry considered Springfield to be the Siberia of hockey, and Shore considered Cherry to be a lousy skater. Shore told Cherry to "visualize" the fact that he had no skating manoeuvrability at all, and harangued Cherry about this and other things. He once had Cherry skate around the rink for four hours and twenty minutes for failing to look him in the eye while talking to him. Cherry played 206 games in an Indians uniform over the course of two full seasons (1957–58 and 1958–59) and parts of two more (1959–60 and 1961–62), and witnessed more than he cared to of Eddie Shore's tyranny.

Cherry recalled that, after a game in which goaltender Claude Evans had posted a 5–0 shutout, Shore walked into the dressing room and "fined Evans $50 because *he didn't bend his knees.*" Once, when he thought the opposition was playing too defensively, Shore told his Indians—under threat of fine—to ice the puck whenever they could, thus bringing the action to a boring halt. The Indians iced the disc seventy-two times before, having made his point, Shore lifted the threat and normal play resumed.

Shore would levy a fine against a player for any infraction. Former Indians recall Shore fining them for eating a piece of pie before a game, for being late for practice, for drinking after hours, and for holding their sticks the wrong way. If he had known about it, Shore would have even fined his players for having sex before a game, because sex, he believed, sapped his warriors of energy. After a 1965 game in Buffalo, Indians goalie Jacques Caron got into a spat with Shore, who had told him he could not spend the night with his wife, who had come down from Toronto to see the game. Caron and Shore bickered all the way into the dressing room, where the argument esca- lated, and it took the referees and all the ushers in the building to separate the two combatants. Once, when the Indians were in a slump, Shore asked the players' wives to attend a special meeting in the Coliseum. Expecting a pleasant evening, the women dressed up for the occasion, but when they got there, it was no party, just Shore gently (because Shore was always gentle with women) requesting that they abstain from marital intimacies, at least during the playoffs.

Shore was not afraid to flout AHL rules. He fired goal judges of his own accord, locked referees in the dressing room, pulled all his men off the ice and dared the referee to continue the game, and berated linesmen over the loudspeakers in that slow voice of his: "Mis-ter-Fon-ta-na-you-do-not-know-how-to . . ." At age sixty-four, Shore escaped the clutches of his police detail to walk out onto the ice in his fedora, business suit, and black shoes in order to help Springfield's Dave Amadio bash Pittsburgh's Ian Cushenan with a Wally.

Shore also thought of himself as a medical man, and his black bag was filled with prairie home remedies. According to those who tried it, his cure for a cold—three drops of iodine—worked. He prescribed laxatives for everything. "The Old Man gave me something called the Marlet Treatment," remembered one of Shore's Indians, Doug McMurdy, who had been suffering from jaundice. "It's a laxative made up of oils. I was scared of it, so I took only half what I was supposed to. I lost 12 pounds in no time, so I cut it out. I think if I'd have taken the whole business it would have been suicide." Dr. Shore recommended that scar tissue be massaged once a day for seven years to make it disappear, treated sprains and bruises with an alternating application of hot and cold water, and counselled his players on "how to screw by the moon" so that their wives had baby boys. In hotel lobbies, he showed strangers how to sit up straight, and, for those interested in veterinary medicine, he would explain how to cut a tumour out of a horse's side or demonstrate, by going through all the motions, how to deliver a calf.

Of all his treatments, though, the one Shore loved best was to adjust a back. "I'm in the dressing room," Albert "Boots" Rossetti, an Indians trainer in the early 1950s, recalled in an interview more than fifty years later, "and in walks Shore. He takes all his clothes off and he tells me, 'Get your clothes off!' I said to myself, what the hell is going on here? He said, 'Get on that table!' He is going to teach me how to crack backs. Now he had hands like a ham and I weigh about 140, and we are stark naked, and he is showing me how to crack a back. Then I am trying to crack his back, and he's a big man, and I can't even move him. We are taking turns on the table, and I start laughing, and he said to me, 'What the heck are you laughing at?' I said, 'It's not a laughing matter, Eddie, I can see the headlines now: Hockey Hall of Famer Caught Naked with Naked Trainer.'"

"Oh that guy Shore was so zany," Sam Pompei, a Shore employee in the 1940s and former sports editor of the Springfield *Daily News*, said in 2007. "One time he claims I misquoted him in the paper or some incidental thing, and he blasted the shit out of me for fifteen minutes, and then the next morning, the phone rang at six o'clock. I thought, Who the hell could be calling me at six in the morning? It's dark. I wasn't used to getting calls at that hour. I answered the phone. It was Shore. He was crying. 'Samuel,' he was sobbing, 'can you find it in your heart to forgive me for what I said last night?' He went on and on, and I didn't say a word. 'It's okay, Eddie,' I finally said. 'Forget it. Forget it Eddie, pretend it never happened.'"

Shore had a reputation, as owner of the Indians, for being incredibly cheap. High-school teams could rent the Coliseum for fifteen dollars an hour—seventeen with the lights turned on. In the United States Hockey League of the 1940s, whenever a referee banished a coach from the game, the coach had to leave the building. In Texas, this happened to one of Shore's coaches, Edwin Murph "Old Hardrock" Chamberlain, and when Old Hardrock tried to re-enter the arena, Shore made him buy a ticket.

"He had NHL-caliber players on his team and prevented them from leaving," said Doug McMurdy, who was an Indian in the 1940s and '50s. "A lot of players from those years, myself included, found out later that NHL teams were really interested in getting us, but Shore wouldn't let us go. He could have traded or sold us, but he wouldn't. He had good players," McMurdy concluded, "and he got them for a good price."

"I hate to say anything bad about him," Jimmy Anderson, an Indian from 1954 to 1967, said of Shore, "but he wouldn't pay any money. His pay was awful, but you couldn't do anything about it. You couldn't go play anywhere else. 'If you don't like it here, go home!' he'd say. 'I don't want you here! Get home! But you can't play for anybody else because I own you,' he'd say. And he was right."

The boys of the Coliseum neighbourhood, which was a close-knit and largely Italian-American community nicknamed the "deadline district," also provided an ample source of free labour. Before he bought a Zamboni, Shore had his unpaid "rink rats" scrape and water the ice; when he did get a Zamboni (it came disassembled with no instructions), he had them shovel the snow out of it. The volunteer rink rats also served as stick and water boys during Indians games, ushered public-skating sessions, officiated at junior hockey league games, and did odd jobs around the building.

"Bend your knees," Shore is telling Sandra Pompei at the Coliseum. First row far right in coat and tie is Shore's nephew and the Indians G.M., Jack Butterfield. *(Courtesy of Edward W. Shore Jr.)*

The boys were terrified of Mr. Shore, and knew that when you were in the Coliseum, his rules had to be obeyed. Take a slap shot against the boards, you go home. Keep your knees bent, even during public skating, or be prepared to be beckoned over to the boards by a crooked finger for a lecture. Off the ice, hockey sticks had to be carried blade down. There was no swearing or fighting on or off the ice, lest you place your entire team at risk of suspension. Every boy played in every junior hockey league game, or else the coach would be at risk of suspension (Shore would not tolerate favouritism). There was no fooling or running around in the halls of the Coliseum, and, while watching a game—and this went for everybody of any age—there was never, *ever,* any putting of feet up on the seats. ("Do you do that in your own house?" Shore would yell as he kicked the offender out of the building.)

The boys had the greatest respect for Shore, and in return for their help around the rink, he gave them free ice time. "We always had an advantage over other teams because we had the ice," a former rink rat, Rudy Basilone, explained. Shore also gave his rink rats, along with any boy interested in hockey, a free spot in the Greater Springfield Junior Hockey League. Shore was responsible for the league from 1939 until 1968. His proudest year was probably 1952, when Rudy Basilone and the rest of the West Springfield High School hockey team, who were all Coliseum rink rats and graduates of the junior hockey league, turned Boston on its head by coming into that larger city and winning the Division 1 state hockey championship. One of those teenage champions, Gene Grazia, later struck gold with the U.S. hockey squad in the 1960 Olympics. Although only a few rink rats made it to the professional ranks, dozens played in college, and some of those can thank Eddie Shore for their education, because without hockey they would not have received college scholarships.

One time, the rink rats heard that their counterparts in New Haven were getting paid real money, and, working up their nerve, they approached Shore's office. Shore, who knew what was up, kept the boys squirming for an hour before granting them an audience. "So we went in there and asked him to pay us," Basilone said, "and he fired all of us on the spot. So we had to go back and apologize to get our jobs back."

But while he was incredibly cheap, Shore could also be very generous. In his Bruins years, whenever the team was in New York and the gang went to the Cotton Club, it was Eddie who picked up the tab, and he was particularly charitable to people in times of need. When Ross Lowe died in a swimming accident the summer after his first fantastic year with the Indians, Shore immediately rushed to Lowe's family in Canada to offer them comfort, support, money, or anything else to ease their burden. If one of Shore's office "girls" got into a car accident, Shore would quietly hand her a wad of bills held tight by rubber bands—and containing hundreds of dollars—to pay for the repairs. He helped his players with personal problems, and provided cash if a member of their family needed an operation, giving Doug McMurdy thousands of dollars when McMurdy's son was ill and in the hospital. And what happened to those fines that Shore deducted from his players' paycheques during the season? He gave them all back the following spring. If any of his Indians had drunk away his salary, Shore would buy him a train ticket home.

Shore expressed his generosity in other ways as well. He made sure the Indians' bus picked up hitchhikers, and even had the driver make detours to get them to their destinations. If a high-school student did not have enough money to buy his date a ticket for an Indians game, Shore might not give him a free pass, but he would give him two dollars to buy a ticket. Besides hockey, Shore's other love was golf, and he wanted his players to embrace the sport as well. So he would take his men down to the country club and buy them equipment. Gerry Ehman, who would later win three Stanley Cups with the Maple Leafs, admired Shore's irons, worth four hundred dollars and the very best because Shore always went first class, and asked his boss if he could buy them. Shore said yes, Ehman asked how much, and Shore replied, "Got a penny in your pocket?"

Shore could certainly have used the good publicity, yet he never allowed a word about any of this to leak out. "He had a

Shore teeing off. He practised relentlessly and
played a scratch game of golf. *(Courtesy of Edward W. Shore Jr.)*

heart of gold, but I often wonder if he wanted to be liked," Pat Egan said. "I don't think he wanted to, so that people wouldn't take advantage of him; but no one was going to take advantage of Eddie."

Shore kept the details of his business affairs confined to those he trusted the most, and these were general manager Jack Butterfield, vice-president Ted Shore, and office manager Carol Ann Gaba. Of the three, only Gaba was not a relative, but Eddie solved that problem by marrying her in 1952. At age fifty, Shore was still full of youth and vitality. He loved hockey and loved driving, fast. Shore's car was a gigantic Cadillac with licence plates that read MR HOCKEY, and he would race teenage hot-rodders down Springfield's Main Street, blowing the kids' doors off. Shore was also still amazingly fast on skates and could outrace his players in an end-to-end dash, skating backwards. The man was, however, mortal, and in 1957, at age fifty-five, and while leading the annual Springfield Country Club Championship by twelve shots, he had the first of what he called "my fatal heart attacks." The heart attacks were soon joined by strokes—over the coming years, he had at least eleven of them. These would subdue Shore for a while, but in time he would be back on his blades to lead practice. During games, he would leave his box to egg his players on as they "engaged" the referee and rival players, which in turn would incite the fans to join in. "If Mr. Shore would just stay put," the West Springfield chief of police complained after his officers responded to one such Coliseum riot, "there wouldn't be all this mess."

The golden era of Indians hockey faded after the 1962 Calder Cup victory, and early in the 1966–67 season the team was struggling. Shore's health had worsened, which made him

With the former Carol Gaba, wedding day, 1952. *(Courtesy of Edward W. Shore Jr.)*

an even more difficult man to deal with. In the first part of the season, Shore once scheduled practice for early Monday morning—after the team had just played games on Friday, Saturday, and Sunday—and the players began to think him demonic. "Had I had to play one more season with Shore," said Dale Rolfe, an Indian that year, "I would have retired. Playing under Shore was unbelievable, almost inhuman . . . terrifying, nauseating, backwards, medieval."

The popular Harry Pidhirny of the golden era was back as the Indians' newest coach for 1966–67, and Pidhirny found himself being second-guessed by Shore at every turn. "He used to phone me up two, three o'clock in the morning to tell me what the guys were doing wrong. After a road trip he asks me, 'How'd it go?' 'Not bad,' I'd say and he says, 'Oh, this guy didn't do this, didn't do that.' He wasn't even there and he's telling me what the guys were doing! During the game, during practices, he would always interfere. He sat right behind us and if he thought something was wrong he'd send Jack Butterfield down to tell me, 'Do this, do that,' which I didn't appreciate too much—I don't think anybody would."

Player morale was dismal. AHL salaries had finally begun to climb, following the trend established by NHL clubs. There were no salary increases in Springfield, though, where some veteran Indians were making less than rookies on other American league teams. The old man was also doling out fines like an angry traffic cop, and in mid-December, after his team had suffered a particularly painful 5–4 loss to the Quebec Aces, he gave his best defencemen—Bill White, Dave Amadio, and Dale Rolfe—a letter informing them that they had been suspended for one week due to "indifferent play." The dreaded "indifferent play" letter was a favourite technique of Shore's to telegraph his dissatisfaction, but in this case White, Rolfe, and Amadio suspected it had more to do with money. At camp that year, all three had successfully held out for more pay, and the meagre raises they'd got were exactly the amounts they would now be losing to the one-week suspensions. It was also remembered that in the final year at Syracuse, where the Warriors were costing Shore dearly, he had suspended seven of his men for the last twenty games of the schedule.

White, Rolfe, and Amadio got their suspension letters on Sunday, December 18, 1966, and the next day, the rest of the Indians decided to do something about it. In the dressing room before practice, the players appointed Brian Kilrea to be their representative. Kilrea went up to Shore's office, where the owner was having his customary cup of tea with two tea bags, and told him that he was there to represent the players. "No one," Shore told Kilrea, "represents my players." Shore then suspended Kilrea for indifferent play.

Following this, the fourth suspension in two days, the players refused to attend afternoon practice, explaining to the Springfield *Union* that Christmas was coming up and they had families to support. "We can't play our best under constant threats of suspension. We've been mistreated too long to back down this time and if we had gone on the ice and practiced then the fellows suspended would have had no support." Kilrea added, "We want to play hockey. That's how we make our living and that's all most of us know what to do." Eddie Shore, however, was unapologetic. "I have no gripes with many of my players," Shore said, "but there are some would-be players who are trying to fool the public while giving only 65 to 70 per cent of their capacity. I decided I wouldn't tolerate it any longer." When asked about the possibility of a player's strike, Shore answered, "Let them. I'll bring in enough players to man two more clubs. We'll have a team here ready to face the Providence Reds Friday night."

On the second day of the walkout, the Coliseum ice was devoid of Indians. Shore warned that replacement players from the Central Hockey League were "on the way" to Springfield from Memphis. Newspapers, television, and radio from coast to coast were covering the drama, which, it was reported, "had shocked the hockey world." In Baltimore, the Clippers of the AHL staged a sit-down sympathy strike before resuming practice two minutes later. Jack Butterfield, who had also just been made acting president of the AHL, walked across the street from the Coliseum to the motel where the Indians were meeting. Butterfield's visit was, according to reports, "for purposes of explaining league rules and the rights of a club owner and the players under contract." Butterfield had the urging of NHL president Clarence Campbell in taking a tough line, and he told the Indians to get back to work or face suspension from hockey for life.

Up in Toronto, a young attorney and ambitious politician named R. Alan Eagleson had just done the unimaginable by negotiating a contract for a hockey player (a kid named Bobby Orr), and the striking Indians asked Eagleson if he could help them. "The Eagle" flew down to Springfield and got his picture on the front pages of the newspapers. Out of sight of the cameras, however, the lawyer bluntly informed his new clients

Number 2, Eddie Shore, and Number 4, Bobby Orr, during a visit to the Shriners Hospital for Children in Springfield, mid-1970s. *(Courtesy of Christopher Hiam.)*

that, contractually, they had no right to strike. He warned the strikers that Butterfield's threat was real and advised them to lace up their skates. Suitably sobered, on Wednesday the players held practice by themselves at the Coliseum while Shore, still having not withdrawn his threat to bring in strike-breakers, said he was undecided as to what steps he might take next. By Thursday, Shore's threats receded, and the following night, two days before Christmas, the former rebels were back in the red, white, and blue uniforms of their employer, demolishing the Providence Reds 9–3. It was a boisterous game, and

Shore was full of holiday cheer, joyfully ejecting a fan who came up to his box and dared confront him about how he treated his players.

After the victory over Providence, however, the holiday spirit evaporated and everything was back to normal. The Indians were still struggling, and Shore was still dishing out fines and suspensions, and giving his coach unwelcome advice. Then, in early January, Harry Pidhirny literally skated off the job. The last straw for Pidhirny came one afternoon during drills, when Shore, for the umpteenth time, told him how to run practice. Pidhirny, perhaps the greatest player in Indians history, jumped over the boards, stomped into the dressing room, and took off his skates. "I'm through," he declared to reporter Sam Pompei, who saw the whole thing. "I've had it up to here. I should have left this job five weeks ago. He's not going to make a fool out of me . . . I just can't take this anymore. Let him run the club, I want no part of it." Shore, who did nothing to stop Pidhirny from walking out to the parking lot, merely remarked, "Generally, a coach informs management either by word or letter of his intentions, but he didn't do either."

Shore took over as coach, and the first thing he did was tell goalie Jacques Caron and forward Roger Côté to "go home." The two were suspended for the rest of the season, and, of course, were unemployable as hockey players while still under contract to Shore. They appealed to Eagleson, and in short order the shocking news came out of the Coliseum that Eddie Shore was stepping down.

Credit for forcing Shore into retirement is generally given to Eagleson, who went on to found the National Hockey League Players' Association and make hockey the first of the four major league sports to be unionized. The Eagle, a self-promoter, did nothing to counter this impression. But Shore's decision to resign had nothing to do with the lawyer from Toronto. Instead, it had everything to do with nephew Jack Butterfield, son Ted, wife Carol, and, especially, personal physician Arthur Gramse. The four met with Shore two days after Pidhirny left to tell him that they were concerned about his health. "The doctor was a great guy," Ted Shore recalled. "He said, 'Ed, your heart, you don't need this, you've had a dozen heart attacks, you don't need any more stress in your life. Turn the hockey team over to someone else.' And everybody agreed that that was the right thing to do. Everybody was worried about Ed; he'd had strokes and heart attacks, and we wanted him around a little longer."

Eddie Shore, the Indians' Super Chief, left the family meeting and gathered his tribe around him, telling his men that he would no longer be their leader, and also that none of them would lose any pay for having gone out on strike. He also promised his Indians a ten-thousand-dollar pool of bonus money if they reached seventy-six points by the end of the season. This meant the Indians would have to win most of the thirty-eight games remaining, and the first opportunity to win one of those games was the next night. After Shore was through with his talk, Ted took him aside and whispered, "Who's going to coach?" "You are," said the old man.

Ted Shore, former senior amateur and college hockey player, was a gentler version of his father. The fines immediately stopped, and Caron and Côté were welcomed back. The day after assuming command, on Friday, January 13, 1967, the new coach stepped in to lead the Indians against the Cleveland

Barons. Nothing went right for Ted. His wife Evelyn (Eddie Shore III was at home with a sitter) sat weeping in the stands, watching as the Indians could not get the puck into the Barons' net no matter how hard they tried, and no matter how often her husband mixed up the lines. At the end of two periods, Springfield was behind 2–1. Then, at 6:31 of the final period, Dave Amadio evened the score with a sizzling shot, and the Indians managed to maintain the tie until the last minute of play, while also looking for a way to put the game away. With forty seconds left, however, the puck became stubbornly stuck in the Indians' zone, and, maddeningly, they could not get it out. Ted Shore rolled the dice and made a line change, but the puck was still stuck in the zone. Throwing caution to the wind, Shore then rolled the dice again and, with twenty seconds left, made yet another line change. This time, something clicked. The Indians' Bill White got possession and, moving on the attack, passed to Brian Kilrea, who outmanoeuvred two Barons to feed the puck to teammate Barclay Plager, who was racing up on the left wing. With two seconds remaining on the clock, Plager neared the Cleveland cage, fired low from a sharp angle, and buried the rubber in the far corner. "Eddie the Elder," sitting in his box seat, was thrilled, there was pandemonium at the Coliseum, and behind the bench, Ted Shore was too stunned to move.

Under Ted Shore, the Indians turned their play around, winning enough games to earn the bonus money promised them, and coming agonizingly close (within four points) to making it into the AHL playoffs. Meanwhile, out in California, Jack Kent Cooke, who'd earned a fortune from cable television and minor-league baseball, had just been granted an NHL expansion franchise that would become the Los Angeles Kings. Now he was in dire need of a couple dozen hockey players. Cooke approached Eddie Shore, and in June, Shore, after long and arduous negotiations, sold Cooke all of the Indians at a handsome profit. In an innovative arrangement, he also leased Cooke the Springfield AHL franchise for five years, with an option for a second five-year term. Renamed the Springfield Kings for the 1967–68 season, the club sent Anderson, Kilrea, White, Caron, Amadio, and Rolfe to Los Angeles to play—at last—in the NHL.

Eddie Shore was now able to devote himself to golf. He had always kept a large net hanging above Section 19 of the Coliseum, into which he could drive golf balls during the cold months, or he would go down to his condo in the Bahamas, where it was warmer and the golfing more lucrative. Shore's pro at the Springfield Golf Club, Harry Mattson, recalled that in the Bahamas Shore's favourite bet was "One-two-three-hundred-dollar Nassau, and he'd win every time. He had a three or four handicap, very good player. Very detailed, very smart . . . a perfectionist. It had to be absolutely perfect every time."

Mattson recalled that "Eddie used to hit golf balls by the hour. His hands would be all calluses, like raw bones. But he was tough, he was a hockey player—I mean, he was tough. You know, everybody feared him, even at that age, because he didn't take any bullshit from anybody. But he was really tough on himself, too. We're playing the second hole one day, and there was Jack Madden, a lawyer, and George Leary, another lawyer, and myself. Shore had the ball on the green for a birdie, just about three feet from the hole, but missed, and he comes up to me and he says, 'Hit me.' 'What do you mean, hit you?'

'Hit me!' 'Eddie, I'm not going to hit you.' So he went over to Jack Madden, and he says, 'Jack, hit me,' and Jack hit him—drew blood."

After striking his deal with Cooke, reportedly worth a million dollars, Shore travelled back to Melville, Saskatchewan, for a reunion of the 1923–24 Millionaires. Those brutal, gory games against the 10th Battalion, Monarchs, and Victorias had caused no lasting damage, as forty-three years later every Millionaire was alive and well and in attendance. Shore was given his accolades, and then he gave the folks of Melville a sizable cheque to keep hockey in the town. Shore was honoured again in 1970, when he received the Lester Patrick Memorial Trophy for his outstanding contributions to hockey in the United States, and in 1974, he attended the fifty-seventh annual NHL meeting, held at the Queen Elizabeth Hotel in Montreal. In the hospitality suite, there was a social gathering, during which the New York Islanders' assistant general manager—and former Bruin—Aut Erickson, age thirty-eight, provoked an argument with Shore, age seventy-two. Erickson told him that his ideas were outmoded and that hockey had passed him by. Shore told Erickson to stop taunting him, there were a couple of shoves between the two men, and in all of this, Erickson missed the classic Shore warning signs—an intense stare and clenched fists. As spectators watched in disbelief, Eddie landed a hard right, followed by a nice left, and Erickson tumbled over a table and landed on the carpet, out cold.

The Springfield Kings had won the Calder Cup in 1971, but had been a financial drain ever since, and in 1974–75 Cooke thought he might as well fold up shop and send his players home. This, Cooke figured, would save him money, even if it left Springfield with no AHL hockey, but Shore reminded Cooke of his commitment to Springfield. Cooke's reply was, "So sue me."

George Maguire, general manager of the Los Angeles Kings, informed his boss that, even if he dismissed Springfield's players, coach, and trainer, he would still have to pay them for the rest of the season. Stuck with those expenses, Cooke agreed to relinquish control of the AHL franchise if Shore would pay for everything else, such as stadium rent, travel, equipment, and league dues. By January 1975, the aging but still mighty Eddie Shore was back in charge, and the Kings were dressed again as Indians in their old colours of red, white, and blue. Thanks to Maguire, there were some player changes, and the team went from being last in the league to making the play-offs. Then they won the Calder Cup, Shore's seventh.

The following season, 1975–76, with Ted Shore as general manager and Jimmy Anderson as coach, and with the Los Angeles Kings no longer affiliated with the team and no longer sending Springfield NHL-calibre talent, the independent Indians had to make do with players no one else wanted. The team finished poorly, and Eddie Shore lost a lot of money. In July 1976, he sold the franchise to his attorney, George Leary. Shore, now officially retired, had more time for the grandchildren, two girls and two boys, giving them the Life Savers that he always carried with him since Dr. Gramse told him to stop smoking. ("You," Gramse had sneered at a protesting Shore, "haven't got the guts to quit." That did the trick.) Shore showed his grandsons how to put up their dukes and land a knockout punch, and, if they missed a blade or two, he would have them mow the lawn again.

Ace Bailey, Harold Ballard (long-time owner of the Maple Leafs), and
Eddie Shore, Toronto, early 1980s. *(Courtesy of Steve Bordeaux.)*

It's unlikely that anyone who saw Shore in action during his
blood-spattered zenith decades earlier could ever have imag-
ined that one day the man from Cupar, Saskatchewan, would
die peacefully in his sleep. Yet this is exactly what happened, on
March 16, 1985. The next morning, newspapers across Canada
and the United States broke the news that Edward William
Shore, the "Edmonton Express," had expired at age eighty-two
after several years of declining health. The funeral was held at
Christ Church Cathedral in Springfield. Family, friends, senators, congressmen, mayors, and hockey players were there.
Ace Bailey was ill in Toronto and could not make it, but King
Clancy went, as did other NHL players spanning the decades:
Pat Egan, Jimmy Anderson, Kent Douglas, and Teddy Harris,

among others, including the man Shore wished he could have taught to skate, if only to have saved his knees, Bobby Orr.

Today, the Coliseum still stands proud, although it would stand much prouder if the ice had not been taken out in 1991. They tore down Boston Garden in 1997, and years before that the city tried to sell the old Boston Arena, but no one was interested. The Arena's future was in doubt (one plan was to turn it into a factory) but then Northeastern University took it over, and on one recent wintry afternoon the weather was so bitterly cold that it drove a horde of frozen students off Huntington Avenue and through the main gates. Inside the grand old building the spirit of Eddie Shore was everywhere as the duelling Huskies of Northeastern and Connecticut universities went at it through three scoreless periods. Then, in the last seconds of play, Connecticut's Michelle Binning took a wicked blast at Northeastern's Florence Schelling. Schelling, that steady Olympian, stood tall before her citadel and saved the day, but U. Conn's dangerous Dominique Thibault was right in front with blade on ice. As the students in the stands screamed like maniacs, she rifled the rebound, bulged the twine, and won the game.

SOURCES

═══

I FOLLOWED EDDIE SHORE's playing career day by day in the pages of the Cupar *Herald*, Regina *Morning Leader*, *Edmonton Journal*, Boston *Evening Transcript*, New York *Herald Tribune*, and Springfield *Daily News*. I also waded deep into the ink of the Edmonton *Bulletin*, Boston *Globe*, Boston *Herald*, Boston *Traveler*, Boston *Post*, Boston *Evening American*, Boston *Record*, Montreal *Daily Star*, Montreal *Herald*, New York *Times*, Springfield *Republican*, and *Toronto Star*. In vintage scrapbook collections I found hundreds of informative newspaper clippings from all over North America, and I consulted countless articles published in recent decades in American and Canadian newspapers.

I read all the magazine articles that I could find on Eddie Shore, including: "Shore—Jekyll and Hyde of Hockey" in the Boston *Sunday Advertiser*, circa 1930; "Hockey: the Return of

Eddie Shore" in *The New Yorker*, February 1934; "Flash and Fury" in *Collier's*, February 24, 1934; "King of Defense Men" in *Open Road for Boys*, January 1935; "Rink Rebel" in *Popular Sports*, February 1938; "One Quick Boo for Shore" in *Newsweek*, November 13, 1939; "Bad Man on Ice" in *Liberty*, November 25, 1939; "Whatever Else . . . You've Seen Shore!" in *Garden-Arena Sports News*, circa December 1939; "Rowdy of the Rinks" in *Sportfolio*, March 1947; "One for the Book" in *Sport*, April 1949; "Eddie Shore: Old Blood and Guts of Hockey" in *Sport*, February 1950; "Mayhem on Ice Skates" in *Saga*, February 1951; "Eddie Shore: Old Blood and Guts" in *Sport*, February 1959; "One of the All Time Great Competitors" in *Hockey Pictorial*, February 1971; "One Lump or Two?" in *Goal*, February 27, 1977; "The Farm Boy Who Became 'Old Blood and Guts'" in *Hockey*, January 1979; "The Darth Vader of Hockey" in *Satellite Entertainment Guide*, February 1994; and "The Toughest of Them All: Eddie Shore" in *Bodycheck*, Vol. 3, No. 4, 1995.

Only four "old-time hockey" memoirs seem to exist, but thankfully all are excellent: *When the Rangers Were Young* by Frank Boucher (New York: Dodd, Mead and Company, 1973); *Clancy: The King's Story as Told to Brian McFarlane* by Brian McFarlane (Toronto: McGraw-Hill, 1968); *Behind the Cheering* by Frank Selke (Toronto: McClelland & Stewart, 1962); and *If You Can't Beat 'Em in the Alley* by Conn Smythe (Toronto: McClelland & Stewart, 1981). I also enjoyed reading two invaluable collections of old-time hockey stories: *Those Were the Days: The Lore of Hockey by the Legends of the Game* by Stan Fischler (New York: Dodd, Mead and Company, 1976), and *The Mad Men of Hockey* by Trent Frayne (New York: Dodd, Mead and Company, 1974).

Other historical books and articles that were very helpful are: *Hockey! The Story of the World's Fastest Sport* by Richard Beddoes, Stan Fischler, and Ira Gitler (New York: Macmillan Publishing, 1973); *The Montreal Maroons: The Forgotten Stanley Cup Champions* by William Brown (Montreal: Véhicule Press, 1999); *Hockey, the Fastest Game on Earth* by Mervyn Dutton (New York: Funk and Wagnalls, 1938); *A Fan for all Seasons* by Tom Gaston (Bolton, Ontario: Fenn Publishing, 2001); *Down the Ice* by Foster Hewitt (Toronto: S.J. Reginald Saunders, 1934); *Hockey: A People's History* by Michael McKinley (Toronto: McClelland & Stewart, 2009); *Superstars: Hockey's Greatest Players* by Andy O'Brien (Toronto: McGraw-Hill Ryerson, 1973); *Players: The Ultimate A–Z Guide of Everyone Who Has Ever Played in the* by Andrew Podnieks (Toronto: Doubleday Canada, 2003); *The Hockey Book: The Great Hockey Stories of All Time* by Wilfrid Roche (Toronto: McClelland & Stewart, 1953); *Cyclone Taylor: A Hockey Legend* by Eric Whitehead (Garden City, New York: Doubleday, 1977); and *The Patricks: Hockey's Royal Family* by Eric Whitehead (Toronto: Doubleday Canada, 1980).

Fortunately, there are also works about the Boston Bruins in particular, and these are: *Boston Bruins: Celebrating 75 Years* by Clark Booth (Del Mar, California: Tehabi Books, 1998); *We Love You Bruins: Boston's Gashouse Gang from Eddie Shore to Bobby Orr* by John Devaney (New York: Sport Magazine Press, 1972); *Bobby Orr and the Big, Bad Bruins* by Stan Fischler (New York: Dell Publishing, 1969); *Champions Remembered: Choice Picks from a Boston Sports Desk* by Ray Fitzgerald (Brattleboro, Vermont: The Stephen Greene Press, 1982); "George Owen: The 'Bobby Orr' of the 1930s" in *Hockey Pictorial*, September 1971; "The Remarkable Boston Bruins" in *Sport*, May 1963; *The Bruins in*

Black and White, 1924–1966 by Richard A. Johnson and Brian Codagnone (Portsmouth, New Hampshire: Arcadia, 2003); and *The Bruins* by Brian McFarlane (Toronto: Stoddart, 1999).

My understanding of regional hockey history was helped greatly by reading *Hockey Towns: Stories of Small Town Hockey in Canada* by Bill Boyd (Toronto: Doubleday Canada, 1999); *Boston's Ballparks and Arenas* by Alan E. Fould (Boston: Northeastern University Press, 2005); "Long Before Orr: Placing Hockey in Boston, 1897–1929" by Stephen Hardy in *The Rock, The Curse and the Hub: A Random History of Boston Sports* (Cambridge, Massachusetts: Harvard University Press, 2005); *Hockey in Syracuse* by Jim Mancuso (Portsmouth, New Hampshire: Arcadia Publishing, 2005); *Green, Black and Gold: A History of Western Canada's Oldest School, 1820–1997* by Samir K. Sinha (provided courtesy of the Martin H. Ainley Archives Centre, St. John's-Ravenscourt School, Winnipeg); and *88 Years of Puck-Chasing in Saskatchewan* by Brenda Zeman (Regina, Saskatchewan: Saskatchewan Sports Hall of Fame, 1983).

Eddie Shore of Springfield Indians fame (or notoriety) is captured in *Grapes: A Vintage View of Hockey* by Don Cherry (Scarborough, Ontario: Prentice-Hall of Canada, 1982); *Hockey in Springfield* by Jim Mancuso (Portsmouth, New Hampshire: Arcadia Publishing, 2005); "Eddie Shore: the Man and the Myth (A Series)" by Sam Pompei in the Springfield *Daily News*, January–March, 1967; "Culture Shock: The Iron Hand of the Legendary Eddie Shore" by Brian Smith in *Canadian Oldtimer's Hockey Association Journal*, November/December 1984; *Springfield Hockey Hall of Fame: Commemorative Program*, February 26, 2000; and the video documentary *Eddie Shore and the Springfield Indians* (Springfield, Massachusetts: WGBY Public Television, 2001).

Other helpful works that I need to mention are *The Proper Bostonians* by Cleveland Amory (New York: E. P. Dutton and Co., 1947); "Boston" in *Fortune*, February 1933; *The Stick: A History, A Celebration, An Elegy* by Bruce Dowbiggin (Toronto: Macfarlane, Walter and Ross, 2001); *The Rajah of Renfrew* by Brant E. Ducey (Edmonton: University of Alberta Press, 1998); and *Boston: The Great Depression and the New Deal* by Charles H. Trout (New York: Oxford University Press, 1977).

Last, but by no means least, were those two reference bibles that never left my side: Dan Diamond's *Total Hockey: The Ultimate Hockey Encyclopedia* (Kingston, New York: Total Sports Publishing, 2000); and Kevin Vautour's *The Bruins Book: The Most Complete Boston Bruins Fact Book Ever Published* (Toronto: ECW Press, 1997).

ACKNOWLEDGEMENTS

My RESEARCH ENDEAVOURS depended upon many people and institutions, and I thank:

Cheryl Adams, Library of Congress; Miragh Addis, Hockey Hall of Fame; Steve Bordeaux, Springfield Hockey Heritage Society; the staff of the Microtext Department, Boston Public Library; Cupar and District Heritage Museum, Saskatchewan; the staff of the reference desk, Edmonton Public Library; Fort Qu'Appelle Museum, Saskatchewan; David Fraser, WGBY Public Television, Springfield; Calla Grabish, Martin H. Ainley Archives Centre, St. John's-Ravenscourt School, Winnipeg; Richard Johnson, The Sports Museum, Boston; John Lorenz, House of Hockey, Morrill, Maine; Ken McCabe, Rural Sports Hall of Fame, Indian Head, Saskatchewan; Melville Heritage Museum, Saskatchewan; the staff of the microfilm room, Montreal Public Library; the staff of the Saskatchewan Archives

Board; Springfield Hockey Hall of Fame; Springfield Falcons; and the staff of the reference desk, Vancouver Public Library.

For generously sharing their memories of Eddie Shore with me, I gratefully acknowledge: Jimmy Anderson, Gary Brown, Thomas Burke, Fred Cusick, Kent Douglas, Ray Getliffe, Brian Kilrea, Rodney Macaulay, Harry Mattson, Ronald Mattson, Hal Passerini, Henry Pidhirny, Pat Pompei, Sam Pompei, Albert Rossetti, Milt Schmidt, Tom Shea, and the Coliseum "rink rats."

Edward William "Ted" Shore Jr. and his wife, Evelyn, were gracious hosts during my several visits to their home. From the outset, Ted told me to feel free to write anything about his father that I wanted to, but to please make it accurate, and he could not have been more helpful in ensuring that what I wrote was accurate. Ted told me stories about his father and provided me with names and contact information of people to interview, he answered my pestering phone calls when I was in need of a fact or two, and he read the manuscript chapter by chapter as it emerged from my printer (and saved me from making some embarrassing mistakes in doing so). He gave me photographs, access to the family records, a tour of the Eastern States Coliseum, and lunches at West Springfield's venerable eating establishment, the White Hut. I additionally wish to thank three other members of the Shore family for their kind assistance: Allen Shore in Saskatchewan and Edward Shore III and Robert Shore in Massachusetts.

Sam Pompei allowed me to copy both his unpublished writings on Eddie Shore and his extensive collection of Eddie Shore material, and David Fraser of WGBY transferred the full interviews done for the Eddie Shore documentary to VHS format for my use. I thank them for their generosity.

At McClelland & Stewart, I thank my editor for her willingness to blow the whistle sparingly and letting me, in a narrative sense, play a wide-open game. Dinah Forbes knows a great deal about hockey, she put a lot of time and thought into the careful reading and editing of my manuscript, and I greatly appreciate all of her help. I thank Lloyd Davis, also a hockey expert, for both his copy editing and his keen eye for the factual error (any errors that remain, however, are mine alone). My agent, Albert LaFarge, has again proved his worth many times over and, again, he has my heartfelt thanks. To my wife, Marina, and our three children, thank you for your understanding, patience, and support during the three years I worked on this book.

INDEX

Abel, Clarence "Taffy," 120, 121-22, 123, 129, 130, 162, 163, 164, 165, 195, 250

Adams, Charles Francis (Navy Secretary), 136-37

Adams, Charles Francis, 69, 73, 79, 81, 89, 91, 95, 99-100, 103, 123, 137-39, 142, 143, 148, 150-51, 162, 165, 169, 172, 178, 188-89, 195, 197, 223, 227, 230-31, 259

Adams, Jack, 85, 198

Adams, John, 136

Adams, John Quincy, 136

Adams, Weston, 147-48, 178, 189, 220, 223, 224, 242-43, 263, 268, 270-71, 286

Alberta Belgian Breeders Association, 203

Allan Cup, 39, 44, 45, 54, 194

Allen, George, 254

Allen, Henry, 90

Amadio, Dave, 291, 300-1, 306, 307

American Hockey League (AHL), 277, 278, 286-87, 291, 300, 302, 306-7, 309

Anderson, Jimmy, 284, 287, 289, 293, 307, 310

Atkinson, LeRoy, 185, 186

Bailey, Irvin Wallace "Ace," 84, 192, 196, 201, 205, 208, 210, 229, 231-32, 310
  benefit game for, 230-31

neurosurgery, 217-19
sucker punched by Shore, 5, 211-16, 221-27

Bailey, Joan, 217, 219, 222, 224

Bailey, Mabel, 217, 218, 219, 222, 229

Baltimore Clippers, 302

Barry, Marty, 177, 199

Basilone, Rudy, 295

"Battle of Richmond," 34-35

Bauer, Bobby, 238, 245, 248, 252, 255, 261, 262, 263

Beattie, John "Red," 200

Bell, Billy, 96, 99

Benedict, Clint, 87, 117, 130, 132

Benson, Bobby, 64

Betts, Frederick E., 26-27

Binning, Michelle, 311

Black Panthers (hockey club), 119

Blair, Andy, 18, 192, 202

Blanchard, Cecil, 226

Blue, Walter, 33, 34

Boston Arena, 90-91, 103, 311

Boston Bruins:
  1924–25 season, 137-39
  1926-27 season, 69-83; Stanley Cup playoffs, 83-84, 87-99
  1927–28 season, 103-13, 117-18, 120-26
  1928–29 season, 142-43, 146-62; Stanley Cup playoffs, 162-69
  1929–30 season, 7-9, 171-73, 176-83
  1930–31 season, 185-87, 189

"Like Bobby Orr a generation later, Eddie Shore was the dominant hockey player of his time. Yet his story has remained untold . . . until now. Michael Hiam remedies this oversight by giving life to the Eddie Shore legend."
—TODD DENAULT, author of *The Greatest Game* and *Jacques Plante*

Eddie Shore was the Babe Ruth and Ty Cobb of hockey, a brilliant player with an unmatched temper. Emerging from the Canadian prairie to join the Boston Bruins in 1926, the man from Saskatchewan invaded every circuit in the NHL like a runaway locomotive on a downgrade. Adoring and hostile fans alike turned out in droves hoping to see him, and in Boston, he was hailed a hero.

During his twenty-year professional career, the controversial Shore personified "that old time hockey" like no other, playing the game with passion, dedication, and a complete disregard for his own safety. One of the most penalized men in the NHL and also a perennial member of its All-Star Team, Shore won the Hart Trophy for the league's most valuable player four times – trailing only Wayne Gretzky and Gordie Howe, and setting a record for a defenseman not since matched – and led Boston to two Stanley Cups in 1929 and 1939. In 1933, he was the instigator of hockey's most infamous event, the tragic "Ace Bailey Incident," which resulted in his polarizing sixteen-game suspension that, to this day, is still talked about.

Spanning his early days in the Western Canada Hockey League to his retirement from the NHL in 1940, to his time as owner and tyrant of the AHL championship-winning Springfield Indians, *Eddie Shore and That Old Time Hockey* is an action-packed and full-throated celebration of the "mighty Eddie Shore" – and also of the sport of hockey as it was gloriously played in a bygone age.

C. MICHAEL HIAM was born in Boston and lives in Newton, Massachusetts, with his wife and three children.

"This is an excellent, long-overdue take on the ground-breaking blueliner's life. . . . Hiam delivers a well-rounded picture of the path from Western Canada's rough-and-tumble leagues to 1930s NHL stardom." – *Straight.com*

McCLELLAND & STEWART
www.mcclelland.com

HOCKEY CAN $21.00 / US $19.95

ISBN 978-0-7710-4129-7

62100

9 780771 041297